Visit classzone.com and get connected

Online resources for students and parents

ClassZone resources provide instruction, practice, and learning support.

eEdition Plus ONLINE

This interactive version of the text encourages students to explore science.

Content Review Online

Interactive review reinforces the big idea and key concepts of each chapter.

SciLinks

NSTA-selected links provide relevant Web resources correlated to the text.

Chapter-Based Support

Math tutorials, news, resources, test practice, and a misconceptions database help students succeed.

Now it all clicks!™

CLASSZONE.COM

McDougal Littell

McDougal Littell Science

Motion and Forces

$F = ma$

GRAVITY

VELOCITY

PHYSICAL SCIENCE

A ▶ Matter and Energy
B ▶ Chemical Interactions
C ▶ Motion and Forces
D ▶ Waves, Sound, and Light
E ▶ Electricity and Magnetism

LIFE SCIENCE

A ▶ Cells and Heredity
B ▶ Life Over Time
C ▶ Diversity of Living Things
D ▶ Ecology
E ▶ Human Biology

EARTH SCIENCE

A ▶ Earth's Surface
B ▶ The Changing Earth
C ▶ Earth's Waters
D ▶ Earth's Atmosphere
E ▶ Space Science

Acknowledgments: Excerpts and adaptations from *National Science Education Standards* by the National Academy of Sciences. Copyright © 1996 by the National Academy of Sciences. Reprinted with permission from the National Academies Press, Washington, D.C.

Excerpts and adaptations from *Benchmarks for Science Literacy: Project 2061.* Copyright © 1993 by the American Association for the Advancement of Science. Reprinted with permission.

Printed in the United States of America

ISBN-13: 978-0-618-84253-7

4500313235

ISBN-10: 0-618-84253-5

6 7 8 - 0914 - 14 13 12 11

Internet Web Site: http://www.mcdougallittell.com

Science Consultants

Chief Science Consultant

James Trefil, Ph.D. is the Clarence J. Robinson Professor of Physics at George Mason University. He is the author or co-author of more than 25 books, including *Science Matters* and *The Nature of Science*. Dr. Trefil is a member of the American Association for the Advancement of Science's Committee on the Public Understanding of Science and Technology. He is also a fellow of the World Economic Forum and a frequent contributor to *Smithsonian* magazine.

Rita Ann Calvo, Ph.D. is Senior Lecturer in Molecular Biology and Genetics at Cornell University, where for 12 years she also directed the Cornell Institute for Biology Teachers. Dr. Calvo is the 1999 recipient of the College and University Teaching Award from the National Association of Biology Teachers.

Kenneth Cutler, M.S. is the Education Coordinator for the Julius L. Chambers Biomedical Biotechnology Research Institute at North Carolina Central University. A former middle school and high school science teacher, he received a 1999 Presidential Award for Excellence in Science Teaching.

Instructional Design Consultants

Douglas Carnine, Ph.D. is Professor of Education and Director of the National Center for Improving the Tools of Educators at the University of Oregon. He is the author of seven books and over 100 other scholarly publications, primarily in the areas of instructional design and effective instructional strategies and tools for diverse learners. Dr. Carnine also serves as a member of the National Institute for Literacy Advisory Board.

Linda Carnine, Ph.D. consults with school districts on curriculum development and effective instruction for students struggling academically. A former teacher and school administrator, Dr. Carnine also co-authored a popular remedial reading program.

Donald Steely, Ph.D. serves as principal investigator at the Oregon Center for Applied Science (ORCAS) on federal grants for science and language arts programs. His background also includes teaching and authoring of print and multimedia programs in science, mathematics, history, and spelling.

Sam Miller, Ph.D. is a middle school science teacher and the Teacher Development Liaison for the Eugene, Oregon, Public Schools. He is the author of curricula for teaching science, mathematics, computer skills, and language arts.

Vicky Vachon, Ph.D. consults with school districts throughout the United States and Canada on improving overall academic achievement with a focus on literacy. She is also co-author of a widely used program for remedial readers.

Content Reviewers

John Beaver, Ph.D.
Ecology
Professor, Director of Science Education Center
College of Education and Human Services
Western Illinois University
Macomb, IL

Donald J. DeCoste, Ph.D.
Matter and Energy, Chemical Interactions
Chemistry Instructor
University of Illinois
Urbana-Champaign, IL

Dorothy Ann Fallows, Ph.D., MSc
Diversity of Living Things, Microbiology
Partners in Health
Boston, MA

Michael Foote, Ph.D.
The Changing Earth, Life Over Time
Associate Professor
Department of the Geophysical Sciences
The University of Chicago
Chicago, IL

Lucy Fortson, Ph.D.
Space Science
Director of Astronomy
Adler Planetarium and Astronomy Museum
Chicago, IL

Elizabeth Godrick, Ph.D.
Human Biology
Professor, CAS Biology
Boston University
Boston, MA

Isabelle Sacramento Grilo, M.S.
The Changing Earth
Lecturer, Department of the Geological Sciences
San Diego State University
San Diego, CA

David Harbster, MSc
Diversity of Living Things
Professor of Biology
Paradise Valley Community College
Phoenix, AZ

Richard D. Norris, Ph.D.
Earth's Waters
Professor of Paleobiology
Scripps Institution of Oceanography
University of California, San Diego
La Jolla, CA

Donald B. Peck, M.S.
Motion and Forces; Waves, Sound, and Light; Electricity and Magnetism
Director of the Center for Science Education (retired)
Fairleigh Dickinson University
Madison, NJ

Javier Penalosa, Ph.D.
Diversity of Living Things, Plants
Associate Professor, Biology Department
Buffalo State College
Buffalo, NY

Raymond T. Pierrehumbert, Ph.D.
Earth's Atmosphere
Professor in Geophysical Sciences (Atmospheric Science)
The University of Chicago
Chicago, IL

Brian J. Skinner, Ph.D.
Earth's Surface
Eugene Higgins Professor of Geology and Geophysics
Yale University
New Haven, CT

Nancy E. Spaulding, M.S.
Earth's Surface, The Changing Earth, Earth's Waters
Earth Science Teacher (retired)
Elmira Free Academy
Elmira, NY

Steven S. Zumdahl, Ph.D.
Matter and Energy, Chemical Interactions
Professor Emeritus of Chemistry
University of Illinois
Urbana-Champaign, IL

Susan L. Zumdahl, M.S.
Matter and Energy, Chemical Interactions
Chemistry Education Specialist
University of Illinois
Urbana-Champaign, IL

Safety Consultant

Juliana Texley, Ph.D.
Former K–12 Science Teacher and School Superintendent
Boca Raton, FL

English Language Advisor

Judy Lewis, M.A.
Director, State and Federal Programs for reading proficiency
and high risk populations
Rancho Cordova, CA

Teacher Panel Members

Carol Arbour
Tallmadge Middle School,
Tallmadge, OH

Patty Belcher
Goodrich Middle School,
Akron, OH

Gwen Broestl
Luis Munoz Marin Middle School,
Cleveland, OH

Al Brofman
Tehipite Middle School,
Fresno, CA

John Cockrell
Clinton Middle School,
Columbus, OH

Jenifer Cox
Sylvan Middle School,
Citrus Heights, CA

Linda Culpepper
Martin Middle School,
Charlotte, NC

Kathleen Ann DeMatteo
Margate Middle School,
Margate, FL

Melvin Figueroa
New River Middle School,
Ft. Lauderdale, FL

Doretha Grier
Kannapolis Middle School,
Kannapolis, NC

Robert Hood
Alexander Hamilton Middle School,
Cleveland, OH

Scott Hudson
Covedale Elementary School,
Cincinnati, OH

Loretta Langdon
Princeton Middle School,
Princeton, NC

Carlyn Little
Glades Middle School,
Miami, FL

Ann Marie Lynn
Amelia Earhart Middle School,
Riverside, CA

James Minogue
Lowe's Grove Middle School,
Durham, NC

Joann Myers
Buchanan Middle School,
Tampa, FL

Barbara Newell
Charles Evans Hughes Middle School,
Long Beach, CA

Anita Parker
Kannapolis Middle School,
Kannapolis, NC

Greg Pirolo
Golden Valley Middle School,
San Bernardino, CA

Laura Pottmyer
Apex Middle School,
Apex, NC

Lynn Prichard
Booker T. Washington Middle Magnet
School, Tampa, FL

Jacque Quick
Walter Williams High School,
Burlington, NC

Robert Glenn Reynolds
Hillman Middle School,
Youngstown, OH

Stacy Rinehart
Lufkin Road Middle School,
Apex, NC

Theresa Short
Abbott Middle School,
Fayetteville, NC

Rita Slivka
Alexander Hamilton Middle School,
Cleveland, OH

Marie Sofsak
B F Stanton Middle School,
Alliance, OH

Nancy Stubbs
Sweetwater Union Unified School District,
Chula Vista, CA

Sharon Stull
Quail Hollow Middle School,
Charlotte, NC

Donna Taylor
Okeeheelee Middle School,
West Palm Beach, FL

Sandi Thompson
Harding Middle School,
Lakewood, OH

Lori Walker
Audubon Middle School & Magnet Center,
Los Angeles, CA

Teacher Lab Evaluators

Andrew Boy
W.E.B. DuBois Academy,
Cincinnati, OH

Jill Brimm-Byrne
Albany Park Academy,
Chicago, IL

Gwen Broestl
Luis Munoz Marin Middle School,
Cleveland, OH

Al Brofman
Tehipite Middle School,
Fresno, CA

Michael A. Burstein
The Rashi School,
Newton, MA

Trudi Coutts
Madison Middle School,
Naperville, IL

Jenifer Cox
Sylvan Middle School,
Citrus Heights, CA

Larry Cwik
Madison Middle School,
Naperville, IL

Jennifer Donatelli
Kennedy Junior High School,
Lisle, IL

Melissa Dupree
Lakeside Middle School,
Evans, GA

Carl Fechko
Luis Munoz Marin Middle School,
Cleveland, OH

Paige Fullhart
Highland Middle School,
Libertyville, IL

Sue Hood
Glen Crest Middle School,
Glen Ellyn, IL

William Luzader
Plymouth Community Intermediate School,
Plymouth, MA

Ann Min
Beardsley Middle School,
Crystal Lake, IL

Aileen Mueller
Kennedy Junior High School,
Lisle, IL

Nancy Nega
Churchville Middle School,
Elmhurst, IL

Oscar Newman
Sumner Math and Science Academy,
Chicago, IL

Lynn Prichard
Booker T. Washington Middle Magnet
School, Tampa, FL

Jacque Quick
Walter Williams High School,
Burlington, NC

Stacy Rinehart
Lufkin Road Middle School,
Apex, NC

Seth Robey
Gwendolyn Brooks Middle School,
Oak Park, IL

Kevin Steele
Grissom Middle School,
Tinley Park, IL

Motion and Forces

Unit Features

1 Motion   6

the **BIG** idea

The motion of an object can be described and predicted.

2 Forces   38

the **BIG** idea

Forces change the motion of objects in predictable ways.

What must happen for a team to win this tug of war? page 38

What forces are acting on this snowboarder? on the snow? page 75

Features

Visual Highlights

Internet Resources @ ClassZone.com

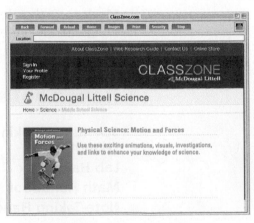

INVESTIGATIONS AND ACTIVITIES

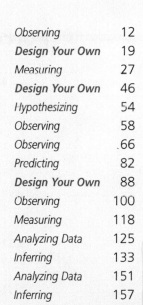

Standards and Benchmarks

Each chapter in **Motion and Forces** covers some of the learning goals that are described in the *National Science Education Standards* (NSES) and the Project 2061 *Benchmarks for Science Literacy*. Selected content and skill standards are shown below in shortened form. The following National Science Education Standards are covered on pages xii–xxvii, in Frontiers in Science, and in Timelines in Science, as well as in chapter features and laboratory investigations: Understandings About Scientific Inquiry (A.9), Understandings About Science and Technology (E.6), Science and Technology in Society (F.5), Science as a Human Endeavor (G.1), Nature of Science (G.2), and History of Science (G.3).

Content Standards

1 Motion

	National Science Education Standards
B.2.a	An object's motion • is described by its position, direction of motion, and speed • can be measured and shown on a graph
	Project 2061 Benchmarks
10.A.1	An object's motion is relative to a certain object or point in space.

2 Forces

	National Science Education Standards
B.2.b	An object will move in a straight line at a constant speed unless a force acts on it.
B.2.c	If more than one force acts on an object, • the forces can act together • the forces can act against each other depending on the size and direction of the forces
	Project 2061 Benchmarks
4.F.3	An unbalanced force • will change an object's speed and/or direction • can cause an object to orbit the center of the force
10.B.1	Newton's Laws describe motion everywhere in the universe.
11.C.2	A system may stay the same because • no forces are acting on the system • forces are acting on the system, but they all cancel each other out

3 Gravity, Friction, and Pressure

	National Science Education Standards
B.1.a	Substances have certain properties, including density.
D.3.c	Gravity is the force that • keeps planets in orbit around the Sun • governs motion within the solar system • holds us to Earth's surface • produces tides

Project 2061 Benchmarks

4.B.3 | Everything on or near Earth is pulled toward Earth's center by the force of gravity.

4.G.1 | Every object exerts the force of gravity, but the force
• depends on the mass and distance of objects
• is difficult to detect unless an object contains a lot of mass

4.G.2 | In the solar system
• the Sun's gravity keeps the planets in orbit around the Sun
• the planets' gravity keeps their moons in orbit around the planets

4 Work and Energy

National Science Education Standards

B.3.a | Energy is transferred in many ways. Energy is often associated with heat, sound, and mechanical motion.

Project 2061 Benchmarks

4.E.1 | Energy cannot be created or destroyed, but it can be changed from one form to another.

4.E.4 | Energy has many different forms, including
• heat—the disorderly motion of particles
• chemical—the arrangement of atoms in matter
• mechanical—the kinetic plus the potential energy of an object
• gravitational—the separation of objects that attract each other

5 Machines

National Science Education Standards

E.6.c | • Science and technology often work together.
• Science helps drive technology.
• Technology is used to improve scientific investigations.

E.6.d | Perfectly designed solutions do not exist. All technology has risks and trade-offs, such as cost, safety, and efficiency

E.6.e | All designs have limits, including those having to do with material properties and availability, safety, and environmental protection.

Project 2061 Benchmarks

8.B.4 | The use of robots has changed the nature of work in many fields, including manufacturing.

Process and Skill Standards

National Science Education Standards

A.2 | Design and conduct a scientific investigation.

A.3 | Use appropriate tools and techniques to gather and interpret data.

A.4 | Use evidence to describe, predict, explain, and model.

A.5 | Use critical thinking to find relationships between results and interpretations.

A.7 | Communicate procedures, results, and conclusions.

A.8 | Use mathematics in scientific investigations.

E.1 | Identify a problem to be solved.

E.2 | Design a solution or product.

E.3 | Implement the proposed solution.

E.4 | Evaluate the solution or design.

Project 2061 Benchmarks

11.C.4 | Use equations to summarize observed changes.

12.C.3 | Using appropriate units, use and read instruments that measure length, volume, weight, time, rate, and temperature.

12.D.1 | Use tables and graphs to organize information and identify relationships.

12.D.2 | Read, interpret, and describe tables and graphs.

12.D.4 | Understand information that includes different types of charts and graphs, including circle charts, bar graphs, line graphs, data tables, diagrams, and symbols.

Introducing Physical Science

Scientists are curious. Since ancient times, they have been asking and answering questions about the world around them. Scientists are also very suspicious of the answers they get. They carefully collect evidence and test their answers many times before accepting an idea as correct.

In this book you will see how scientific knowledge keeps growing and changing as scientists ask new questions and rethink what was known before. The following sections will help get you started.

What Is Physical Science?

In the simplest terms, physical science is the study of what things are made of and how they change. It combines the studies of both physics and chemistry. Physics is the science of matter, energy, and forces. It includes the study of topics such as motion, light, and electricity and magnetism. Chemistry is the study of the structure and properties of matter, and it especially focuses on how substances change into different substances.

The text and pictures in this book will help you learn key concepts and important facts about physical science. A variety of activities will help you investigate these concepts. As you learn, it helps to have a big picture of physical science as a framework for this new information. The four unifying principles listed below will give you this big picture. Read the next few pages to get an overview of each of these principles and a sense of why they are so important.

- **Matter is made of particles too small to see.**

- **Matter changes form and moves from place to place.**

- **Energy changes from one form to another, but it cannot be created or destroyed.**

- **Physical forces affect the movement of all matter on Earth and throughout the universe.**

the **BIG** idea

Each chapter begins with a big idea. Keep in mind that each big idea relates to one or more of the unifying principles.

Matter is made of particles too small to see.

This simple statement is the basis for explaining an amazing variety of things about the world. For example, it explains why substances can exist as solids, liquids, and gases, and why wood burns but iron does not. Like the tiles that make up this mosaic picture, the particles that make up all substances combine to make patterns and structures that can be seen. Unlike these tiles, the individual particles themselves are far too small to see.

What It Means

To understand this principle better, let's take a closer look at the two key words: *matter* and *particles*.

Matter

Objects you can see and touch are all around you. The materials that these objects are made of are called **matter.** All living things—even you—are also matter. Even though you can't see it, the air around you is matter too. Scientists often say that matter is anything that has mass and takes up space. **Mass** is a measure of the amount of matter in an object. We use the word **volume** to refer to the amount of space an object or a substance takes up.

Particles

The tiny particles that make up all matter are called **atoms.** Just how tiny are atoms? They are far too small to see, even through a powerful microscope. In fact, an atom is more than a million times smaller than the period at the end of this sentence.

There are more than 100 basic kinds of matter called **elements.** For example, iron, gold, and oxygen are three common elements. Each element has its own unique kind of atom. The atoms of any element are all alike but different from the atoms of any other element.

Many familiar materials are made of particles called molecules. In a **molecule,** two or more atoms stick together to form a larger particle. For example, a water molecule is made of two atoms of hydrogen and one atom of oxygen.

Why It's Important

Understanding atoms and molecules makes it possible to explain and predict the behavior of matter. Among other things, this knowledge allows scientists to

- explain why different materials have different characteristics
- predict how a material will change when heated or cooled
- figure out how to combine atoms and molecules to make new and useful materials

Matter changes form and moves from place to place.

You see matter change form every day. You see the ice in your glass of juice disappear without a trace. You see a black metal gate slowly develop a flaky, orange coating. Matter is constantly changing and moving.

What It Means

Remember that matter is made of tiny particles called atoms. Atoms are constantly moving and combining with one another. All changes in matter are the result of atoms moving and combining in different ways.

Matter Changes and Moves

You can look at water to see how matter changes and moves. A block of ice is hard like a rock. Leave the ice out in sunlight, however, and it changes into a puddle of water. That puddle of water can eventually change into water vapor and disappear into the air. The water vapor in the air can become raindrops, which may fall on rocks, causing them to weather and wear away. The water that flows in rivers and streams picks up tiny bits of rock and carries them from one shore to another. Understanding how the world works requires an understanding of how matter changes and moves.

Matter Is Conserved

No matter was lost in any of the changes described above. The ice turned to water because its molecules began to move more quickly as they got warmer. The bits of rock carried away by the flowing river were not gone forever. They simply ended up farther down the river. The puddles of rainwater didn't really disappear; their molecules slowly mixed with molecules in the air.

Under ordinary conditions, when matter changes form, no matter is created or destroyed. The water created by melting ice has the same mass as the ice did. If you could measure the water vapor that mixes with the air, you would find it had the same mass as the water in the puddle did.

Why It's Important

Understanding how mass is conserved when matter changes form has helped scientists to

- describe changes they see in the world
- predict what will happen when two substances are mixed
- explain where matter goes when it seems to disappear

Energy changes from one form to another, but it cannot be created or destroyed.

When you use energy to warm your food or to turn on a flashlight, you may think that you "use up" the energy. Even though the camp-stove fuel is gone and the flashlight battery no longer functions, the energy they provided has not disappeared. It has been changed into a form you can no longer use. Understanding how energy changes forms is the basis for understanding how heat, light, and motion are produced.

What It Means

Changes that you see around you depend on energy. **Energy,** in fact, means the ability to cause change. The electrical energy from an outlet changes into light and heat in a light bulb. Plants change the light energy from the Sun into chemical energy, which animals use to power their muscles.

Energy Changes Forms

Using energy means changing energy. You probably have seen electric energy changing into light, heat, sound, and mechanical energy in household appliances. Fuels like wood, coal, and oil contain chemical energy that produces heat when burned. Electric power plants make electrical energy from a variety of energy sources, including falling water, nuclear energy, and fossil fuels.

Energy Is Conserved

Energy can be converted into forms that can be used for specific purposes. During the conversion, some of the original energy is converted into unwanted forms. For instance, when a power plant converts the energy of falling water into electrical energy, some of the energy is lost to friction and sound.

Similarly, when electrical energy is used to run an appliance, some of the energy is converted into forms that are not useful. Only a small percentage of the energy used in a light bulb, for instance, produces light; most of the energy becomes heat. Nonetheless, the total amount of energy remains the same through all these conversions.

The fact that energy does not disappear is a law of physical science. The **law of conservation of energy** states that energy cannot be created or destroyed. It can only change form.

Why It's Important

Understanding that energy changes form but does not disappear has helped scientists to

• predict how energy will change form
• manage energy conversions in useful ways
• build and improve machines

Physical forces affect the movement of all matter on Earth and throughout the universe.

What makes the world go around? The answer is simple: forces. Forces allow you to walk across the room, and forces keep the stars together in galaxies. Consider the forces acting on the rafts below. The rushing water is pushing the rafts forward. The force from the people paddling helps to steer the rafts.

What It Means

A **force** is a push or a pull. Every time you push or pull an object, you're applying a force to that object, whether or not the object moves. There are several forces—several pushes and pulls—acting on you right now. All these forces are necessary for you to do the things you do, even sitting and reading.

- You are already familiar with the force of gravity. **Gravity** is the force of attraction between two objects. Right now gravity is at work pulling you to Earth and Earth to you. The Moon stays in orbit around Earth because gravity holds it close.

- A contact force occurs when one object pushes or pulls another object by touching it. If you kick a soccer ball, for instance, you apply a contact force to the ball. You apply a contact force to a shopping cart that you push down a grocery aisle or a sled that you pull up a hill.

- **Friction** is the force that resists motion between two surfaces pressed together. If you've ever tried to walk on an icy sidewalk, you know how important friction can be. If you lightly rub your finger across a smooth page in a book and then across a piece of sandpaper, you can feel how the different surfaces produce different frictional forces. Which is easier to do?

- There are other forces at work in the world too. For example, a compass needle responds to the magnetic force exerted by Earth's magnetic field, and objects made of certain metals are attracted by magnets. In addition to magnetic forces, there are electrical forces operating between particles and between objects. For example, you can demonstrate electrical forces by rubbing an inflated balloon on your hair. The balloon will then stick to your head or to a wall without additional means of support.

Why It's Important

Although some of these forces are more obvious than others, physical forces at work in the world are necessary for you to do the things you do. Understanding forces allows scientists to

- predict how objects will move
- design machines that perform complex tasks
- predict where planets and stars will be in the sky from one night to the next

The Nature of Science

You may think of science as a body of knowledge or a collection of facts. More important, however, science is an active process that involves certain ways of looking at the world.

Scientific Habits of Mind

Scientists are curious. They are always asking questions. Scientists have asked questions such as, "What is the smallest form of matter?" and "How do the smallest particles behave?" These and other important questions are being investigated by scientists around the world.

Scientists are observant. They are always looking closely at the world around them. Scientists once thought the smallest parts of atoms were protons, neutrons, and electrons. Later, protons and neutrons were found to be made of even smaller particles called quarks.

Scientists are creative. They draw on what they know to form possible explanations for a pattern, an event, or an interesting phenomenon that they have observed. Then scientists create a plan for testing their ideas.

Scientists are skeptical. Scientists don't accept an explanation or answer unless it is based on evidence and logical reasoning. They continually question their own conclusions and the conclusions suggested by other scientists. Scientists trust only evidence that is confirmed by other people or methods.

Scientists cannot always make observations with their own eyes. They have developed technology, such as this particle detector, to help them gather information about the smallest particles of matter.

Scientists ask questions about the physical world and seek answers through carefully controlled procedures. Here a researcher works with supercooled magnets.

Science Processes at Work

You can think of science as a continuous cycle of asking and seeking answers to questions about the world. Although there are many processes that scientists use, scientists typically do each of the following:

- Observe and ask a question
- Determine what is known
- Investigate
- Interpret results
- Share results

Ask a question → Determine what is known → Investigate → Interpret results → Share results

Observe and Ask a Question

It may surprise you that asking questions is an important skill. A scientific process may start when a scientist asks a question. Perhaps scientists observe an event or a process that they don't understand, or perhaps answering one question leads to another.

Determine What Is Known

When beginning an inquiry, scientists find out what is already known about a question. They study results from other scientific investigations, read journals, and talk with other scientists. A scientist working on subatomic particles is most likely a member of a large team using sophisticated equipment. Before beginning original research, the team analyzes results from previous studies.

Investigate

Investigating is the process of collecting evidence. Two important ways of investigating are observing and experimenting.

Observing is the act of noting and recording an event, a characteristic, or anything else detected with an instrument or with the senses. A researcher may study the properties of a substance by handling it, finding its mass, warming or cooling it, stretching it, and so on. For information about the behavior of subatomic particles, however, a researcher may rely on technology such as scanning tunneling microscopes, which produce images of structures that cannot be seen with the eye.

An **experiment** is an organized procedure to study something under controlled conditions. In order to study the effect of wing shape on the motion of a glider, for instance, a researcher would need to conduct controlled studies in which gliders made of the same materials and with the same masses differed only in the shape of their wings.

Scanning tunneling microscopes create images that allow scientists to observe molecular structure.

Physical chemists have found a way to observe chemical reactions at the atomic level. Using lasers, they can watch bonds breaking and new bonds forming.

Forming hypotheses and making predictions are two of the skills involved in scientific investigations. A **hypothesis** is a tentative explanation for an observation, a phenomenon, or a scientific problem that can be tested by further investigation. For example, in the mid-1800s astronomers noticed that the planet Uranus departed slightly from its expected orbit. One astronomer hypothesized that the irregularities in the planet's orbit were due to the gravitational effect of another planet—one that had not yet been detected. A **prediction** is an expectation of what will be observed or what will happen. A prediction can be used to test a hypothesis. The astronomers predicted that they would discover a new planet in the position calculated, and their prediction was confirmed with the discovery of the planet Neptune.

Interpret Results

As scientists investigate, they analyze their evidence, or data, and begin to draw conclusions. **Analyzing data** involves looking at the evidence gathered through observations or experiments and trying to identify any patterns that might exist in the data. Scientists often need to make additional observations or perform more experiments before they are sure of their conclusions. Many times scientists make new predictions or revise their hypotheses.

Often scientists use computers to help them analyze data. Computers reveal patterns that might otherwise be missed.

Scientists use computers to create models of objects or processes they are studying. This model shows carbon atoms forming a sphere.

Share Results

An important part of scientific investigation is sharing results of experiments. Scientists read and publish in journals and attend conferences to communicate with other scientists around the world. Sharing data and procedures gives them a way to test one another's results. They also share results with the public through newspapers, television, and other media.

The Nature of Technology

When you think of technology, you may think of cars, computers, and cell phones, as well as refrigerators, radios, and bicycles. Technology is not only the machines and devices that make modern lives easier, however. It is also a process in which new methods and devices are created. Technology makes use of scientific knowledge to design solutions to real-world problems.

Science and Technology

Science and technology go hand in hand. Each depends upon the other. Even designing a device as simple as a toaster requires knowledge of how heat flows and which materials are the best conductors of heat. Just as technology based on scientific knowledge makes our lives easier, some technology is used to advance scientific inquiry itself. For example, researchers use a number of specialized instruments to help them collect data. Microscopes, telescopes, spectrographs, and computers are just a few of the tools that help scientists learn more about the world. The more information these tools provide, the more devices can be developed to aid scientific research and to improve modern lives.

The Process of Technological Design

The process of technology involves many choices. For example, how does an automobile engineer design a better car? Is a better car faster? safer? cheaper? Before designing any new machine, the engineer must decide exactly what he or she wants the machine to do as well as what may be given up for the machine to do it. A faster car may get people to their destinations more quickly, but it may cost more and be less safe. As you study the technological process, think about all the choices that were made to build the technologies you use.

Identify a Need

Successful technology fills a need; it helps us perform a task we need or want to do. For example, as more cars appear on the road, noise and air pollution become serious threats to the environment and to people's health. Gas consumption also depletes precious petroleum resources. There is a need to find a fuel source for a car that will not pollute the air and that will never run out.

Design and Develop

Hydrogen fuel cells are a potential solution to this need. These cells combine hydrogen and oxygen into water, producing electricity in the process. Engineers have found a way to make fuel cells small enough to fit into a car, yet able to produce enough electricity to power an electric motor. Before arriving at this final design, engineers tried many others.

Test and Improve

Just because a technology works doesn't mean it cannot be improved. A fuel-cell-powered car has been driven from San Francisco to Washington, D.C., but it probably will be a while before it's in dealer showrooms. Engineers won't know how these cars will perform until they're driven in real-world conditions. Engineers also won't know if the average driver will be able to handle the necessary maintenance on the car until the car is made available to ordinary drivers. Improvements in the future may well bring cars powered by fuel cells into garages everywhere.

Using McDougal Littell Science

Reading Text and Visuals

This book is organized to help you learn. Use these boxed pointers as a path to help you learn and remember the **Big Ideas** and **Key Concepts**.

Read the Big Idea.

As you read **Key Concepts** for the chapter, relate them to **the Big Idea.**

Take notes.

Use the strategies on the **Getting Ready to Learn** page.

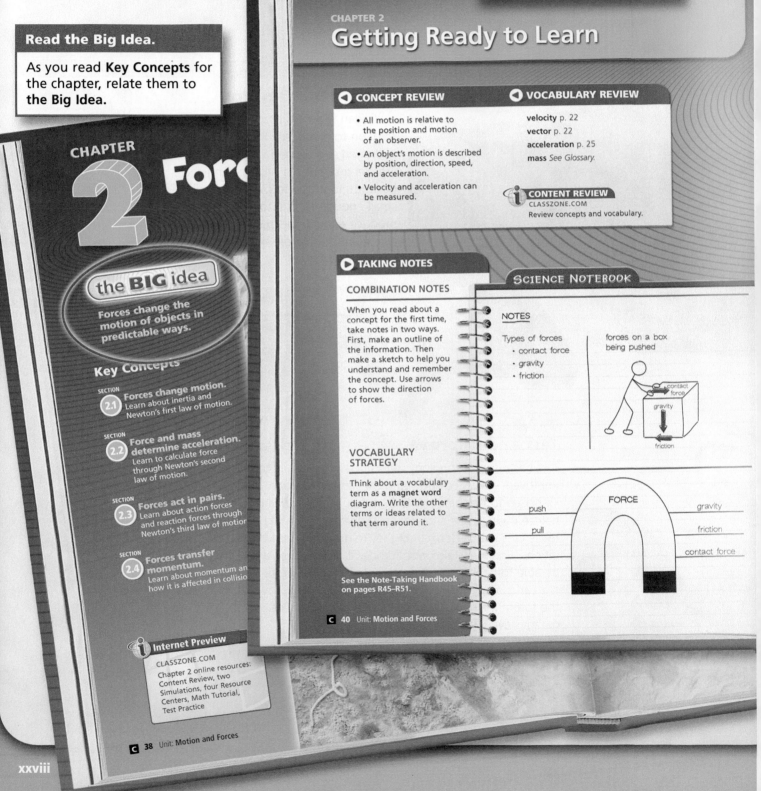

CHAPTER 2

2 Forces

the BIG idea

Forces change the motion of objects in predictable ways.

Key Concepts

SECTION
2.1 Forces change motion.
Learn about inertia and Newton's first law of motion.

SECTION
2.2 Force and mass determine acceleration.
Learn to calculate force through Newton's second law of motion.

SECTION
2.3 Forces act in pairs.
Learn about action forces and reaction forces through Newton's third law of motion.

SECTION
2.4 Forces transfer momentum.
Learn about momentum and how it is affected in collisions.

Internet Preview

CLASSZONE.COM
Chapter 2 online resources: Content Review, two Simulations, four Resource Centers, Math Tutorial, Test Practice

C **38** Unit: Motion and Forces

CHAPTER 2
Getting Ready to Learn

CONCEPT REVIEW

- All motion is relative to the position and motion of an observer.
- An object's motion is described by position, direction, speed, and acceleration.
- Velocity and acceleration can be measured.

VOCABULARY REVIEW

velocity p. 22
vector p. 22
acceleration p. 25
mass *See Glossary.*

CONTENT REVIEW
CLASSZONE.COM
Review concepts and vocabulary.

TAKING NOTES

COMBINATION NOTES

When you read about a concept for the first time, take notes in two ways. First, make an outline of the information. Then make a sketch to help you understand and remember the concept. Use arrows to show the direction of forces.

VOCABULARY STRATEGY

Think about a vocabulary term as a **magnet word** diagram. Write the other terms or ideas related to that term around it.

See the Note-Taking Handbook on pages R45–R51.

SCIENCE NOTEBOOK

NOTES

Types of forces
- contact force
- gravity
- friction

forces on a box being pushed

contact force
gravity
friction

FORCE
push — gravity
pull — friction
— contact force

C **40** Unit: Motion and Forces

Read each heading.

See how it fits into the outline of the chapter.

Remember what you know.

Think about concepts you learned earlier and preview what you'll learn now.

KEY CONCEPT

2.1 Matter has observable properties.

◀ **BEFORE,** you learned

- Matter has mass and volume
- Matter is made of atoms
- Matter exists in different states

▶ **NOW,** you will learn

- About physical and chemical properties
- About physical changes
- About chemical changes

VOCABULARY

physical property p. 41
density p. 43
physical change p. 44
chemical property p. 46
chemical change p. 46

EXPLORE Physical Properties

How can a substance be changed?

PROCEDURE

① Observe the clay. Note its physical characteristics, such as color, shape, texture, and size.

② Change the shape of the clay. Note which characteristics changed and which ones stayed the same.

WHAT DO YOU THINK?

- How did reshaping the clay change its physical characteristics?
- How were the mass and the volume of the clay affected?

MATERIAL
rectangular piece of clay

Try the activities.

They will introduce you to science concepts.

VOCABULARY
Make a magnet word diagram in your notebook for *physical property*.

Physical properties describe a substance.

What words would you use to describe a table? a chair? the sandwich you ate for lunch? You would probably say something about the shape, color, and size of each item. Next you might consider whether it is hard or soft, smooth or rough to the touch. Normally, when describing an object, you identify the characteristics of the object that you can observe without changing the identity of the object.

The characteristics of a substance that can be observed without changing the identity of the substance are called **physical properties.** In science, observation can include measuring and handling a substance. All of your senses can be used to detect physical properties. Color, shape, size, texture, volume, and mass are a few of the physical properties you probably have encountered.

CHECK YOUR READING Describe some of the physical properties of your desk.

Learn the vocabulary.

Take notes on each term.

Answer the questions.

Check Your Reading questions will help you remember what you read.

Chapter 2: **Properties of Matter** 41 **A**

Reading Text and Visuals

Read one paragraph at a time.

Look for a topic sentence that explains the main idea of the paragraph. Figure out how the details relate to that idea. One paragraph might have several important ideas; you may have to reread to understand.

Answer the questions.

Check Your Reading questions will help you remember what you read.

Study the visuals.

- Read the title.
- Read all labels and captions.
- Figure out what the picture is showing. Notice colors, arrows, and lines.
- Answer the question. **Reading Visuals** questions will help you understand the picture.

REMINDER

Because all formulas for volume involve the multiplication of three measurements, volume has a unit that is cubed (such as cm^3).

Physical Properties

How do you know which characteristics are physical properties? Just ask yourself whether observing the property involves changing the substance to a different substance. For example, you can stretch a rubber band. Does stretching the rubber band change what it is made of? No. The rubber band is still a rubber band before and after it is stretched. It may look a little different, but it is still a rubber band.

Mass and volume are two physical properties. Measuring these properties does not change the identity of a substance. For example, a lump of clay might have a mass of 200 grams (g) and a volume of 100 cubic centimeters (cm^3). If you were to break the clay in half, you would have two 100 g pieces of clay, each with a volume of 50 cm^3. You can bend and shape the clay too. Even if you were to mold a realistic model of a car out of the clay, it still would be a piece of clay. Although you have changed some of the properties of the object, such as its shape and volume, you have not changed the fact that the substance you are observing is clay.

CHECK YOUR READING Which physical properties listed above are found by taking measurements? Which are not?

Physical Properties

Physical properties of clay—such as volume, mass, color, texture, and shape—can be observed without changing the fact that the substance is clay.

Block of Clay

Shaped Clay

READING VISUALS COMPARE AND CONTRAST Which physical properties do the two pieces of clay have in common? Which are different?

Doing Labs

To understand science, you have to see it in action. Doing labs helps you understand how things really work.

① Read the entire lab first.

② Form a hypothesis.

③ Follow the procedure.

④ Record the data.

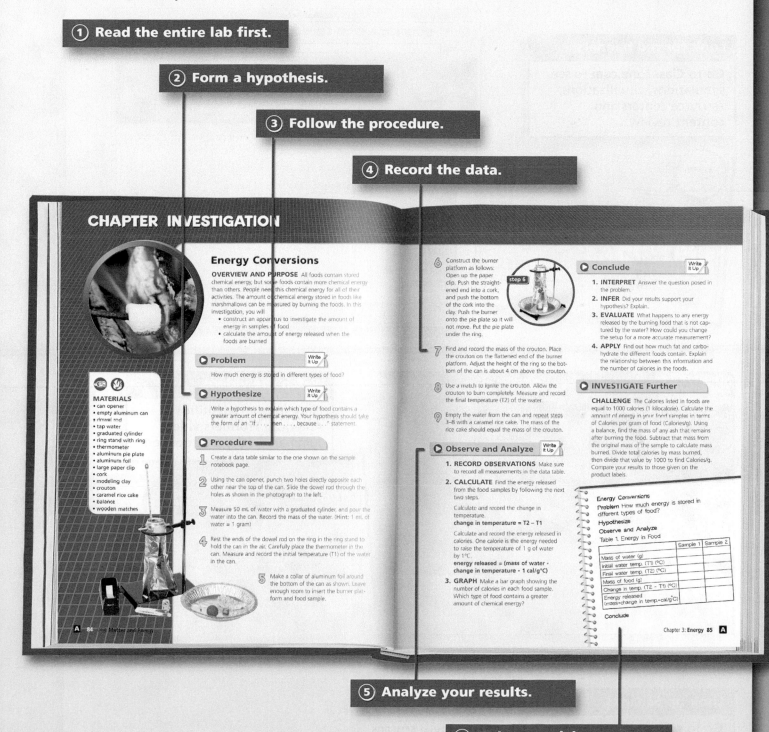

CHAPTER INVESTIGATION

Energy Conversions

OVERVIEW AND PURPOSE All foods contain stored chemical energy, but some foods contain more chemical energy than others. People need this chemical energy for all of their activities. The amount of chemical energy stored in foods like marshmallows can be measured by burning the foods. In this investigation, you will
• construct an apparatus to investigate the amount of energy in samples of food
• calculate the amount of energy released when the foods are burned

▶ Problem   Write It Up

How much energy is stored in different types of food?

▶ Hypothesize   Write It Up

Write a hypothesis to explain which type of food contains a greater amount of chemical energy. Your hypothesis should take the form of an "If . . . , then . . . , because . . ." statement.

▶ Procedure

1. Create a data table similar to the one shown on the sample notebook page.

2. Using the can opener, punch two holes directly opposite each other near the top of the can. Slide the dowel rod through the holes as shown in the photograph to the left.

3. Measure 50 mL of water with a graduated cylinder, and pour the water into the can. Record the mass of the water. (Hint: 1 mL of water = 1 gram)

4. Rest the ends of the dowel rod on the ring in the ring stand to hold the can in the air. Carefully place the thermometer in the can. Measure and record the initial temperature (T1) of the water in the can.

5. Make a collar of aluminum foil around the bottom of the can as shown. Leave enough room to insert the burner platform and food sample.

MATERIALS
• can opener
• empty aluminum can
• dowel rod
• tap water
• graduated cylinder
• ring stand with ring
• thermometer
• aluminum pie plate
• aluminum foil
• large paper clip
• cork
• modeling clay
• crouton
• caramel rice cake
• balance
• wooden matches

6. Construct the burner platform as follows: Open up the paper clip. Push the straightened end into a cork, and push the bottom of the cork into the clay. Push the burner onto the pie plate so it will not move. Put the pie plate under the ring.

step 6

7. Find and record the mass of the crouton. Place the crouton on the flattened end of the burner platform. Adjust the height of the ring so the bottom of the can is about 4 cm above the crouton.

8. Use a match to ignite the crouton. Allow the crouton to burn completely. Measure and record the final temperature (T2) of the water.

9. Empty the water from the can and repeat steps 3–8 with a caramel rice cake. The mass of the rice cake should equal the mass of the crouton.

▶ Observe and Analyze   Write It Up

1. **RECORD OBSERVATIONS** Make sure to record all measurements in the data table.

2. **CALCULATE** Find the energy released from the food samples by following the next two steps.

   Calculate and record the change in temperature.
   change in temperature = T2 – T1

   Calculate and record the energy released in calories. One calorie is the energy needed to raise the temperature of 1 g of water by 1°C.
   energy released = (mass of water · change in temperature · 1 cal/g°C)

3. **GRAPH** Make a bar graph showing the number of calories in each food sample. Which type of food contains a greater amount of chemical energy?

▶ Conclude   Write It Up

1. **INTERPRET** Answer the question posed in the problem.

2. **INFER** Did your results support your hypothesis? Explain.

3. **EVALUATE** What happens to any energy released by the burning food that is not captured by the water? How could you change the setup for a more accurate measurement?

4. **APPLY** Find out how much fat and carbohydrate the different foods contain. Explain the relationship between this information and the number of calories in the foods.

▶ INVESTIGATE Further

CHALLENGE The Calories listed in foods are equal to 1000 calories (1 kilocalorie). Calculate the amount of energy in your food samples in terms of Calories per gram of food (Calories/g). Using a balance, find the mass of any ash that remains after burning the food. Subtract that mass from the original mass of the sample to calculate mass burned. Divide total calories by mass burned, then divide that value by 1000 to find Calories/g. Compare your results to those given on the product labels.

Energy Conversions
Problem How much energy is stored in different types of food?
Hypothesize
Observe and Analyze
Table 1. Energy in Food

	Sample 1	Sample 2
Mass of water (g)		
Initial water temp. (T1) (°C)		
Final water temp. (T2) (°C)		
Mass of food (g)		
Change in temp. (T2 – T1) (°C)		
Energy released (mass·change in temp.·cal/g°C)		

Conclude

⑤ Analyze your results.

⑥ Write your lab report.

Using Technology

The Internet is a great source of information about up-to-date science. The ClassZone Web site and SciLinks have exciting sites for you to explore. Video clips and simulations can make science come alive.

Look for red banners.

Go to **ClassZone.com** to see simulations, visualizations, resource centers and content review.

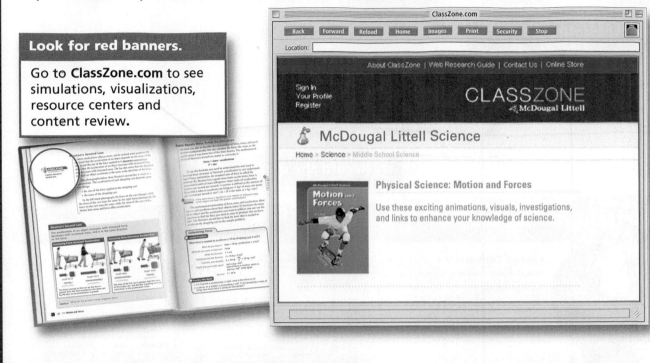

Watch the videos.

Look for the **Scientific American Frontiers video** summary in the unit opener.

Look up SciLinks.

Go to **scilinks.org** to explore the topic.

Forces **Code: MDL005**

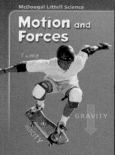

McDougal Littell Science
Motion and Forces

Motion and Forces
Contents Overview

Unit Features

1 Motion   6

the BIG idea

The motion of an object can be
described and predicted.

2 Forces   38

the BIG idea

Forces change the motion of objects
in predictable ways.

3 Gravity, Friction, and Pressure   74

the BIG idea

Newton's laws apply to all forces.

4 Work and Energy   112

the BIG idea

Energy is transferred when a force
moves an object.

5 Machines   142

the BIG idea

Machines help people do work
by changing the force applied to
an object.

ROBOTS on Mars

If you could design a robot to explore Mars, what would you want it to be able to do?

SCIENTIFIC AMERICAN FRONTIERS

Watch the video segment "Teetering to Victory" to learn about a competition that challenges students to use their knowledge of motion and forces to design a machine.

The surface of Mars looks rocky and barren today, but scientists have long wondered if life might have existed on Mars long ago. That would have been possible only if Mars once had water, which is necessary for all forms of life.

NASA's Mars Exploration Rover (MER) shown in a computer-simulated Martian landscape

Searching for Water

We know that Mars is now a cold, dry world, but was that always true? Images from spacecraft in orbit around Mars show land formations that seem to be dried-up lakes and riverbeds. Was Mars more like Earth in the past, warmer and wetter than it is today? We know water is a necessary ingredient for life on Earth. Could a warmer and wetter Mars have also supported life? To answer these questions, in 2003 NASA launched two robotic rovers. They would take six months to reach Mars. The first rover, named *Spirit*, was sent to a crater that looked like a dried-up lake. The second rover, named *Opportunity*, was launched about a month later. *Opportunity*'s landing site was chosen because it contained the mineral hematite, which usually forms in water.

Robot Geologists

To discover the history of water on Mars, *Spirit* and *Opportunity* would have to do the work of a human geologist. They were well equipped to navigate Mars and find interesting spots. Each rover has eight cameras which are used to avoid rocks and make detailed color images of its surroundings. Six-wheel drive gives them solid traction in the sandy Martian soil. Once a rover spots an interesting rock, it can analyze the rock using its RAT (rock abrasion tool) to grind away the rock's surface. The rover can then take a closer look with its microscopic imager, or use its other scientific instruments to see what the rock is made of.

Spirit's Mission

Spirit landed safely on Mars in January 2004. Based on the orbital images, it looked as if the landing site might once have been a lake. *Spirit* soon determined that this could not have been the case. The soil contained volcanic minerals that are destroyed even by small amounts of water. There could not have been a significant amount of water at this spot for a very long time. Perhaps the rocks at a different location would tell a different story. The most promising location was a geologic feature named Columbia Hills, but it was 2.7 kilometers away.

Could the rover drive that far? On average, *Spirit* was able to drive 60 meters each sol. A sol is a Martian day, about 40 minutes longer than an Earth day. The time the rover would take to reach the hills can be found by dividing the distance by the average speed—2700 meters divided by 60 meters per sol, which equals 45 sols. The distance was within the rover's range, and *Spirit* accomplished the journey. Once there, *Spirit* found older rocks with a different history. These rocks did indeed show evidence that there had been some liquid water in the past—but not very large amounts.

This rock, nicknamed El Capitan, shows rippled layering and embedded "blueberries." El Capitan provided evidence that Mars contained an ancient sea.

Opportunity's Mission

In an incredible stroke of luck, *Opportunity* landed in a small crater that was only 22 meters across. Craters form when a meteorite crashes into the surface of a planet. The resulting hole exposes layers of rock that would normally be hard to reach. When *Opportunity*'s first images were transmitted back to Earth, it became clear just how lucky the landing was. The images showed layered rocks and small round pebbles. The scientists called these round rocks blueberries.

SCIENTIFIC AMERICAN FRONTIERS

View the "Teetering to Victory" segment of your Scientific American Frontiers video to learn how some students solved a robotic design challenge.

IN THIS SCENE FROM THE VIDEO ▶
MIT students prepare to test their machines.

BATTLE OF MACHINES Each year more than 100 engineering students at the Massachusetts Institute of Technology (MIT) compete in a contest to see who can design and build the best machine. The challenge this time is to build a machine that starts out sitting on a teeter-totter beam and within 45 seconds manages to tilt its end down against an opponent trying to do the same thing.

Just as the Mars rover designers had to consider the constraints of space travel and Mars' harsh environment, the students had constraints on their designs. They all started with the same kit of materials, and their finished machines had to weigh less than 10 pounds as well as fit inside the box the materials came in. Within these constraints, the student designers came up with an amazing variety of solutions.

Upon closer examination, scientists saw ripples in the rock layers. After a month of exploration, it was determined that the layered rocks, the blueberries, and the large amount of salts in the rocks all meant that this spot had once been a salty sea. *Opportunity* had made the discovery that it had been sent to Mars to make. Mars did have liquid water in the past.

Having made that discovery, *Opportunity* still had more work to do. Unfortunately, it failed in its first attempt to drive out of the crater. It is hard for the rovers to drive up a steep crater wall. When a surface is flat, gravity pushes the rover against the surface, which gives the tires a better grip on the surface. When the crater is steep, however, the rover must use its own force to balance the downward pull of gravity. Also, the tires are more likely to slip. On its second try, *Opportunity* followed a shallower route out of the crater and was successful in climbing out.

They Keep Going and Going . . .

Spirit and *Opportunity* had been designed to last only 90 sols, but they were still going as late as December 2005. In addition to exploring hills and craters, they provided data for movies of dust devils, found a small iron meteorite, and investigated parts of the spacecraft discarded during landing. The more the rovers explore, the more their information prepares us for the day when explorers on Mars will include not only robots but people as well.

UNANSWERED Questions

As scientists learn more and more about Mars, new questions always arise.

- What role, if any, did water, wind, or volcanoes play in shaping the landscape of Mars?
- Were the conditions necessary to support life ever present on Mars?
- Could there be bacteria-like life forms surviving below the surface of Mars today?

UNIT PROJECTS

As you study this unit, work alone or with a group on one of these projects.

Build a Mechanical Arm (8.2.b)

Design and build a mechanical arm to perform a simple task.

- Plan and sketch an arm that could lift a pencil from the floor at a distance of one meter.
- Collect materials and assemble your arm.
- Conduct trials and improve your design.

Multimedia Presentation (8.2.g)

Create an informative program on the forces involved in remote exploration.

- Collect information about the Mars rover mission or a similar expedition.
- Learn how engineers use air resistance, gravity, and rocket thrusters to maneuver the orbiter close to the planet and its moons.
- Give a presentation describing what you learned, using mixed media, such as a computer slide show and a model.

Design an Experiment (8.2.a)

Design an experiment to determine the pressure needed to crush a small object.

- Select a small object, such as a vitamin C tablet, to use in your experiment.
- Collect other materials of your choosing.
- Plan and conduct a procedure to test the pressure required to crush the object. Vary the procedure until you can crush the object using the least amount of force.

CAREER CENTER
CLASSZONE.COM

Learn more about careers in physics and engineering.

1 Motion

the BIG idea

The motion of an object can be described and predicted.

Where will these people be in a few seconds? How do you know?

Key Concepts

Internet Preview

CLASSZONE.COM

Chapter 1 online resources: Content Review, Visualization, Simulation, two Resource Centers, Math Tutorial, Test Practice

Off the Wall

Roll a rubber ball toward a wall. Record the time from the starting point to the wall. Change the distance between the wall and the starting point. Adjust the speed at which you roll the ball until it takes the same amount of time to hit the wall as before.

Observe and Think How did the speed of the ball over the longer distance compare with the speed over the shorter distance?

Rolling Along

Make a ramp by leaning the edge of one book on two other books. Roll a marble up the ramp. Repeat several times and notice what happens each time.

Observe and Think How does the speed of the marble change? At what point does its direction of motion change?

Internet Activity: Relative Motion

Go to **ClassZone.com** to examine motion from different points of view. Learn how your motion makes a difference in what you observe.

Observe and Think How does the way you see motion depend on your point of view?

NSTA
scilinks.org
SCiLINKS

Velocity **Code: MDL004**

Getting Ready to Learn

◀ CONCEPT REVIEW

- Objects can move at different speeds and in different directions.
- Pushing or pulling on an object will change how it moves.

◀ VOCABULARY REVIEW

See Glossary for definitions.

horizontal

meter

second

vertical

ⓘ CONTENT REVIEW
CLASSZONE.COM
Review concepts and vocabulary.

▶ TAKING NOTES

OUTLINE

As you read, copy the headings onto your paper in the form of an outline. Then add notes in your own words that summarize what you read.

VOCABULARY STRATEGY

Place each new vocabulary term at the center of a **description wheel** diagram. As you read about the term, write some words on the spokes describing the term.

See the Note-Taking Handbook on pages R45–R51.

SCIENCE NOTEBOOK

OUTLINE

I. Position describes the location of an object.

　A. Describing a position

　　1. A position is compared to a reference point.

　　2. Position can be described using distance and direction.

can change
with time   **MOTION**   is a change
in position

KEY CONCEPT

An object in motion changes position.

1.1

◀ **BEFORE,** you learned

- Objects can move in different ways
- An object's position can change

▶ **NOW,** you will learn

- How to describe an object's position
- How to describe an object's motion

VOCABULARY

position p. 9
reference point p. 10
motion p. 11

EXPLORE Location

How do you describe the location of an object?

PROCEDURE

① Choose an object in the classroom that is easy to see.

② Without pointing to, describing, or naming the object, give directions to a classmate for finding it.

③ Ask your classmate to identify the object using your directions. If your classmate does not correctly identify the object, try giving directions in a different way. Continue until your classmate has located the object.

WHAT DO YOU THINK?
What kinds of information must you give another person when you are trying to describe a location?

Position describes the location of an object.

VOCABULARY
Make a description wheel in your notebook for *position*.

Have you ever gotten lost while looking for a specific place? If so, you probably know that accurately describing where a place is can be very important. The **position** of a place or an object is the location of that place or object. Often you describe where something is by comparing its position with where you currently are. You might say, for example, that a classmate sitting next to you is about a meter to your right, or that a mailbox is two blocks south of where you live. Each time you identify the position of an object, you are comparing the location of the object with the location of another object or place.

 CHECK YOUR READING Why do you need to discuss two locations to describe the position of an object?

Describing a Position

You might describe the position of a city based on the location of another city. A location to which you compare other locations is called a **reference point.** You can describe where Santiago, Chile, is from the reference point of the city Brasília, Brazil, by saying that Santiago is about 3000 kilometers (1860 mi) southwest of Brasília.

You can also describe a position using a method that is similar to describing where a point on a graph is located. For example, in the longitude and latitude system, locations are given by two numbers—longitude and latitude. Longitude describes how many degrees east or west a location is from the prime meridian, an imaginary line running north-south through Greenwich, England. Latitude describes how many degrees north or south a location is from the equator, the imaginary circle that divides the northern and southern hemispheres. Having a standard way of describing location, such as longitude and latitude, makes it easier for people to compare locations.

New knowledge

Describing Position

There are several different ways to describe a position.
The way you choose may depend on your reference point.

① **Reference Point: Brasília**

To describe where Santiago is, using Brasília as a reference point, you would need to know how far Santiago is from Brasília and in what direction it is.

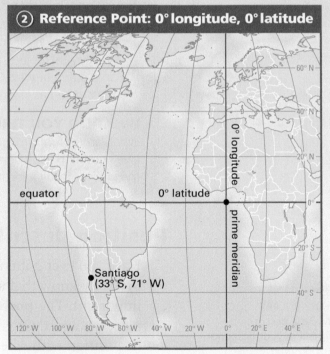

② **Reference Point: 0° longitude, 0° latitude**

In the longitude and latitude system, a location is described by how many degrees north or south it is from the equator and how many degrees east or west it is from the prime meridian.

READING VISUALS Compare and contrast the two ways of describing the location of Santiago as shown here.

Measuring Distance

If you were to travel from Brasília to Santiago, you would end up about 3000 kilometers from where you started. The actual distance you traveled, however, would depend on the exact path you took. If you took a route that had many curves, the distance you traveled would be greater than 3000 kilometers.

The way you measure distance depends on the information you want. Sometimes you want to know the straight-line distance between two positions. Sometimes, however, you might need to know the total length of a certain path between those positions. During a hike, you are probably more interested in how far you have walked than in how far you are from your starting point.

When measuring either the straight-line distance between two points or the length of a path between those points, scientists use a standard unit of measurement. The standard unit of length is the meter (m), which is 3.3 feet. Longer distances can be measured in kilometers (km), and shorter distances in centimeters (cm).

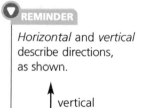

COMPARE How does the distance each person has walked compare with the distance each is from the start of the maze?

those are the same so why is there a difference in opinion

Motion is a change in position.

The illustration below shows an athlete at several positions during a long jump. If you were to watch her jump, you would see that she is in motion. **Motion** is the change of position over time. As she jumps, both her horizontal and vertical positions change. If you missed the motion of the jump, you would still know that motion occurred because of the distance between her starting and ending positions. A change in position is evidence that motion happened.

▼ **REMINDER**

Horizontal and *vertical* describe directions, as shown.

↕ vertical

←→ horizontal

starting position

ending position

How are changes in position observed?

PROCEDURE

SKILL FOCUS
Observing

MATERIALS
• small ball
• paper
• pencil

TIME
20 minutes

1. Begin walking while tossing a ball straight up and catching it as it falls back down toward your hand. Observe the changes in the position of the ball as you toss it while walking a distance of about 4 m.

2. Make a sketch showing how the position of the ball changed as you walked. Use your own position as a reference point for the ball's position.

3. Watch while a classmate walks and tosses the ball. Observe the changes in the position of the ball using your own position as a reference point. Make a sketch showing how the ball moved based on your new point of view.

WHAT DO YOU THINK?

• Compare your two sketches. How was the change in position of the ball you tossed different from the change in position of the ball that your partner tossed?

• How did your change in viewpoint affect what you observed? Explain.

CHALLENGE How would the change in position of the ball appear to a person standing 4 m directly in front of you?

Describing Motion

A change in an object's position tells you that motion took place, but it does not tell you how quickly the object changed position. The speed of a moving object is a measure of how quickly or slowly the object changes position. A faster object moves farther than a slower moving object would in the same amount of time.

The way in which an object moves can change. As a raft moves along a river, its speed changes as the speed of the river changes. When the raft reaches a calm area of the river, it slows down. When the raft reaches rapids, it speeds up. The rafters can also change the motion of the raft by using paddles. You will learn more about speed and changing speed in the following sections.

APPLY Describe the different directions in which the raft is moving.

Relative Motion

If you sit still in a chair, you are not moving. Or are you? The answer depends on the position and motion of the person observing you. You do not notice your position changing compared with the room and the objects in it. But if an observer could leave Earth and look at you from outer space, he could see that you are moving along with Earth as it travels around the Sun. How an observer sees your motion depends on how it compares with his own motion. Just as position is described by using a reference point, motion is described by using a frame of reference. You can think of a frame of reference as the location of an observer, who may be in motion.

Consider a student sitting behind the driver of a moving bus. The bus passes another student waiting at a street sign to cross the street.

① To the observer on the bus, the driver is not changing his position compared with the inside of the bus. The street sign, however, moves past the observer's window. From this observer's point of view, the driver is not moving, but the street sign is.

② To the observer on the sidewalk, the driver is changing position along with the bus. The street sign, on the other hand, is not changing position. From this observer's point of view, the street sign is not moving, but the driver is.

OUTLINE
Add relative motion to your outline, along with supporting details.

I. Main idea
   A. Supporting idea
      1. Detail
      2. Detail
   B. Supporting idea

Relative Motion

An observer on the bus would say that the sign is changing position, but the driver is not.

An observer on the sidewalk would say that the driver is changing position, but the sign is not.

READING VISUALS Describe the motion of an object on a moving bus to both a person on the bus and a person on the sidewalk.

When you ride in a train, a bus, or an airplane, you think of yourself as moving and the ground as standing still. That is, you usually consider the ground as the frame of reference for your motion. If you traveled between two cities, you would say that you had moved, not that the ground had moved under you in the opposite direction.

If you cannot see the ground or objects on it, it is sometimes difficult to tell if a train you are riding in is moving. If the ride is very smooth and you do not look out the window at the scenery, you might never realize you are moving at all.

Suppose you are in a train, and you cannot tell if you are stopped or moving. Outside the window, another train is slowly moving forward. Could you tell which of the following situations is happening?

- Your train is stopped, and the other train is moving slowly forward.

- The other train is stopped, and your train is moving slowly backward.

- Both trains are moving forward, with the other train moving a little faster.

- Your train is moving very slowly backward, and the other train is moving very slowly forward.

Actually, all four of these possibilities would look exactly the same to you. Unless you compared the motion to the motion of something outside the train, such as the ground, you could not tell the difference between these situations.

APPLY In the top picture, the train is moving compared with the camera and the ground. Describe the relative motion of the train, camera, and ground in the bottom picture.

CHECK YOUR READING How does your observation of motion depend on your own motion?

1.1 Review

KEY CONCEPTS

1. What information do you need to describe an object's location?

2. Describe how your position changes as you jump over an object.

3. Give an example of how the apparent motion of an object depends on the observer's motion.

CRITICAL THINKING

4. **Infer** Kyle walks 3 blocks south from his home to school, and Jana walks 2 blocks north from her home to Kyle's home. How far and in what direction is the school from Jana's home?

5. **Predict** If you sit on a moving bus and toss a coin straight up into the air, where will it land?

◐ CHALLENGE

6. **Infer** Jamal is in a car going north. He looks out his window and thinks that the northbound traffic is moving very slowly. Ellen is in a car going south. She thinks the northbound traffic is moving quickly. Explain why Jamal and Ellen have different ideas about the motion of the traffic.

COAST GUARD RESCUE

Physics for Rescuers

Performing a rescue operation is often difficult and risky because the person in trouble is in a dangerous situation. Coast Guard Search and Rescue Teams have an especially difficult problem to deal with. As a rescue ship or helicopter approaches a stranded boat, the team must get close enough to help but avoid making the problem worse by colliding with the boat. At the same time, wind, waves, and currents cause changes in the motion of both crafts.

Finding the Problem

A stranded boater fires a flare to indicate his location. The observer on the Coast Guard ship tracks the motion of the flare to its source.

Avoiding Collision

As the boats move closer together, the captain assesses their motion relative to each other. The speeds of the boats must match, and the boats must be close enough that a rope can be thrown across the gap. If the sea is rough, both boats will move up and down, making the proper positioning even more difficult.

Rescue from Above

The helicopter pilot determines where to hover so that the rescue basket lands on target. A mistake could be disastrous for the rescuers as well as the people being rescued.

EXPLORE

1. **PREDICT** Tie a washer to a 30 cm piece of string. Using your hand as a helicopter, lower the rescue washer to a mark on the floor. Turn on a fan to create wind. Predict where you will need to hold the string to land the washer on the mark. Place the fan at a different location and try again. How accurate was your prediction? Does your accuracy improve with practice?

2. **CHALLENGE** Have a partner throw a baseball into the air from behind the corner of a wall. Using the motion of the ball, try to determine the position from which it was thrown. When is it easier—when the ball is thrown in a high arc or lower one?

1.2 Speed measures how fast position changes.

◀ **BEFORE, you learned**

- An object's position is measured from a reference point
- To describe the position of an object, you can use distance and direction
- An object in motion changes position with time

▶ **NOW, you will learn**

- How to calculate an object's speed
- How to describe an object's velocity

VOCABULARY

speed p. 16
velocity p. 22
vector p. 22

EXPLORE Speed

How can you measure speed?

PROCEDURE

1. Place a piece of tape on the floor. Measure a distance on the floor 2 m away from the tape. Mark this distance with a second piece of tape.

2. Roll a tennis ball from one piece of tape to the other, timing how long it takes to travel the 2 m.

3. Roll the ball again so that it travels the same distance in less time. Then roll the ball so that it takes more time to travel that distance than it did the first time.

WHAT DO YOU THINK?

- How did you change the time it took the ball to travel 2 m?
- How did changing the time affect the motion of the ball?

MATERIALS

- tape
- meter stick
- tennis ball
- stopwatch

Position can change at different rates.

When someone asks you how far it is to the library, you can answer in terms of distance or time. You can say it is several blocks, or you can say it is a five-minute walk. When you give a time instead of a distance, you are basing your time estimate on the distance to the library and the person's speed. **Speed** is a measure of how fast something moves or the distance it moves, in a given amount of time. The greater the speed an object has, the faster it changes position.

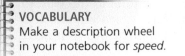

VOCABULARY
Make a description wheel in your notebook for *speed*.

 CHECK YOUR READING   How are speed and position related?

The way in which one quantity changes compared to another quantity is called a rate. Speed is the rate at which the distance an object moves changes compared to time. If you are riding a bike to a movie, and you think you might be late, you increase the rate at which your distance changes by pedaling harder. In other words, you increase your speed.

Calculating Speed

To calculate speed, you need to know both distance and time measurements. Consider the two bike riders below.

1 The two bikes pass the same point at the same time.

2 After one second, the first bike has traveled four meters, while the second has traveled only two meters. Because the first bike has traveled four meters in one second, it has a speed of four meters per second. The second bike has a speed of two meters per second.

3 If each bike continues moving at the same speed as before, then after two seconds the first rider will have traveled eight meters, while the second one will have traveled only four meters.

Comparing Speed

Objects that travel at different speeds move different distances in the same amount of time.

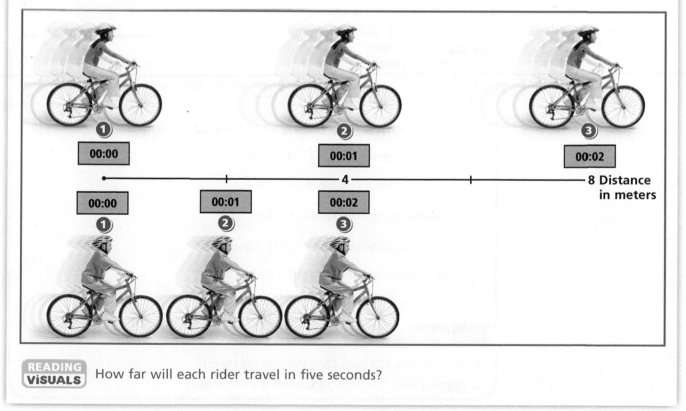

READING VISUALS How far will each rider travel in five seconds?

Racing wheelchairs are specially designed to reach higher speeds than regular wheelchairs.

Speed can be calculated by dividing the distance an object travels by the time it takes to cover the distance. The formula for finding speed is

$$\text{Speed} = \frac{\text{distance}}{\text{time}} \qquad S = \frac{d}{t}$$

Speed is shown in the formula as the letter S, distance as the letter d, and time as the letter t. The formula shows how distance, time, and speed are related. If two objects travel the same distance, the object that took a shorter amount of time will have the greater speed. Similarly, an object with a greater speed will travel a longer distance in the same amount of time than an object with a lower speed will.

The standard unit for speed is meters per second (m/s). Speed is also given in kilometers per hour (km/h). In the United States, where the English system of measurement is still used, speeds are often given in miles per hour (mi/h or mph). One mile per hour is equal to 0.45 m/s.

The man participating in the wheelchair race, at left, will win if his speed is greater than the speed of the other racers. You can use the formula to calculate his speed.

CHECK YOUR READING If two runners cover the same distance in different amounts of time, how do their speeds compare?

Calculating Speed

▶ Sample Problem

A wheelchair racer completes a 100-meter course in 20 seconds. What is his speed?

What do you know?	distance = 100 m, time = 20 s
What do you want to find out?	speed
Write the formula:	$S = \frac{d}{t}$
Substitute into the formula:	$S = \frac{100 \text{ m}}{20 \text{ s}}$
Calculate and simplify:	$S = 5$ m/s
Check that your units agree:	Unit is m/s. Unit of speed is m/s. Units agree.
Answer:	$S = 5$ m/s

▶ Practice the Math

1. A man runs 200 m in 25 s. What is his speed?
2. If you travel 100 m in 50 s, what is your speed?

Average Speed

Speed is not constant. When you run, you might slow down to pace yourself, or speed up to win a race. At each point as you are running, you have a specific speed. This moment-to-moment speed is called your instantaneous speed. Your instantaneous speed can be difficult to measure; however, it is easier to calculate your average speed over a distance.

READING TiP

The root of *instantaneous* is *instant,* meaning "moment."

In a long race, runners often want to know their times for each lap so that they can pace themselves. For example, an excellent middle school runner might have the following times for the four laps of a 1600-meter race: 83 seconds, 81 seconds, 79 seconds, 77 seconds. The lap times show the runner is gradually increasing her speed throughout the race.

The total time for the four laps can be used to calculate the runner's average speed for the entire race. The total time is 320 seconds (5 min 20 s) for the entire distance of 1600 meters. The runner's average speed is 1600 meters divided by 320 seconds, or 5.0 meters per second.

INVESTIGATE Speed and Distance

How does design affect speed?

Cars are built in different shapes. How does the shape of the car affect the way it moves? Design your own car, and see how fast it can go.

DESIGN
— YOUR OWN —
EXPERIMENT

PROCEDURE

(1) Use the clay, film container lids, and toothpicks to design a car that rolls when it is pushed. The car should have a total mass of 150 g or less.

(2) Using any or all of the other materials, design an experiment to measure and compare the speed of your car with the speed of someone else's car. Your experiment should be designed so that the design of the car is the only variable being tested. Write up your procedure.

(3) Perform the experiment using your car and another student's car. Record the data you need to calculate the speed of both cars.

(4) Calculate the speed of each car, and record which car went faster.

WHAT DO YOU THINK?

- What were the constants in your experiment?
- How would you improve your design if you were to repeat the experiment?

SKILL FOCUS
Designing experiments

MATERIALS
- clay
- film container lids
- toothpicks
- beam balance
- board
- books
- string
- straw
- scissors
- stopwatch

TIME
20 minutes

Distance-Time Graphs

A convenient way to show the motion of an object is by using a graph that plots the distance the object has traveled against time. This type of graph, called a distance-time graph, shows how speed relates to distance and time. You can use a distance-time graph to see how both distance and speed change with time.

The distance-time graph on page 21 tracks the changing motion of a zebra. At first the zebra looks for a spot to graze. Its meal is interrupted by a lion, and the zebra starts running to escape.

In a distance-time graph, time is on the horizontal axis, or *x*-axis, and distance is on the vertical axis, or *y*-axis.

1 As an object moves, the distance it travels increases with time. This can be seen as a climbing, or rising, line on the graph.

2 A flat, or horizontal, line shows an interval of time where the speed is zero meters per second.

3 Steeper lines show intervals where the speed is greater than intervals with less steep lines.

You can use a distance-time graph to determine the speed of an object. The steepness, or slope, of the line is calculated by dividing the change in distance by the change in time for that time interval.

REMINDER

The *x*-axis and *y*-axis are arranged as shown:

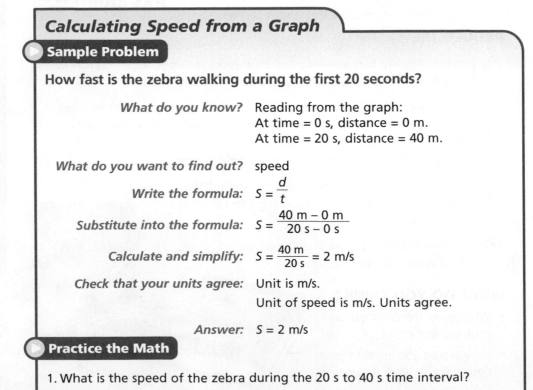

Calculating Speed from a Graph

▶ Sample Problem

How fast is the zebra walking during the first 20 seconds?

What do you know?	Reading from the graph: At time = 0 s, distance = 0 m. At time = 20 s, distance = 40 m.
What do you want to find out?	speed
Write the formula:	$S = \dfrac{d}{t}$
Substitute into the formula:	$S = \dfrac{40 \text{ m} - 0 \text{ m}}{20 \text{ s} - 0 \text{ s}}$
Calculate and simplify:	$S = \dfrac{40 \text{ m}}{20 \text{ s}} = 2 \text{ m/s}$
Check that your units agree:	Unit is m/s. Unit of speed is m/s. Units agree.
Answer:	$S = 2 \text{ m/s}$

▶ Practice the Math

1. What is the speed of the zebra during the 20 s to 40 s time interval?
2. What is the speed of the zebra during the 40 s to 60 s interval?

Distance-Time Graph

A zebra's speed will change throughout the day, especially if a hungry lion is nearby. You can use a distance-time graph to compare the zebra's speed over different time intervals.

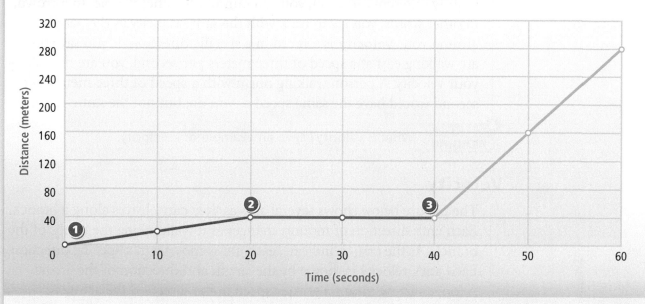

1 When the zebra is walking, its distance from its starting point increases. You can see this motion on the graph as a climbing line.

2 When the zebra stops to graze, it no longer changes its distance from the starting point. Time, however, continues to pass. Therefore, the graph shows a flat, or horizontal, line.

3 As soon as the zebra notices the lion, it stops grazing and starts to run for its life. The zebra is covering a greater distance in each time interval than it was before the chase started, so the line is steeper.

READING VISUALS   How do the distances change over each 10-second time interval?

Velocity includes speed and direction.

Sometimes the direction of motion is as important as its speed. In large crowds, for example, you probably always try to walk in the same direction the crowd is moving and at the same speed. If you walk in even a slightly different direction, you can bump into other people. In a crowd, in other words, you try to walk with the same velocity as the people around you. **Velocity** is a speed in a specific direction. If you say you are walking east at a speed of three meters per second, you are describing your velocity. A person walking north with a speed of three meters per second would have the same speed as you do, but not the same velocity.

CHECK YOUR READING What is velocity? Give an example of a velocity.

Velocity

The picture below shows several ants as they carry leaves along a branch. Each ant's direction of motion changes as it walks along the bends of the branch. As the arrows indicate, each ant is moving in a specific direction. Each ant's velocity is shown by the length and direction of the arrow. A longer arrow means a greater speed in the direction the arrow is pointing. In this picture, for example, the ant moving up the branch is traveling more slowly than the ant moving down the branch.

To determine the velocity of an ant as it carries a leaf, you need to know both its speed and its direction. A change in either speed or direction results in a change in velocity. For example, the velocity of an ant changes if it slows down but continues moving in the same direction. Velocity also changes if the ant continues moving at the same speed but changes direction.

Velocity is an example of a vector. A **vector** is a quantity that has both size and direction. Speed is not a vector because speed is a measure of how fast or slow an object moves, not which direction it moves in. Velocity, however, has a size—the speed—and a direction, so it is a vector quantity.

READING TiP

Green arrows show velocity.

A longer arrow indicates a faster speed than a shorter arrow. The direction of the arrow indicates the direction of motion.

ant moving slowly upward

ant moving quickly downward

INFER How does this ant's velocity compare with those of the other ants?

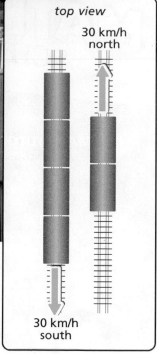

top view

30 km/h
north

30 km/h
south

INFER How do the speeds and velocities of these trains compare?

Velocity Versus Speed

Because velocity includes direction, it is possible for two objects to have the same speed but different velocities. If you traveled by train to visit a friend, you might go 30 kilometers per hour (km/h) north on the way there and 30 km/h south on the way back. Your speed is the same both going and coming back, but your velocity is different because your direction of motion has changed.

Another difference between speed and velocity is the way the average is calculated. Your average speed depends on the total distance you have traveled. The average velocity depends on the total distance you are from where you started. Going north, your average speed would be 30 km/h, and your average velocity would be 30 km/h north. After the round trip ride, your average traveling speed would still be 30 km/h. Your average velocity, however, would be 0 km/h because you ended up exactly where you started.

CHECK YOUR READING Use a Venn diagram to compare and contrast speed and velocity.

1.2 Review

KEY CONCEPTS

1. How is speed related to distance and time?

2. How would decreasing the time it takes you to run a certain distance affect your speed?

3. What two things do you need to know to describe the velocity of an object?

CRITICAL THINKING

4. **Compare** Amy and Ellie left school at the same time. Amy lives farther away than Ellie, but she and Ellie arrived at their homes at the same time. Compare the girls' speeds.

5. **Calculate** Carlos lives 100 m away from his friend's home. What is his average speed if he reaches his friend's home in 50 s?

⊙ CHALLENGE

6. **Synthesize** If you watch a train go by at 20 m/s, at what speed will the people sitting on the train be moving relative to you? Would someone walking toward the back of the train have a greater or lesser speed relative to you? Explain.

MATH TUTORIAL
CLASSZONE.COM
Click on Math Tutorial for
more help with units and rates.

A cheetah can reach a speed
of 30 meters per second, but
only in short bursts.

Time, Distance, and Speed

If someone tells you the store is "five" from the school, you would probably ask, "Five what? Five meters? Five blocks?" You typically describe a distance using standard units of measurement, such as meters, miles, or kilometers. By using units, you help other people understand exactly what your measurement means.

When you work with a formula, the numbers that you substitute into the formula have units. When you calculate with a number, you also calculate with the unit associated with that number.

Example

A cheetah runs at a speed of 30 meters per second. How long does the cheetah take to run 90 meters?

The formula for time in terms of speed and distance is

$$\text{time} = \frac{\text{distance}}{\text{Speed}} \qquad t = \frac{d}{S}$$

(1) Start by substituting the numbers into the formula. Include the units with the numbers.

$$t = \frac{90 \text{ m}}{30 \text{ m/s}}$$

(2) When the units or calculations include fractions, write out the units as fractions as well:

$$t = \frac{90 \text{ m}}{\frac{30 \text{ m}}{\text{s}}}$$

(3) Do the calculation and simplify the units by cancellation:

$$t = 90 \text{ m} \cdot \frac{\text{s}}{30 \text{ m}} = \frac{90}{30} \cdot \frac{\text{m} \cdot \text{s}}{\text{m}} = 3 \cdot \frac{\text{m} \cdot \text{s}}{\text{m}} = 3 \text{ s}$$

ANSWER 3 seconds

Note that the answer has a unit of time. Use the units to check that your answer is reasonable. An answer that is supposed to have a unit of time, for example, should not have a unit of distance.

Answer the following questions.

1. How long would it take an object traveling 12 m/s to go 60 m? What unit of time is your answer in?

2. If a car travels 60 km/h, how long would it take the car to travel 300 km? What unit of time is your answer in?

3. If a man walks 3 miles in 1 hour, what is his speed? What unit of speed is your answer in? (Use the formula on page 18.)

CHALLENGE Show that the formula *distance = speed • time* has a unit for distance on both sides of the equal sign.

Acceleration measures how fast velocity changes.

◀ BEFORE, you learned	▶ NOW, you will learn
• Speed describes how far an object travels in a given time	• How acceleration is related to velocity
• Velocity is a measure of the speed and direction of motion	• How to calculate acceleration

VOCABULARY

acceleration p. 25

THINK ABOUT

How does velocity change?

The photograph at right shows the path that a bouncing ball takes. The time between each image of the ball is the same during the entire bounce. Is the ball moving the same distance in each time interval? Is the ball moving the same direction in each time interval?

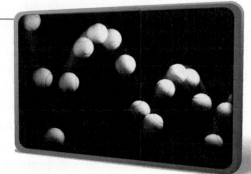

Speed and direction can change with time.

OUTLINE

Remember to use the blue and red headings in this chapter to help you make notes on acceleration.

I. Main idea
  A. Supporting idea
    1. Detail
    2. Detail
  B. Supporting idea

When you throw a ball into the air, it leaves your hand at a certain speed. As the ball rises, it slows down. Then, as the ball falls back toward the ground, it speeds up again. When the ball hits the ground, its direction of motion changes and it bounces back up into the air. The speed and direction of the ball do not stay the same as the ball moves. The ball's velocity keeps changing.

You can find out how much an object's position changes during a certain amount of time if you know its velocity. In a similar way, you can measure how an object's velocity changes with time. The rate at which velocity changes with time is called **acceleration.** Acceleration is a measure of how quickly the velocity is changing. If velocity does not change, there is no acceleration.

Important Information icon

 CHECK YOUR READING What is the relationship between velocity and acceleration?

The word *acceleration* is commonly used to mean "speeding up." In physics, however, acceleration refers to any change in velocity. A driver slowing down to stop at a light is accelerating. A runner turning a corner at a constant speed is also accelerating because the direction of her velocity is changing as she turns.

Like velocity, acceleration is a vector, which means it has both size and direction. The direction of the acceleration determines whether an object will slow down, speed up, or turn.

READING TiP

Orange arrows are used to show acceleration.

Remember that green arrows show velocity.

A longer arrow means greater acceleration or velocity.

① Acceleration in the Same Direction as Motion When the acceleration is in the same direction as the object is moving, the speed of the object increases. The car speeds up.

② Acceleration in the Opposite Direction of Motion When the acceleration is opposite to the motion, the speed of the object decreases. The car slows down. Slowing down is also called negative acceleration.

③ Acceleration at a Right Angle to Motion When the acceleration is at a right angle to the motion, the direction of motion changes. The car changes the direction in which it is moving by some angle, but its speed does not change.

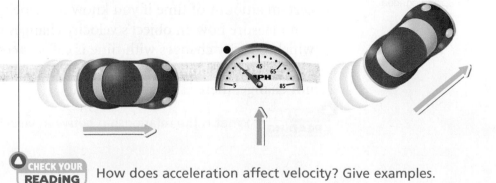

CHECK YOUR READING How does acceleration affect velocity? Give examples.

INVESTIGATE Acceleration

When does an object accelerate?

PROCEDURE

1. Use the template and materials to construct an acceleration measuring tool.

2. Hold the tool in your right hand so that the string falls over the 0 m/s^2 mark. Move the tool in the direction of the arrow. Try to produce both positive and negative acceleration without changing the direction of motion.

3. With the arrow pointing ahead of you, start to walk. Observe the motion of the string while you increase your speed.

4. Repeat step 3, but this time observe the string while slowing down.

5. Repeat step 3 again, but observe the string while walking at a steady speed.

WHAT DO YOU THINK?

• When could you measure an acceleration?

• What was the largest acceleration (positive or negative) that you measured?

CHALLENGE If you moved the acceleration measuring tool backward, how would the measuring scale change?

Acceleration can be calculated from velocity and time.

Suppose you are racing a classmate. In one second, you go from standing still to running at six meters per second. In the same time, your classmate goes from standing still to running at three meters per second. How does your acceleration compare with your classmate's acceleration? To measure acceleration, you need to know how velocity changes with time.

• The change in velocity can be found by comparing the initial velocity and the final velocity of the moving object.

• The time interval over which the velocity changed can be measured.

In one second, you increase your velocity by six meters per second, and your friend increases her velocity by three meters per second. Because your velocity changes more, you have a greater acceleration during that second of time than your friend does. Remember that acceleration measures the change in velocity, not velocity itself. As long as your classmate increases her current velocity by three meters per second, her acceleration will be the same whether she is going from zero to three meters per second or from three to six meters per second.

Calculating Acceleration

If you know the starting velocity of an object, the final velocity, and the time interval during which the object changed velocity, you can calculate the acceleration of the object. The formula for acceleration is shown below.

$$\textbf{acceleration} = \frac{\textbf{final velocity} - \textbf{initial velocity}}{\textbf{time}}$$

$$a = \frac{v_{final} - v_{initial}}{t}$$

Remember that velocity is expressed in units of meters per second. The standard units for acceleration, therefore, are meters per second over time, or meters per second per second. This is simplified to meters per second squared, which is written as m/s^2.

As the girl in the photograph at left sleds down the sandy hill, what happens to her velocity? At the bottom of the hill, her velocity will be greater than it was at the top. You can calculate her average acceleration down the hill if you know her starting and ending velocities and how long it took her to get to the bottom. This calculation is shown in the sample problem below.

Calculating Acceleration

Sample Problem

Ama starts sliding with a velocity of 1 m/s. After 3 s, her velocity is 7 m/s. What is Ama's acceleration?

What do you know?   initial velocity = 1 m/s, final velocity = 7 m/s, time = 3 s

What do you want to find out?   acceleration

Write the formula: $a = \dfrac{v_{final} - v_{initial}}{t}$

Substitute into the formula: $a = \dfrac{7 \text{ m/s} - 1 \text{ m/s}}{3 \text{ s}}$

Calculate and simplify: $a = \dfrac{6 \text{ m/s}}{3 \text{ s}} = 2 \dfrac{m/s}{s} = 2 \text{ m/s}^2$

Check that your units agree: $\dfrac{m/s}{s} = \dfrac{m}{s} \cdot \dfrac{1}{s} = \dfrac{m}{s^2}$

Unit of acceleration is m/s^2. Units agree.

Answer: $a = 2 \text{ m/s}^2$

Practice the Math

1. A man walking at 0.5 m/s accelerates to a velocity of 0.6 m/s in 1 s. What is his acceleration?

2. A train traveling at 10 m/s slows down to a complete stop in 20 s. What is the acceleration of the train?

The sledder's final velocity was greater than her initial velocity. If an object is slowing down, on the other hand, the final velocity is less than the initial velocity. Suppose a car going 10 meters per second takes 2 seconds to stop for a red light. In this case, the initial velocity is 10 m/s and the final velocity is 0 m/s. The formula for acceleration gives a negative answer, -5 m/s^2. The negative sign indicates a negative acceleration—that is, an acceleration that decreases the velocity.

RESOURCE CENTER
CLASSZONE.COM
Learn more about acceleration.

 CHECK YOUR READING What would be true of the values for initial velocity and final velocity if the acceleration were zero?

Acceleration over Time

Even a very small positive acceleration can lead to great speeds if an object accelerates for a long enough period. In 1998, NASA launched the *Deep Space 1* spacecraft. This spacecraft tested a new type of engine—one that gave the spacecraft an extremely small acceleration. The new engine required less fuel than previous spacecraft engines. However, the spacecraft needed a great deal of time to reach its target velocity.

The acceleration of the *Deep Space 1* spacecraft is less than 2/10,000 of a meter per second per second (0.0002 m/s^2). That may not seem like much, but over 20 months, the spacecraft could increase its speed by 4500 meters per second (10,000 mi/h).

By carefully adjusting both the amount and the direction of the acceleration of *Deep Space 1*, scientists were able to control its flight path. In 2001, the spacecraft successfully flew by a comet, sending back images from about 230 million kilometers (140 million mi) away.

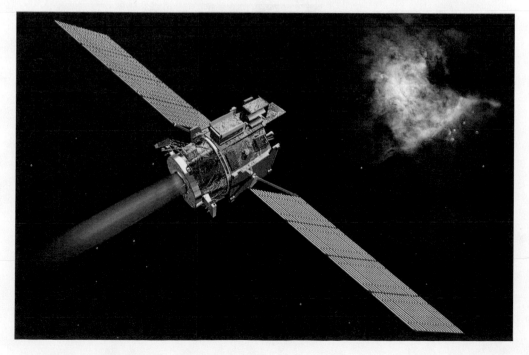

APPLY What makes the new engine technology used by *Deep Space 1* more useful for long-term missions than for short-term ones?

Velocity-Time Graphs

Velocity-time graphs and distance-time graphs are related. This is because the distance an object travels depends on its velocity. Compare the velocity-time graph on the right with the distance-time graph below it.

Velocity-Time Graph

1 As the student starts to push the scooter, his velocity increases. His acceleration is positive, so he moves forward a greater distance with each second that passes.

2 He coasts at a constant velocity. Because his velocity does not change, he has no acceleration, and he continues to move forward the same distance each second.

3 As he slows down, his velocity decreases. His acceleration is negative, and he moves forward a smaller distance with each passing second until he finally stops.

Distance-Time Graph

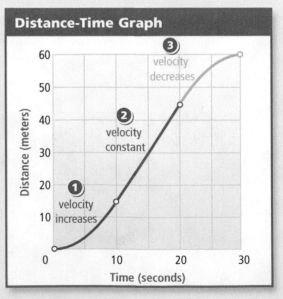

READING VISUALS What velocity does the student have after five seconds? About how far has he moved in that time?

Velocity-Time Graphs

Acceleration, like position and velocity, can change with time. Just as you can use a distance-time graph to understand velocity, you can use a velocity-time graph to understand acceleration. Both graphs tell you how something is changing over time. In a velocity-time graph, time is on the horizontal axis, or x-axis, and velocity is on the vertical axis, or y-axis.

SIMULATION
CLASSZONE.COM

Explore how changing the acceleration of an object changes its motion.

The two graphs on page 30 show a velocity-time graph and a distance-time graph of a student riding on a scooter. He first starts moving and speeds up. He coasts, and then he slows down to a stop.

① The rising line on the velocity-time graph shows where the acceleration is positive. The steeper the line, the greater the acceleration. The distance-time graph for the same interval is curving upward more and more steeply as the velocity increases.

② The flat line on the velocity-time graph shows an interval of no acceleration. The distance-time graph has a straight line during this time, since the velocity is not changing.

③ The falling line on the velocity-time graph shows where the acceleration is negative. The same interval on the distance-time graph shows a curve that becomes less and less steep as the velocity decreases. Notice that the overall distance still increases.

Velocity-time graphs and distance-time graphs can provide useful information. For example, scientists who study earthquakes create these graphs in order to study the up-and-down and side-to-side movement of the ground during an earthquake. They produce the graphs from instruments that measure the acceleration of the ground.

CHECK YOUR READING What does a flat line on a velocity-time graph represent?

1.3 Review

KEY CONCEPTS

1. What measurements or observations tell you that a car is accelerating?

2. If an object accelerates in the same direction in which it is moving, how is its speed affected?

3. What measurements do you need in order to calculate acceleration?

CRITICAL THINKING

4. **Calculate** A car goes from 20 m/s to 30 m/s in 10 seconds. What is its acceleration?

5. **Infer** Two runners start a race. After 2 seconds, they both have the same velocity. If they both started at the same time, how do their average accelerations compare?

◆ CHALLENGE

6. **Analyze** Is it possible for an object that has a constant negative acceleration to change the direction in which it is moving? Explain why or why not.

CHAPTER INVESTIGATION

Acceleration and Slope

OVERVIEW AND PURPOSE When a downhill skier glides down a mountain without using her ski poles, her velocity increases and she experiences acceleration. How would gliding down a hill with a greater slope affect her acceleration? In this investigation you will

- calculate the acceleration of an object rolling down two ramps of different slopes
- determine how the slope of the ramp affects the acceleration of the object

▶ Problem

How does the slope of a ramp affect the acceleration of an object rolling down the ramp?

▶ Hypothesize

Write a hypothesis to explain how changing the slope of the ramp will affect acceleration. Your hypothesis should take the form of an "If . . . , then . . . , because . . ." statement.

▶ Procedure

1. Make a data table like the one shown on the sample notebook page.

2. Make a ramp by laying two meter sticks side by side. Leave a small gap between the meter sticks.

3. Use masking tape as shown in the photograph to join the meter sticks. The marble should be able to roll freely along the groove.

4. Set up your ramp on a smooth, even surface, such as a tabletop. Raise one end of the ramp on top of one of the books. The other end of the ramp should remain on the table.

5. Make a finish line by putting a piece of tape on the tabletop 30 cm from the bottom of the ramp. Place a ruler just beyond the finish line to keep your marble from rolling beyond your work area.

MATERIALS
- 2 meter sticks
- masking tape
- marble
- 2 paperback books
- ruler
- stopwatch
- calculator

6 Test your ramp by releasing the marble from the top of the ramp. Make sure that the marble rolls freely. Do not push on the marble.

7 Release the marble and measure the time it takes for it to roll from the release point to the end of the ramp. Record this time under Column A for trial 1.

8 Release the marble again from the same point, and record the time it takes the marble to roll from the end of the ramp to the finish line. Record this time in Column B for trial 1. Repeat and record three more trials.

9 Raise the height of the ramp by propping it up with both paperback books. Repeat steps 7 and 8.

▶ Observe and Analyze Write It Up

1. **RECORD OBSERVATIONS** Draw the setup of your procedures. Be sure your data table is complete.

2. **IDENTIFY VARIABLES AND CONSTANTS** Identify the variables and constants in the experiment. List them in your notebook.

3. **CALCULATE**

Average Time For ramps 1 and 2, calculate and record the average time it took for the marble to travel from the end of the ramp to the finish line.

Final Velocity For ramps 1 and 2, calculate and record v_{final} using the formula below.

$$v_{final} = \frac{\text{distance from end of ramp to finish line}}{\text{average time from end of ramp to finish line}}$$

Acceleration For ramps 1 and 2, calculate and record acceleration using the formula below. (**Hint:** Speed at the release of the marble is 0 m/s.)

$$a = \frac{v_{final} - v_{initial} \text{ (speed at release)}}{\text{average time from release to bottom of ramp}}$$

▶ Conclude Write It Up

1. **COMPARE** How did the acceleration of the marble on ramp 1 compare with the acceleration of the marble on ramp 2?

2. **INTERPRET** Answer the question posed in the problem.

3. **ANALYZE** Compare your results with your hypothesis. Do your data support your hypothesis?

4. **EVALUATE** Why was it necessary to measure how fast the marble traveled from the end of the ramp to the finish line?

5. **IDENTIFY LIMITS** What possible limitations or sources of error could have affected your results? Why was it important to perform four trials for each measurement of speed?

▶ INVESTIGATE Further

CHALLENGE Design your own experiment to determine how the marble's mass affects its acceleration down a ramp.

Acceleration and Slope

Problem How does the slope of a ramp affect the acceleration of an object rolling down the ramp?

Hypothesize

Observe and Analyze

Table 1. Times for Marble to Travel down Ramp

Height of Ramp (cm)	Trial Number	Column A Time from release to end of ramp	Column B Time from end of ramp to finish line
Ramp 1	1		
	2		
	3		
	4		
	Totals		
		Average	Average

Chapter Review

the **BIG** idea

The motion of an object can be described and predicted.

CONTENT REVIEW
CLASSZONE.COM

KEY CONCEPTS SUMMARY

1.1 An object in motion changes position.

Position is measured from a reference point.

Motion is measured relative to an observer.

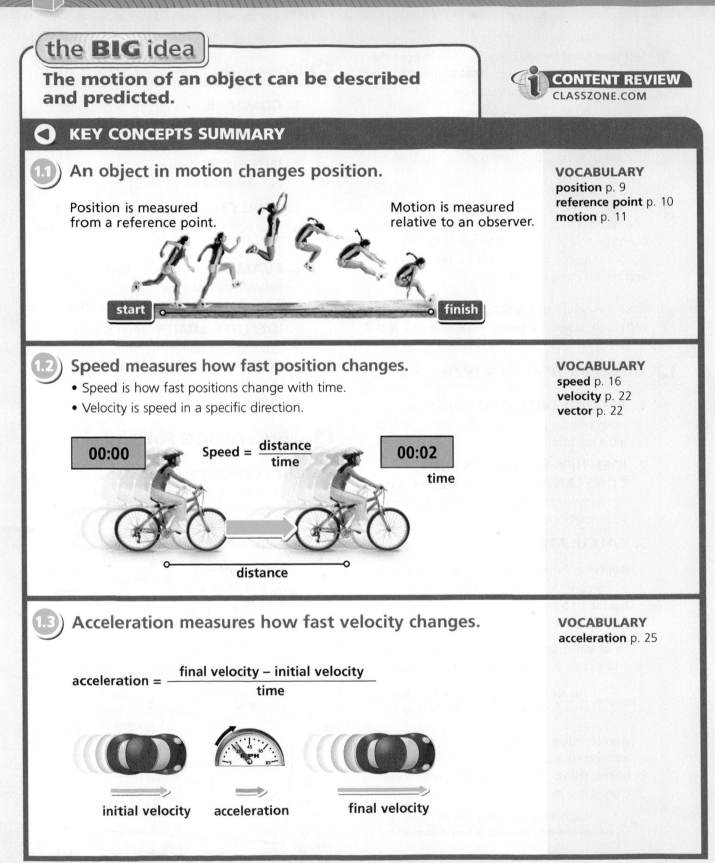

start   finish

VOCABULARY
position p. 9
reference point p. 10
motion p. 11

1.2 Speed measures how fast position changes.

• Speed is how fast positions change with time.
• Velocity is speed in a specific direction.

00:00 $\text{Speed} = \dfrac{\text{distance}}{\text{time}}$ 00:02

time

distance

VOCABULARY
speed p. 16
velocity p. 22
vector p. 22

1.3 Acceleration measures how fast velocity changes.

$$\text{acceleration} = \frac{\text{final velocity} - \text{initial velocity}}{\text{time}}$$

initial velocity   acceleration   final velocity

VOCABULARY
acceleration p. 25

Reviewing Vocabulary

Copy and complete the chart below. If the left column is blank, give the correct term. If the right column is blank, give a brief description.

Term	Description
1.	speed in a specific direction
2.	a change of position over time
3. speed	
4.	an object's location
5. reference point	
6.	the rate at which velocity changes over time
7.	a quantity that has both size and direction

Reviewing Key Concepts

Multiple Choice *Choose the letter of the best answer.*

8. A position describes an object's location compared to
   a. its motion
   b. a reference point
   c. its speed
   d. a vector

9. Maria walked 2 km in half an hour. What was her average speed during her walk?
   a. 1 km/h
   b. 2 km/h
   c. 4 km/h
   d. 6 km/h

10. A vector is a quantity that has
    a. speed
    b. acceleration
    c. size and direction
    d. position and distance

11. Mary and Keisha run with the same constant speed but in opposite directions. The girls have
    a. the same position
    b. different accelerations
    c. different speeds
    d. different velocities

12. A swimmer increases her speed as she approaches the end of the pool. Her acceleration is
    a. in the same direction as her motion
    b. in the opposite direction of her motion
    c. at right angles to her motion
    d. zero

13. A cheetah can go from 0 m/s to 20 m/s in 2 s. What is the cheetah's acceleration?
    a. 5 m/s^2
    b. 10 m/s^2
    c. 20 m/s^2
    d. 40 m/s^2

14. Jon walks for a few minutes, then runs for a few minutes. During this time, his average speed is
    a. the same as his final speed
    b. greater than his final speed
    c. less than his final speed
    d. zero

15. A car traveling at 40 m/s slows down to 20 m/s. During this time, the car has
    a. no acceleration
    b. positive acceleration
    c. negative acceleration
    d. constant velocity

Short Answer *Write a short answer to each question.*

16. Suppose you are biking with a friend. How would your friend describe your relative motion as he passes you?

17. Describe a situation where an object has a changing velocity but constant speed.

18. Give two examples of an accelerating object.

Use the following graph to answer the next three questions.

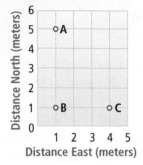

Distance East (meters)

19. **OBSERVE** Describe the location of point A. Explain what you used as a reference point for your location.

20. **COMPARE** Copy the graph into your notebook. Draw two different paths an object could take when moving from point B to point C. How do the lengths of these two paths compare?

21. **ANALYZE** An object moves from point A to point C in the same amount of time that another object moves from point B to point C. If both objects traveled in a straight line, which one had the greater speed?

Read the following paragraph and use the information to answer the next three questions.

In Aesop's fable of the tortoise and the hare, a slow-moving tortoise races a fast-moving hare. The hare, certain it can win, stops to take a long nap. Meanwhile, the tortoise continues to move toward the finish line at a slow but steady speed. When the hare wakes up, it runs as fast as it can. Just as the hare is about to catch up to the tortoise, however, the tortoise wins the race.

22. **ANALYZE** How does the race between the tortoise and the hare show the difference between average speed and instantaneous speed?

23. **MODEL** Assume the racetrack was 100 meters long and the race took 40 minutes. Create a possible distance-time graph for both the tortoise and the hare.

24. **COMPARE** If the racetrack were circular, how would the tortoise's speed be different from its velocity?

25. **APPLY** How might a person use a floating stick to measure the speed at which a river flows?

26. **CONNECT** Describe a frame of reference other than the ground that you might use to measure motion. When would you use it?

27. José skated 50 m in 10 s. What was his speed?

28. Use the information in the photograph below to calculate the speed of the ant as it moves down the branch.

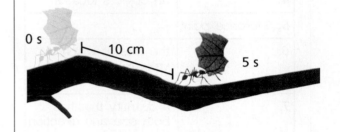

0 s   10 cm   5 s

29. While riding her bicycle, Jamie accelerated from 7 m/s to 2 m/s in 5 s. What was her acceleration?

the BIG idea

30. **PREDICT** Look back at the picture at the beginning of the chapter on pages 6–7. Predict how the velocity of the roller coaster will change in the next moment.

31. **WRITE** A car is traveling east at 40 km/h. Use this information to predict where the car will be in one hour. Discuss the assumptions you made to reach your conclusion and the factors that might affect it.

If you are doing a unit project, make a folder for your project. Include in your folder a list of the resources you will need, the date on which the project is due, and a schedule to keep track of your progress. Begin gathering data.

Interpreting Graphs

The graph below is a distance-time graph showing a 50-meter race.

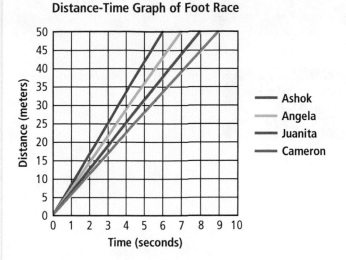

Distance-Time Graph of Foot Race

— Ashok
— Angela
— Juanita
— Cameron

Study the graph and then answer the questions that follow.

1. Which runner reached the finish line first?

   a. Ashok   **c.** Juanita

   b. Angela   **d.** Cameron

2. How far did Juanita run in the first 4 seconds of the race?

   a. 5 m   **c.** 25 m

   b. 15 m   **d.** 35 m

3. How much time passed between the time Angela finished the race and Cameron finished the race?

   a. 1 s   **c.** 3 s

   b. 2 s   **d.** 4 s

4. Which of the following setups would you use to calculate Angela's average speed during the race?

   a. $\dfrac{7 \text{ m}}{50 \text{ s}}$ **c.** $\dfrac{50 \text{ m}}{6 \text{ s}}$

   b. $\dfrac{7 \text{ s}}{50 \text{ m}}$ **d.** $\dfrac{50 \text{ m}}{7 \text{ s}}$

5. What can you say about the speed of all of the runners?

   a. They ran at the same speed.

   b. They ran at a steady pace but at different speeds.

   c. They sped up as they reached the finish line.

   d. They slowed down as they reached the finish line.

Extended Response

Answer the two questions below in detail.

6. Suppose you are biking. What is the difference between your speed at any given moment during your bike ride and your average speed for the entire ride? Which is easier to measure? Why?

7. Suppose you are riding your bike along a path that is also used by in-line skaters. You pass a skater, and another biker passes you, both going in the same direction you're going. You pass a family having a picnic on the grass. Describe your motion from the points of view of the skater, the other biker, and the family.

CHAPTER 2 Forces

the **BIG** idea

Forces change the motion of objects in predictable ways.

What must happen for a team to win this tug of war?

Key Concepts

SECTION
2.1 **Forces change motion.**
Learn about inertia and Newton's first law of motion.

SECTION
2.2 **Force and mass determine acceleration.**
Learn to calculate force through Newton's second law of motion.

SECTION
2.3 **Forces act in pairs.**
Learn about action forces and reaction forces through Newton's third law of motion.

SECTION
2.4 **Forces transfer momentum.**
Learn about momentum and how it is affected in collisions.

Internet Preview

CLASSZONE.COM

Chapter 2 online resources: Content Review, two Simulations, four Resource Centers, Math Tutorial, Test Practice

Popping Ping-Pong Balls

Place a Ping-Pong ball in front of a flexible ruler. Carefully bend the ruler back and then release it. Repeat with a golf ball or another heavier ball. Be sure to bend the ruler back to the same spot each time. Predict which ball will go farther.

Observe and Think
Which ball went farther? Why?

Take Off!

Blow up a balloon and hold the end closed. Tape the balloon to the top of a small model car. (Put the tape around the car and the balloon.) Predict what will happen to the car when you set it down and let go of the balloon. Will the car move? If so, in what direction? How far?

Observe and Think
What happened to the car? If you try it again, will you get the same results? What do you think explains the motion of the car?

Internet Activity: Forces

Go to **ClassZone.com** to change the sizes and directions of forces on an object. Predict how the object will move, and then run the simulation to see if you were right.

Observe and Think What happens if two forces are applied to the object in the same direction? in opposite directions? Why?

NSTA
scilinks.org

SCI
LINKS

Forces **Code: MDL005**

Getting Ready to Learn

◀ CONCEPT REVIEW

- All motion is relative to the position and motion of an observer.
- An object's motion is described by position, direction, speed, and acceleration.
- Velocity and acceleration can be measured.

◀ VOCABULARY REVIEW

velocity p. 22

vector p. 22

acceleration p. 25

mass *See Glossary.*

CONTENT REVIEW

CLASSZONE.COM

Review concepts and vocabulary.

▶ TAKING NOTES

COMBINATION NOTES

When you read about a concept for the first time, take notes in two ways. First, make an outline of the information. Then make a sketch to help you understand and remember the concept. Use arrows to show the direction of forces.

VOCABULARY STRATEGY

Think about a vocabulary term as a **magnet word** diagram. Write the other terms or ideas related to that term around it.

See the Note-Taking Handbook on pages R45–R51.

SCIENCE NOTEBOOK

NOTES

Types of forces
- contact force
- gravity
- friction

forces on a box being pushed

contact force

gravity

friction

FORCE

push

pull

gravity

friction

contact force

2.1 Forces change motion.

> **BEFORE, you learned**
> - The velocity of an object is its change in position over time
> - The acceleration of an object is its change in velocity over time

> **NOW, you will learn**
> - What a force is
> - How unbalanced forces change an object's motion
> - How Newton's first law allows you to predict motion

VOCABULARY

force p. 41
net force p. 43
Newton's first law p. 45
inertia p. 46

EXPLORE Changing Motion

How can you change an object's motion?

PROCEDURE

1. Choose an object from the materials list and change its motion in several ways, from
   - not moving to moving
   - moving to not moving
   - moving to moving faster
   - moving to moving in a different direction

2. Describe the actions used to change the motion.

3. Experiment again with another object. First, decide what you will do; then predict how the motion of the object will change.

WHAT DO YOU THINK?

In step 3, how were you able to predict the motion of the object?

MATERIALS
- quarter
- book
- tennis ball
- cup
- feather

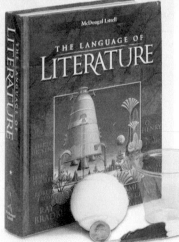

A force is a push or a pull.

> **REMINDER**
>
> Motion is a change in position over time.

Think about what happens during an exciting moment at the ballpark. The pitcher throws the ball across the plate, and the batter hits it high up into the stands. A fan in the stands catches the home-run ball. In this example, the pitcher sets the ball in motion, the batter changes the direction of the ball's motion, and the fan stops the ball's motion. To do so, each must use a **force**, or a push or a pull.

You use forces all day long to change the motion of objects in your world. You use a force to pick up your backpack, to open or close a car door, and even to move a pencil across your desktop. Any time you change the motion of an object, you use a force.

Types of Forces

A variety of forces are always affecting the motion of objects around you. For example, take a look at how three kinds of forces affect the skater in the photograph on the left.

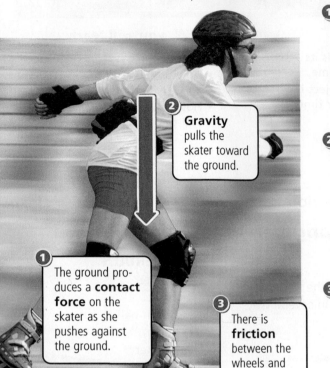

Gravity pulls the skater toward the ground.

The ground produces a **contact force** on the skater as she pushes against the ground.

There is **friction** between the wheels and the ground.

① Contact Force When one object pushes or pulls another object by touching it, the first object is applying a contact force to the second. The skater applies a contact force as she pushes against the ground. The ground applies a contact force that pushes the skater forward.

② Gravity Gravity is the force of attraction between two masses. Earth's gravity is pulling on the skater, holding her to the ground. The strength of the gravitational force between two objects depends on their masses. For example, the pull between you and Earth is much greater than the pull between you and a book.

③ Friction Friction is a force that resists motion between two surfaces that are pressed together. Friction between the surface of the ground and the wheels of the skates exerts a force that resists the skater's forward motion.

You will learn more about gravity and friction in Chapter 3. In this chapter, most of the examples involve contact forces. You use contact forces constantly. Turning a page, pulling a chair, using a pencil to write, pushing your hair away from your eyes—all involve contact forces.

CHECK YOUR READING What is a contact force? Give an example of a contact force.

Size and Direction of Forces

Like velocity, force is a vector. That means that force has both size and direction. For example, think about what happens when you try to make a shot in basketball. To get the ball through the hoop, you must apply the right amount of force to the ball and aim the force in the right direction. If you use too little force, the ball will not reach the basket. If you use too much force, the ball may bounce off the backboard and into your opponent's hands.

In the illustrations in this book, red arrows represent forces. The direction of an arrow shows the direction of the force, and the length of the arrow indicates the amount, or size, of the force. A blue box represents mass.

Balanced and Unbalanced Forces

Considering the size and the direction of all the forces acting on an object allows you to predict changes in the object's motion. The overall force acting on an object when all the forces are combined is called the **net force**.

If the net force on an object is zero, the forces acting on the object are balanced. Balanced forces have the same effect as no force at all. That is, the motion of the object does not change. For example, think about the forces on the basketball when one player attempts a shot and another blocks it. In the photograph below on the left, the players are pushing on the ball with equal force but from opposite directions. The forces on the ball are balanced, and so the ball does not move.

Only an unbalanced force can change the motion of an object. If one of the basketball players pushes with greater force than the other player, the ball will move in the direction that player is pushing. The motion of the ball changes because the forces on the ball become unbalanced.

It does not matter whether the ball started at rest or was already moving. Only an unbalanced force will change the ball's motion.

COMBINATION NOTES
Make an outline and draw a diagram about balanced and unbalanced forces.

balanced forces

unbalanced forces

READING VISUALS **COMPARE** Compare the net force on the balls in these two photographs. Which photograph shows a net force of zero?

Forces on Moving Objects

An object with forces acting on it can be moving at a constant velocity as long as those forces are balanced. For example, if you ride a bike straight ahead at a constant speed, the force moving the bike forward exactly balances the forces of friction that would slow the bike down. If you stop pedaling, the forces are no longer balanced, and frictional forces slow you down until you eventually stop.

Balanced forces cannot change an object's speed or its direction. An unbalanced force is needed to change an object's motion.

- To increase the speed of your bike, you may exert more forward force by pedaling harder or changing gears. The net force moves the bike ahead faster.
- To turn your bike, you apply an unbalanced force by leaning to one side and turning the handlebars.
- To stop the bike, you use the extra force of friction that your bike brakes provide.

CHECK YOUR READING What happens to a moving object if all the forces on it are balanced? Which sentence above tells you?

Newton's first law relates force and motion.

In the mid-1600s, the English scientist Sir Isaac Newton studied the effects of forces on objects. He formulated three laws of motion that are still helping people describe and predict the motions of objects today. Newton's ideas were built on those of other scientists, in particular the Italian scientist Galileo Galilei (gal-uh-LEE-oh gal-uh-LAY). Both Galileo and Newton overturned thinking that had been accepted since the times of the ancient Greek philosophers.

The ancient Greeks had concluded that it was necessary to apply a continuous force to keep an object in motion. For example, if you set a book on a table and give the book a quick push, the book slides a short way and then stops. To keep the book moving, you need to keep pushing it. The Greeks reasoned that the book stops moving because you stop pushing it.

Galileo's Thought Experiment

In the early 1600s, Galileo suggested a different way of interpreting such observations. He imagined a world without friction and conducted a thought experiment in this ideal world. He concluded that, in the absence of friction, a moving object will continue moving even if there is no force acting on it. In other words, it does not take a force to keep an object moving; it takes a force—friction—to stop an object that is already moving.

READING TIP

Contrast the last sentence of this paragraph with the last sentence of the previous paragraph.

Objects at rest and objects in motion both resist changes in motion. That is, objects at rest tend to stay at rest, and objects that are moving tend to continue moving unless a force acts on them. Galileo reasoned there was no real difference between an object that is moving at a constant velocity and an object that is standing still. An object at rest is simply an object with zero velocity.

CHECK YOUR READING How were Galileo's ideas about objects in motion different from the ideas of the ancient Greeks?

Newton's First Law

Newton restated Galileo's conclusions as his first law of motion. **Newton's first law** states that objects at rest remain at rest, and objects in motion remain in motion with the same velocity, unless acted upon by an unbalanced force. You can easily observe the effects of unbalanced forces, both on the ball at rest and the ball in motion, in the pictures below.

Newton's First Law

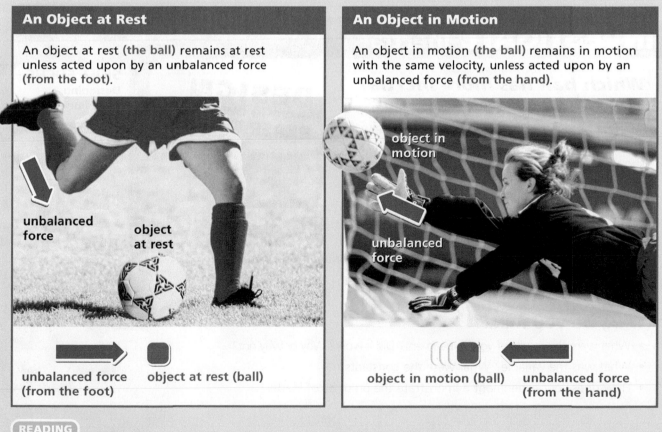

Objects at rest remain at rest, and objects in motion remain in motion with the same velocity, unless acted upon by an unbalanced force.

An Object at Rest

An object at rest (the ball) remains at rest unless acted upon by an unbalanced force (from the foot).

unbalanced force

object at rest

unbalanced force (from the foot)   object at rest (ball)

An Object in Motion

An object in motion (the ball) remains in motion with the same velocity, unless acted upon by an unbalanced force (from the hand).

object in motion

unbalanced force

object in motion (ball)   unbalanced force (from the hand)

READING VISUALS What will happen to the ball's motion in each picture? Why?

You will find many examples of Newton's first law around you. For instance, if you throw a stick for a dog to catch, you are changing the motion of the stick. The dog changes the motion of the stick by catching it and by dropping it at your feet. You change the motion of a volleyball when you spike it, a tennis racket when you swing it, a paintbrush when you make a brush stroke, and an oboe when you pick it up to play or set it down after playing. In each of these examples, you apply a force that changes the motion of the object.

Inertia

Inertia (ih-NUR-shuh) is the resistance of an object to a change in the speed or the direction of its motion. Newton's first law, which describes the tendency of objects to resist changes in motion, is also called the law of inertia. Inertia is closely related to mass. When you measure the mass of an object, you are also measuring its inertia. You know from experience that it is easier to push or pull an empty box than it is to push or pull the same box when it is full of books. Likewise, it is easier to stop or to turn an empty wagon than to stop or turn a wagon full of sand. In both of these cases, it is harder to change the motion of the object that has more mass.

INVESTIGATE Inertia

Which ball has more inertia?

Two balls have different masses and therefore different amounts of inertia. Use what you know about force and inertia to design an experiment that shows which ball has more inertia. Your procedure cannot include lifting the balls, weighing the balls, or touching the balls with your hands.

DESIGN — YOUR OWN — EXPERIMENT

PROCEDURE

1. Figure out how to use the meter stick or other materials to compare the inertia of the two balls.

2. Write up your procedure.

3. Test your procedure.

WHAT DO YOU THINK?

- What were the results of your experiment? Did it work? Why or why not?
- What was the variable? What were the constants?
- How does your experiment demonstrate the property of inertia?

SKILL FOCUS
Designing experiments

MATERIALS
- 2 balls of unknown masses
- string
- block
- meter stick

TIME
30 minutes

Inertia is the reason that people in cars need to wear seat belts. A moving car has inertia, and so do the riders inside it. When the driver applies the brakes, an unbalanced force is applied to the car. Normally, the bottom of the seat applies an unbalanced force—friction—which slows the riders down as the car slows. If the driver stops the car suddenly, however, this force is not exerted over enough time to stop the motion of the riders. Instead, the riders continue moving forward with most of their original speed because of their inertia.

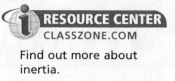
RESOURCE CENTER
CLASSZONE.COM
Find out more about inertia.

① As a car moves forward, the driver—shown here as a crash-test dummy—moves forward with the same velocity as the car.

② When the driver hits the brakes, the car stops. If the stop is sudden and the driver is not wearing a seat belt, the driver keeps moving forward.

③ Finally, the windshield applies an unbalanced force that stops the driver's forward motion.

If the driver is wearing a seat belt, the seat belt rather than the windshield applies the unbalanced force that stops the driver's forward motion. The force from the seat belt is applied over a longer time, so the force causes less damage. In a collision, seat belts alone are sometimes not enough to stop the motion of drivers or passengers. Air bags further cushion people from the effects of inertia in an accident.

CHECK YOUR READING If a car makes a sudden stop, what happens to a passenger riding in the back seat who is not wearing a seat belt?

2.1 Review

KEY CONCEPTS

1. Explain the difference between balanced and unbalanced forces.

2. What is the relationship between force and motion described by Newton's first law?

3. What is inertia? How is the inertia of an object related to its mass?

CRITICAL THINKING

4. **Infer** Once a baseball has been hit into the air, what forces are acting upon it? How can you tell that any forces are acting upon the ball?

5. **Predict** A ball is at rest on the floor of a car moving at a constant velocity. What will happen to the ball if the car swerves suddenly to the left?

☢ CHALLENGE

6. **Synthesize** What can the changes in an object's position tell you about the forces acting on that object? Describe an example from everyday life that shows how forces affect the position of an object.

A playa was once a shallow lake. The water in it evaporated, leaving a dry lakebed.

Think SCIENCE

SKILL: EVALUATING HYPOTHESES

Why Do These Rocks Slide?

In Death Valley, California, there is a dry lakebed known as Racetrack Playa. Rocks are mysteriously moving across the ground there, leaving tracks in the clay. These rocks can have masses as great as 320 kilograms (corresponding to 700 lb). No one has ever observed the rocks sliding, even though scientists have studied their tracks for more than 50 years. What force moves these rocks? Scientists do not yet know.

◗ Observations

Scientists made these observations.

> a. Some rocks left trails that are almost parallel.
> b. Some rocks left trails that took abrupt turns.
> c. Sometimes a small rock moved while a larger rock did not.
> d. Most of the trails are on level surfaces. Some trails run slightly uphill.
> e. The temperature in that area sometimes drops below freezing.

This rock made a U-turn.

◗ Hypotheses

Scientists formed these hypotheses about how the rocks move.

> • When the lakebed gets wet, it becomes so slippery that gravity causes the rocks to slide.
> • When the lakebed gets wet, it becomes so slippery that strong winds can move the rocks.
> • When the lakebed gets wet and cold, a sheet of ice forms and traps the rocks. Strong winds move both the ice sheet and the trapped rocks.

◗ Evaluate Each Hypothesis

On Your Own Think about whether all the observations support each hypothesis. Some facts may rule out some hypotheses. Some facts may neither support nor contradict a particular hypothesis.

As a Group Decide which hypotheses are reasonable. Discuss your thinking and conclusions in a small group, and list the reasonable hypotheses.

CHALLENGE What further observations would you make to test any of these hypotheses? What information would each observation add?

RESOURCE CENTER Learn more about the moving rocks.
CLASSZONE.COM

2.2 Force and mass determine acceleration.

<table>
<tr><td>

▶ **BEFORE**, you learned

- Mass is a measure of inertia
- The motion of an object will not change unless the object is acted upon by an unbalanced force

</td><td>

▶ **NOW**, you will learn

- How Newton's second law relates force, mass, and acceleration
- How force works in circular motion

</td></tr>
</table>

VOCABULARY

Newton's second law p. 50
centripetal force p. 54

EXPLORE Acceleration

How are force and acceleration related?

PROCEDURE

1. Tie a paper clip to each end of a long string. Hook two more paper clips to one end.

2. Hold the single paper clip in the middle of a smooth table; hang the other end of the string over the edge. Let go and observe.

3. Add one more paper clip to the hanging end and repeat the experiment. Observe what happens. Repeat.

MATERIALS
- paper clips
- string

WHAT DO YOU THINK?
- What happened each time that you let go of the single paper clip?
- Explain the relationship between the number of hanging paper clips and the motion of the paper clip on the table.

Newton's second law relates force, mass, and acceleration.

Suppose you are eating lunch with a friend and she asks you to pass the milk container. You decide to slide it across the table to her. How much force would you use to get the container moving? You would probably use a different force if the container were full than if the container were empty.

If you want to give two objects with different masses the same acceleration, you have to apply different forces to them. You must push a full milk container harder than an empty one to slide it over to your friend in the same amount of time.

REMINDER

Acceleration is a change in velocity over time.

CHECK YOUR READING What three concepts are involved in Newton's second law?

Newton's Second Law

Newton studied how objects move, and he noticed some patterns. He observed that the acceleration of an object depends on the mass of the object and the size of the force applied to it. **Newton's second law** states that the acceleration of an object increases with increased force and decreases with increased mass. The law also states that the direction in which an object accelerates is the same as the direction of the force.

The photographs below show Newton's second law at work in a supermarket. The acceleration of each shopping cart depends upon two things:

- the size of the force applied to the shopping cart
- the mass of the shopping cart

In the left-hand photograph, the force on the cart changes, while the mass of the cart stays the same. In the right-hand photograph, the force on the cart stays the same, while the mass of the cart varies. Notice how mass and force affect acceleration.

Newton's Second Law

The acceleration of an object increases with increased force, decreases with increased mass, and is in the same direction as the force.

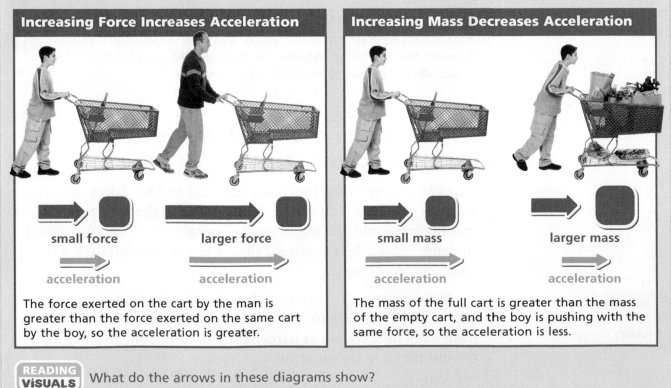

Increasing Force Increases Acceleration

small force   larger force

acceleration   acceleration

The force exerted on the cart by the man is greater than the force exerted on the same cart by the boy, so the acceleration is greater.

Increasing Mass Decreases Acceleration

small mass   larger mass

acceleration   acceleration

The mass of the full cart is greater than the mass of the empty cart, and the boy is pushing with the same force, so the acceleration is less.

READING VISUALS What do the arrows in these diagrams show?

Force Equals Mass Times Acceleration

Newton was able to describe the relationship of force, mass, and acceleration mathematically. You can calculate the force, the mass, or the acceleration if you know two of the three factors. The mathematical form of Newton's second law, stated as a formula, is

$$\textbf{Force} = \textbf{mass} \cdot \textbf{acceleration}$$
$$\textbf{\textit{F} = \textit{ma}}$$

To use this formula, you need to understand the unit used to measure force. In honor of Newton's contribution to our understanding of force and motion, the standard unit of force is called the newton (N). Because force equals mass times acceleration, force is measured in units of mass (kilograms) times units of acceleration (meters per second per second). A newton is defined as the amount of force that it takes to accelerate one kilogram (1 kg) of mass one meter per second per second (1 m/s²). So 1 N is the same as 1 kg • m/s².

REMINDER

Meters per second per second is the same as *m/s²*, which can be read "meters per second squared."

CHECK YOUR READING If the same force is applied to two objects of different mass, which object will have the greater acceleration?

The mathematical relationship of force, mass, and acceleration allow you to solve problems about how objects move. If you know the mass of an object and the acceleration you want to achieve, you can use the formula to find the force you need to exert to produce that acceleration. Use Newton's second law to find the force that is needed to accelerate the shopping cart in the sample problem.

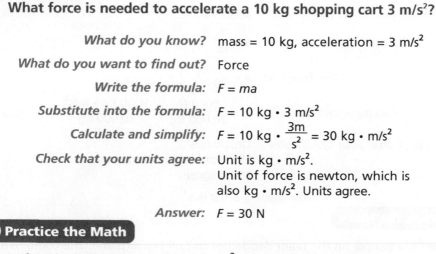

Calculating Force

Sample Problem

What force is needed to accelerate a 10 kg shopping cart 3 m/s²?

What do you know?	mass = 10 kg, acceleration = 3 m/s²
What do you want to find out?	Force
Write the formula:	$F = ma$
Substitute into the formula:	$F = 10 \text{ kg} \cdot 3 \text{ m/s}^2$
Calculate and simplify:	$F = 10 \text{ kg} \cdot \dfrac{3m}{s^2} = 30 \text{ kg} \cdot \text{m/s}^2$
Check that your units agree:	Unit is kg • m/s². Unit of force is newton, which is also kg • m/s². Units agree.
Answer:	$F = 30 \text{ N}$

Practice the Math

1. If a 5 kg ball is accelerating 1.2 m/s², what is the force on it?
2. A person on a scooter is accelerating 2 m/s². If the person has a mass of 50 kg, how much force is acting on that person?

This team of 20 people pulled a 72,000-kilogram (159,000 lb) Boeing 727 airplane 3.7 meters (12 ft) in 6.74 seconds.

The photograph above shows people who are combining forces to pull an airplane. Suppose you knew the mass of the plane and how hard the people were pulling. How much would the plane accelerate? The sample problem below shows how Newton's second law helps you calculate the acceleration.

Calculating Acceleration

Sample Problem

If a team pulls with a combined force of 9000 N on an airplane with a mass of 30,000 kg, what is the acceleration of the airplane?

What do you know?	mass = 30,000 kg, force = 9000 N
What do you want to find out?	acceleration
Rearrange the formula:	$a = \dfrac{F}{m}$
Substitute into the formula:	$a = \dfrac{9000 \text{ N}}{30,000 \text{ kg}}$
Calculate and simplify:	$a = \dfrac{9000 \text{ N}}{30,000 \text{ kg}} = \dfrac{9000 \text{ kg} \cdot \text{m/s}^2}{30,000 \text{ kg}} = 0.3 \text{ m/s}^2$
Check that your units agree:	Unit is m/s². Unit for acceleration is m/s². Units agree.
Answer:	$a = 0.3 \text{ m/s}^2$

Practice the Math

1. Half the people on the team decide not to pull the airplane. The combined force of those left is 4500 N, while the airplane's mass is still 30,000 kg. What will be the acceleration?

2. A girl pulls a wheeled backpack with a force of 3 N. If the backpack has a mass of 6 kg, what is its acceleration?

Mass and Acceleration

Mass is also a variable in Newton's second law. If the same force acts on two objects, the object with less mass will have the greater acceleration. For instance, if you push a soccer ball and a bowling ball with equal force, the soccer ball will have a greater acceleration.

If objects lose mass, they can gain acceleration if the force remains the same. When a rocket is first launched, most of its mass is the fuel it carries. As the rocket burns fuel, it loses mass. As the mass continually decreases, the acceleration continually increases.

APPLY This NASA launch rocket accelerates with enough force to lift about 45 cars off the ground. As the rocket loses fuel, will it accelerate more or less? Why?

Calculating Mass

> **Sample Problem**

A model rocket is accelerating at 2 m/s². The force on it is 1 N. What is the mass of the rocket?

What do you know?	acceleration = 2 m/s², force = 1 N
What do you want to find out?	mass
Rearrange the formula:	$m = \dfrac{F}{a}$
Substitute into the formula:	$m = \dfrac{1\ N}{2\ m/s^2}$
Calculate and simplify:	$m = \dfrac{1\ N}{2\ m/s^2} = \dfrac{1\ kg \cdot m/s^2}{2\ m/s^2} = 0.5\ kg$
Check that your units agree:	Unit is kg. Unit of mass is kg. Units agree.
Answer:	$m = 0.5\ kg$

> **Practice the Math**

1. Another model rocket is accelerating at a rate of 3 m/s² with a force of 1 N. What is the mass of the rocket?
2. A boy pushes a shopping cart with a force of 10 N, and the cart accelerates 1 m/s². What is the mass of the cart?

Forces can change the direction of motion.

Usually, we think of a force as either speeding up or slowing down the motion of an object, but force can also make an object change direction. If an object changes direction, it is accelerating. Newton's second law says that if you apply a force to an object, the direction in which the object accelerates is the same as the direction of the force. You can change the direction of an object without changing its speed. For example, a good soccer player can control the motion of a soccer ball by applying a force that changes the ball's direction but not its speed.

CHECK YOUR READING   How can an object accelerate when it does not change speed?

INVESTIGATE Motion and Force

What affects circular motion?

PROCEDURE

1. Spread newspaper over your work surface. Place the paper plate down on the newspaper.

2. Practice rolling the marble around the edge of the plate until you can roll it around completely at least once.

3. Cut out a one-quarter slice of the paper plate. Put a dab of paint on the edge of the plate where the marble will leave it. Place the plate back down on the newspaper.

4. Hypothesize: How will the marble move once it rolls off the plate? Why?

5. Roll the marble all the way around the paper plate into the cut-away section and observe the resulting motion as shown by the trail of paint.

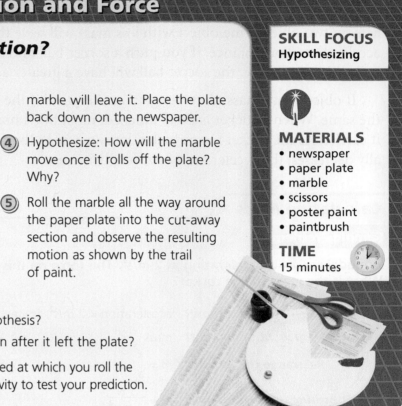

WHAT DO YOU THINK?

- Did your observations support your hypothesis?
- What forces affected the marble's motion after it left the plate?

CHALLENGE How will changing the speed at which you roll the marble change your results? Repeat the activity to test your prediction.

Centripetal Force

VOCABULARY
Remember to make a magnet word diagram for *centripetal force*.

When you were younger, you may have experimented with using force to change motion. Perhaps you and a friend took turns swinging each other in a circle. If you remember this game, you may also remember that your arms got tired because they were constantly pulling your friend as your friend spun around. It took force to change the direction of your friend's motion. Without that force, your friend could not have kept moving in a circle.

Any force that keeps an object moving in a circle is known as a **centripetal force** (sehn-TRIHP-ih-tuhl). This force points toward the center of the circle. Without the centripetal force, the object would go flying off in a straight line. When you whirl a ball on a string, what keeps the ball moving in a circle? The force of the string turns the ball, changing the ball's direction of motion. When the string turns, so does the ball. As the string changes direction, the force from the string also changes direction. The force is always pointing along the string toward your hand, the center of the circle. The centripetal force on the whirling ball is the pull from the string. If you let go of the string, the ball would fly off in the direction it was headed when you let go.

 CHECK YOUR READING How does centripetal force change the motion of an object?

centripetal force

top view

Centripetal force
The force that keeps the female skater moving in a circle is the pull exerted by her partner. The diagram shows the direction of the centripetal force.

Circular Motion and Newton's Second Law

Suppose the male skater shown above spins his partner faster. Her direction changes more quickly than before, so she accelerates more. To get more acceleration, he must apply more force. The same idea holds for a ball you whirl on a string. You have to pull harder on the string when you whirl the ball faster, because it takes more centripetal force to keep the ball moving at the greater speed.

You can apply the formula for Newton's second law even to an object moving in a circle. If you know the size of the centripetal force acting upon the object, you can find its acceleration. A greater acceleration requires a greater centripetal force. A more massive object requires a greater centripetal force to have the same circular speed as a less massive object. But no matter what the mass of an object is, if it moves in a circle, its force and acceleration are directed toward the center of the circle.

CHECK YOUR READING How does increasing the centripetal force on an object affect its acceleration?

2.2 Review

KEY CONCEPTS

1. If the force acting upon an object is increased, what happens to the object's acceleration?

2. How does the mass of an object affect its acceleration?

3. What force keeps an object moving in a circle? In what direction does this force act?

CRITICAL THINKING

4. **Infer** Use Newton's second law to determine how much force is being applied to an object that is traveling at a constant velocity.

5. **Calculate** What force is needed to accelerate an object 5 m/s² if the object has a mass of 10 kg?

⬥ CHALLENGE

6. **Synthesize** Carlos pushes a 3 kg box with a force of 9 N. The force of friction on the box is 3 N in the opposite direction. What is the acceleration of the box? **Hint:** Combine forces to find the net force.

Meaningful Numbers

MATH TUTORIAL
CLASSZONE.COM

Click on Math Tutorial for more help with rounding decimals.

A student doing a science report on artificial hearts reads that a certain artificial heart weighs about 2 pounds. The student then writes that the mass of the artificial heart is 0.907185 kilograms. Someone reading this report might think that the student knows the mass to a high precision, when actually he knows it only to one meaningful number.

When you make calculations, the number of digits to include in your answer depends in part on the number of meaningful digits, or significant figures, in the numbers you are working with.

The AbioCor artificial heart, which has a mass of about 0.9 kg, is designed to fit entirely inside the human body.

Example

In an experiment to find acceleration, a scientist might record the following data.

Force = 3.1 N   mass = 1.450 kg

In this example, force is given to two significant figures, and mass is given to four significant figures.

(1) Use a calculator and the formula $a = F/m$ to find the acceleration. The display on the calculator shows

2.1379310345

(2) To determine how many of the digits in this answer are really meaningful, look at the measurement with the least number of significant figures. In this example, force is given to two significant figures. Therefore, the answer is meaningful only to two significant figures.

(3) Round the calculated number to two digits.

ANSWER acceleration = 2.1 m/s²

Answer the following questions.

For each pair of measurements, calculate the acceleration to the appropriate number of digits.

1. Force = 3.100 N   mass = 3.1 kg

2. Force = 2 N   mass = 4.2 kg

3. Force = 1.21 N   mass = 1.1000 kg

CHALLENGE Suppose a scientist measures a force of 3.25 N and a mass of 3.3 kg. She could round the force to two significant figures and then divide, or she could divide and then round the answer. Compare these two methods. Which method do you think is more accurate?

KEY CONCEPT

2.3 Forces act in pairs.

BEFORE, you learned

- A force is a push or a pull
- Increasing the force on an object increases the acceleration
- The acceleration of an object depends on its mass and the force applied to it

NOW, you will learn

- How Newton's third law relates action/reaction pairs of forces
- How Newton's laws work together

VOCABULARY

Newton's third law p. 57

THINK ABOUT

How do jellyfish move?

Jellyfish do not have much control over their movements. They drift with the current in the ocean. However, jellyfish do have some control over their up-and-down motion. By squeezing water out of
its umbrella-like body, the jellyfish shown here applies a force in one direction to move in the opposite direction. If the water is forced downward, the jellyfish moves upward. How can a person or an object move in one direction by exerting a force in the opposite direction?

Newton's third law relates action and reaction forces.

COMBINATION NOTES
In your notebook, make an outline and draw a diagram about Newton's third law.

Newton made an important observation that explains the motion of the jellyfish. He noticed that forces always act in pairs. **Newton's third law** states that every time one object exerts a force on another object, the second object exerts a force that is equal in size and opposite in direction back on the first object. As the jellyfish contracts its body, it applies a downward force on the water. The water applies an equal force back on the jellyfish. It is this equal and opposite force on the jellyfish that pushes it up. This is similar to what happens when a blown-up balloon is released. The balloon pushes air out the end, and the air pushes back on the balloon and moves it forward.

 CHECK YOUR READING What moves the jellyfish through the water?

Action and Reaction Pairs

The force that is exerted on an object and the force that the object exerts back are known together as an action/reaction force pair. One force in the pair is called the action force, and the other is called the reaction force. For instance, if the jellyfish pushing on the water is the action force, the water pushing back on the jellyfish is the reaction force. Likewise, if the balloon pushing the air backward is the action force, the air pushing the balloon forward is the reaction force.

You can see many examples of action and reaction forces in the world around you. Here are three:

- You may have watched the liftoffs of the space shuttle on television. When the booster rockets carrying the space shuttle take off, their engines push fuel exhaust downward. The exhaust pushes back on the rockets, sending them upward.

- When you bang your toe into the leg of a table, the same amount of force that you exert on the table is exerted back on your toe.

- Action and reaction forces do not always result in motion. For example, if you press down on a table, the table resists the push with the same amount of force, even though nothing moves.

CHECK YOUR READING Identify the action/reaction forces in each example described above.

INVESTIGATE Newton's Third Law

How do action and reaction forces compare?

PROCEDURE

1. With a partner, hook the two spring scales together.

2. Pull gently on your spring scale while your partner holds but does not pull on the other scale.

3. Observe and record the amount of force that is shown on your scale and on your partner's scale.

4. Both of you pull together. Observe the force shown on each scale.

WHAT DO YOU THINK?

- What happened to your partner's force as your force increased?
- What happened when you both pulled?
- Explain why you think what you observed in each case happened.

CHALLENGE Can you think of a way to use the scales to show Newton's first or second law?

SKILL FOCUS
Observing

MATERIALS
2 spring scales

TIME
15 minutes

Action and Reaction Forces Versus Balanced Forces

Because action and reaction forces are equal and opposite, they may be confused with balanced forces. Keep in mind that balanced forces act on a single object, while action and reaction forces act on different objects.

Balanced Forces If you and a friend pull on opposite sides of a backpack with the same amount of force, the backpack doesn't move, because the forces acting on it are balanced. In this case, both forces are exerted on one object—the backpack.

Action and Reaction As you drag a heavy backpack across a floor, you can feel the backpack pulling on you with an equal amount of force. The action force and the reaction force are acting on two different things—one is acting on the backpack, and the other is acting on you.

The illustration below summarizes Newton's third law. The girl exerts an action force on the boy by pushing him. Even though the boy is not trying to push the girl, an equal and opposite reaction force acts upon the girl, causing her to move as well.

Newton's Third Law

When one object exerts a force on another object, the second object exerts an equal and opposite force on the first object.

① One Skater Pushes

reaction force   action force

The action force from the girl sets the boy in motion.

② Both Skaters Move

Even though the boy does not do anything, the reaction force from him sets the girl in motion as well.

READING VISUALS How does the direction of the force on the girl relate to her motion?

Newton's Three Laws of Motion

All three of Newton's laws work together to help describe how an object will move.

Newton's First Law

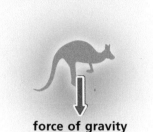

force of gravity

This kangaroo has jumped, setting itself in motion. If no other forces acted on it, the kangaroo would continue to move through the air with the same motion. Instead, the force of gravity will bring this kangaroo back to the ground.

Newton's Second Law

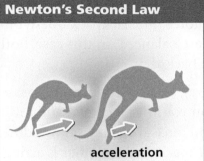

acceleration

The large kangaroo does not have as much acceleration as a less massive kangaroo would if it used the same force to jump. However, the more massive kangaroo can increase its acceleration by increasing the force of its jump.

Newton's Third Law

action force   **reaction force**

A kangaroo applies an action force on the ground with its powerful back legs. The reaction force from the ground can send the kangaroo as far as 8 meters (26 ft) through the air.

READING VISUALS What forces are involved in a kangaroo jump?

Common Name: Red kangaroo
Scientific Name: *Macropus rufus*
Home: Australia
Top Speed: 65 km/h (40 mi/h)
Maximum Leap: 8 m (26 ft)

AUSTRALIA

Newton's three laws describe and predict motion.

Newton's three laws can explain the motion of almost any object, including the motion of animals. The illustrations on page 60 show how all three of Newton's laws can be used to describe how kangaroos move. The three laws are not independent of one another; they are used together to explain the motion of objects.

You can use the laws of motion to explain how other animals move as well. For example, Newton's laws explain why a squid moves forward while squirting water out behind it. These laws also explain that a bird is exerting force when it speeds up to fly away or when it changes its direction in the air.

You can also use Newton's laws to make predictions about motion. If you know the force acting upon an object, then you can predict how that object's motion will change. For example, if you want to send a spacecraft to Mars, you must be able to predict exactly where Mars will be by the time the spacecraft reaches it. You must also be able to control the force on your spacecraft so that it will arrive at the right place at the right time.

Knowing how Newton's three laws work together can also help you win a canoe race. In order to start the canoe moving, you need to apply a force to overcome its inertia. Newton's second law might affect your choice of canoes, because a less massive canoe is easier to accelerate than a more massive one. You can also predict the best position for your paddle in the water. If you want to move straight ahead, you push backward on the paddle so that the canoe moves forward. Together, Newton's laws can help you explain and predict how the canoe, or any object, will move.

RESOURCE CENTER
CLASSZONE.COM

Find out more about Newton's laws of motion.

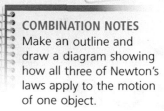

COMBINATION NOTES
Make an outline and draw a diagram showing how all three of Newton's laws apply to the motion of one object.

2.3 Review

KEY CONCEPTS

1. Identify the action/reaction force pair involved when you catch a ball.

2. Explain the difference between balanced forces and action/reaction forces.

3. How do Newton's laws of motion apply to the motion of an animal, such as a cat that is running?

CRITICAL THINKING

4. **Apply** A man pushes on a wall with a force of 50 N. What are the size and the direction of the force that the wall exerts on the man?

5. **Evaluate** Jim will not help push a heavy box. He says, "My force will produce an opposite force and cancel my effort." Evaluate Jim's statement.

⬥ CHALLENGE

6. **Calculate** Suppose you are holding a basketball while standing still on a skateboard. You and the skateboard have a mass of 50 kg. You throw the basketball with a force of 10 N. What is your acceleration before and after you throw the ball?

CHAPTER INVESTIGATION

Newton's Laws of Motion

OVERVIEW AND PURPOSE As you know, rocket engineers consider Newton's laws when designing rockets and planning rocket flights. In this investigation you will use what you have learned about Newton's laws to
- build a straw rocket
- improve the rocket's performance by modifying one design element

▶ Problem `Write It Up`

What aspects of a model rocket affect the distance it flies?

▶ Hypothesize `Write It Up`

After step 8 in the procedure, write a hypothesis to explain what you predict will happen during the second set of trials. Your hypothesis should take the form of an "If . . . , then . . . , because . . ." statement.

▶ Procedure

1. Make a data table like the one shown on the sample notebook page.

2. Insert the straw with the smaller diameter into one of the bottles. Seal the mouth of the bottle tightly with modeling clay so that air can escape only through the straw. This is the rocket launcher.

3. Cut two thin strips of paper, one about 8 cm long and the other about 12 cm long. Connect the ends of the strips to make loops.

4. To create the rocket, place the straw with the larger diameter through the smaller loop and tape the loop to the straw at one end. Attach the other loop to the other end of the straw in the same way. Both loops should be attached to the same side of the straw to stabilize your rocket in flight.

MATERIALS

- 2 straws with different diameters
- several plastic bottles, in different sizes
- modeling clay
- scissors
- construction paper
- meter stick
- tape

5. Use a small ball of modeling clay to seal the end of the straw near the smaller loop.

6. Slide the open end of the rocket over the straw on the launcher. Place the bottle on the edge of a table so that the rocket is pointing away from the table.

7. Test launch your rocket by holding the bottle with two hands and squeezing it quickly. Measure the distance the rocket lands from the edge of the table. Practice the launch several times. Remember to squeeze with equal force each time.

8. Launch the rocket four times. Keep the amount of force you use constant. Measure the distance the rocket travels each time, and record the results in your data table.

9. List all the variables that may affect the distance your rocket flies. Change the rocket or launcher to alter one variable. Launch the rocket and measure the distance it flies. Repeat three more times, and record the results in your data table.

▶ Observe and Analyze Write It Up

1. **RECORD OBSERVATIONS** Draw a diagram of both of your bottle rockets. Make sure your data table is complete.

2. **IDENTIFY VARIABLES** What variables did you identify, and what variable did you modify?

▶ Conclude Write It Up

1. **COMPARE** How did the flight distances of the original rocket compare with those of the modified rocket?

2. **ANALYZE** Compare your results with your hypothesis. Do the results support your hypothesis?

3. **IDENTIFY LIMITS** What possible limitations or errors did you experience or could you have experienced?

4. **APPLY** Use Newton's laws to explain why the rocket flies.

5. **APPLY** What other real-life example can you think of that demonstrates Newton's laws?

▶ INVESTIGATE Further

CHALLENGE Why does the rocket have paper loops taped to it? Determine how the flight of the rocket is affected if one or both loops are completely removed. Hypothesize about the function of the paper loops and design an experiment to test your hypothesis.

Newton's Laws of Motion

Problem What aspects of a model rocket affect the distance it flies?

Hypothesize

Observe and Analyze

Table 1. Flight Distances of Original and Modified Rocket

Trial Number	Original Rocket Distance Rocket Flew (cm)	Modified Rocket Distance Rocket Flew (cm)
1		
2		
3		
4		

Conclude

2.4 Forces transfer momentum.

◁ **BEFORE, you learned**

- A force is a push or a pull
- Newton's laws help to describe and predict motion

▷ **NOW, you will learn**

- What momentum is
- How to calculate momentum
- How momentum is affected by collisions

VOCABULARY

momentum p. 64
collision p. 66
conservation of momentum p. 67

EXPLORE Collisions

What happens when objects collide?

PROCEDURE

① Roll the two balls toward each other on a flat surface. Try to roll them at the same speed. Observe what happens. Experiment by changing the speeds of the two balls.

② Leave one ball at rest, and roll the other ball so that it hits the first ball. Observe what happens. Then repeat the experiment with the balls switched.

WHAT DO YOU THINK?

- How did varying the speed of the balls affect the motion of the balls after the collision?
- What happened when one ball was at rest? Why did switching the two balls affect the outcome?

MATERIALS
2 balls of different masses

Objects in motion have momentum.

If you throw a tennis ball at a wall, it will bounce back toward you. What would happen if you could throw a wrecking ball at the wall at the same speed that you threw the tennis ball? The wall would most likely break apart. Why would a wrecking ball have a different effect on the wall than the tennis ball?

A moving object has a property that is called momentum. **Momentum** (moh-MEHN-tuhm) is a measure of mass in motion; the momentum of an object is the product of its mass and its velocity. At the same velocity, the wrecking ball has more momentum than the tennis ball because the wrecking ball has more mass. However, you could increase the momentum of the tennis ball by throwing it faster.

VOCABULARY
Make a magnet word diagram for *momentum*.

Momentum is similar to inertia. Like inertia, the momentum of an object depends on its mass. Unlike inertia, however, momentum takes into account how fast the object is moving. A wrecking ball that is moving very slowly, for example, has less momentum than a fast-moving wrecking ball. With less momentum, the slower-moving wrecking ball would not be able to do as much damage to the wall.

To calculate an object's momentum, you can use the following formula:

$$\textbf{momentum} = \textbf{mass} \cdot \textbf{velocity}$$
$$\boldsymbol{p = mv}$$

In this formula, p stands for momentum, m for mass, and v for velocity. In standard units, the mass of an object is given in kilograms (kg), and velocity is given in meters per second (m/s). Therefore, the unit of momentum is the kilogram-meter per second (kg · m/s). Notice that the unit of momentum combines mass, length, and time.

Like force, velocity, and acceleration, momentum is a vector—it has both a size and a direction. The direction of an object's momentum is the same as the direction of its velocity. You can use speed instead of velocity in the formula as long as you do not need to know the direction of motion. As you will read later, it is important to know the direction of the momentum when you are working with more than one object.

REMINDER
Inertia is the resistance of an object to changes in its motion.

RESOURCE CENTER
CLASSZONE.COM
Explore momentum.

CHECK YOUR READING How do an object's mass and velocity affect its momentum?

Calculating Momentum

Sample Problem

What is the momentum of a 1.5 kg ball moving at 2 m/s?

What do you know?	mass = 1.5 kg, velocity = 2 m/s
What do you want to find out?	momentum
Write the formula:	$p = mv$
Substitute into the formula:	$p = 1.5 \text{ kg} \cdot 2 \text{ m/s}$
Calculate and simplify:	$p = 3 \text{ kg} \cdot \text{m/s}$
Check that your units agree:	Unit is kg · m/s. Unit of momentum is kg · m/s. Units agree.
Answer:	$p = 3 \text{ kg} \cdot \text{m/s}$

Practice the Math

1. A 3 kg ball is moving with a velocity of 1 m/s. What is the ball's momentum?
2. What is the momentum of a 0.5 kg ball moving 0.5 m/s?

What happens when objects collide?

PROCEDURE

1. Set up two parallel rulers separated by one centimeter. Place a line of five marbles, each touching the next, in the groove between the rulers.

2. Roll a marble down the groove so that it collides with the line of marbles, and observe the results.

3. Repeat your experiment by rolling two and then three marbles at the line of marbles. Observe the results.

WHAT DO YOU THINK?

- What did you observe when you rolled the marbles?
- Why do you think the marbles moved the way they did?

CHALLENGE Use your answers to write a hypothesis explaining your observations. Design your own marble experiment to test this hypothesis. Do your results support your hypothesis?

SKILL FOCUS
Observing

MATERIALS
- 2 rulers
- 8 marbles

TIME
20 minutes

Momentum can be transferred from one object to another.

If you have ever ridden in a bumper car, you have experienced collisions. A **collision** is a situation in which two objects in close contact exchange energy and momentum. As another car bumps into the back of yours, the force pushes your car forward. Some of the momentum of the car behind you is transferred to your car. At the same time, the car behind you slows because of the reaction force from your car. You gain momentum from the collision, and the other car loses momentum. The action and reaction forces in collisions are one way in which objects transfer momentum.

If two objects involved in a collision have very different masses, the one with less mass has a greater change in velocity. For example, consider what happens if you roll a tennis ball and a bowling ball toward each other so that they collide. Not only will the speed of the tennis ball change, but the direction of its motion will change as it bounces back. The bowling ball, however, will simply slow down. Even though the forces acting on the two balls are the same, the tennis ball will be accelerated more during the collision because it has less mass.

CHECK YOUR READING How can a collision affect the momentum of an object?

Momentum is conserved.

During a collision between two objects, each object exerts a force on the other. The colliding objects make up a system—a collection of objects that affect one another. As the two objects collide, the velocity and the momentum of each object change. However, as no other forces are acting on the objects, the total momentum of both objects is unchanged by the collision. This is due to the conservation of momentum. The principle of **conservation of momentum** states that the total momentum of a system of objects does not change, as long as no outside forces are acting on that system.

READING TiP

A light blue-green arrow shows the momentum of an individual object.

A dark blue-green arrow shows the total momentum.

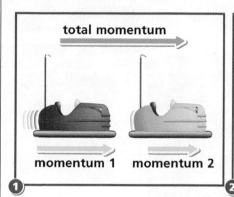

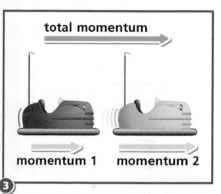

①

Before the collision The momentum of the first car is greater than the momentum of the second car. Their combined momentum is the total momentum of the system.

②

During the collision The forces on the two cars are equal and opposite, as described by Newton's third law. Momentum is transferred from one car to the other during the collision.

③

After the collision The momentum lost by one car was gained by the other car. The total momentum of the system remains the same as it was before the collision.

How much an object's momentum changes when a force is applied depends on the size of the force and how long that force is applied. Remember Newton's third law—during a collision, two objects are acted upon by equal and opposite forces for the same length of time. This means that the objects receive equal and opposite changes in momentum, and the total momentum does not change.

You can find the total momentum of a system of objects before a collision by combining the momenta of the objects. Because momentum is a vector, like force, the direction of motion is important. To find the total momentum of objects moving in the same direction, add the momenta of the objects. For two objects traveling in opposite directions, subtract one momentum from the other. Then use the principle of conservation of momentum and the formula for momentum to predict how the objects will move after they collide.

READING TiP

The plural of *momentum* is *momenta*.

CHECK YOUR READING What is meant by "conservation of momentum"? What questions do you have about the application of this principle?

Two Types of Collisions

When bumper cars collide, they bounce off each other. Most of the force goes into changing the motion of the cars. The two bumper cars travel separately after the collision, just as they did before the collision. The combined momentum of both cars after the collision is the same as the combined momentum of both cars before the collision.

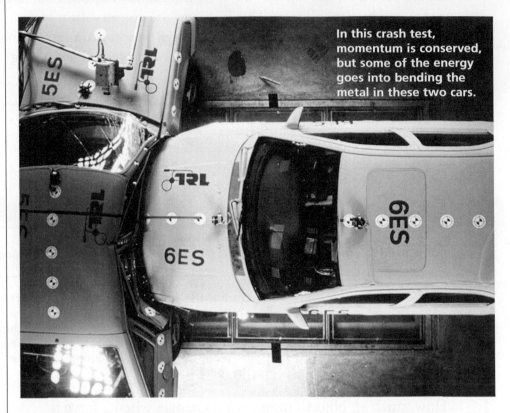

In this crash test, momentum is conserved, but some of the energy goes into bending the metal in these two cars.

When two cars collide during a crash test, momentum is also conserved during the collision. Unlike the bumper cars, however, which separate, the two cars shown in the photograph above stick and move together after the collision. Even in this case, the total momentum of both cars together is the same as the total momentum of both cars before the collision. Before the crash shown in the photograph, the yellow car had a certain momentum, and the blue car had no momentum. After the crash, the two cars move together with a combined momentum equal to the momentum the yellow car had before the collision.

CHECK YOUR READING Compare collisions in which objects separate with collisions in which objects stick together.

Momentum and Newton's Third Law

Collisions are not the only events in which momentum is conserved. In fact, momentum is conserved whenever the only forces acting on objects are action/reaction force pairs. Conservation of momentum is really just another way of looking at Newton's third law.

When a firefighter turns on a hose, water comes out of the nozzle in one direction, and the hose moves back in the opposite direction. You can explain why by using Newton's third law. The water is forced out of the hose. A reaction force pushes the hose backward. You can also use the principle of conservation of momentum to explain why the hose moves backward:

- Before the firefighter turns on the water, the hose and the water are not in motion, so the hose/water system has no momentum.

- Once the water is turned on, the water has momentum in the forward direction.

- For the total momentum of the hose and the water to stay the same, the hose must have an equal amount of momentum in the opposite direction. The hose moves backward.

If the hose and the water are not acted on by any other forces, momentum is conserved. Water is pushed forward, and the hose is pushed backward. However, the action and reaction force pair acting on the hose and the water are not usually the only forces acting on the hose/water system, as shown in the photograph above. There the firefighters are holding the hose steady.

The force the firefighters apply is called an outside force because it is not being applied by the hose or the water. When there is an outside force on a system, momentum is not conserved. Because the firefighters hold the hose, the hose does not move backward, even though the water has a forward momentum.

Firefighters must apply a force to the water hose to prevent it from flying backward when the water comes out.

CHECK YOUR READING Under what condition is momentum not conserved? What part of the paragraph above tells you?

2.4 Review

KEY CONCEPTS

1. How does increasing the speed of an object change its momentum?

2. A car and a truck are traveling at the same speed. Which has more momentum? Why?

3. Give two examples showing the conservation of momentum. Give one example where momentum is not conserved.

CRITICAL THINKING

4. **Predict** A performing dolphin speeds through the water and hits a rubber ball originally at rest. Describe what happens to the velocities of the dolphin and the ball.

5. **Calculate** A 50 kg person is running at 2 m/s. What is the person's momentum?

CHALLENGE

6. **Apply** A moving train car bumps into another train car with the same mass. After the collision, the two cars are coupled and move off together. How does the final speed of the two train cars compare with the initial speed of the moving train cars before the collision?

the **BIG** idea

Forces change the motion of objects in predictable ways.

CONTENT REVIEW
CLASSZONE.COM

KEY CONCEPTS SUMMARY

2.1 Forces change motion.

Newton's first law
Objects at rest remain at rest, and objects in motion remain in motion with the same velocity, unless acted upon by an unbalanced force.

unbalanced force — object at rest

object in motion — unbalanced force

VOCABULARY
force p. 41
net force p. 43
Newton's first law p. 45
inertia p. 46

2.2 Force and mass determine acceleration.

Newton's second law
The acceleration of an object increases with increased force and decreases with increased mass, and is in the same direction as the force.

small force   larger force   small mass   larger mass

same mass, larger force = increased acceleration   larger mass, same force = decreased acceleration

VOCABULARY
Newton's second law p. 50
centripetal force p. 54

2.3 Forces act in pairs.

Newton's third law
When one object exerts a force on another object, the second object exerts an equal and opposite force on the first object.

reaction force   action force

VOCABULARY
Newton's third law p. 57

2.4 Forces transfer momentum.

• Momentum is a property of a moving object.
• Forces in collisions are equal and opposite.
• Momentum is conserved in collisions.

VOCABULARY
momentum p. 64
collision p. 66
conservation of momentum p. 67

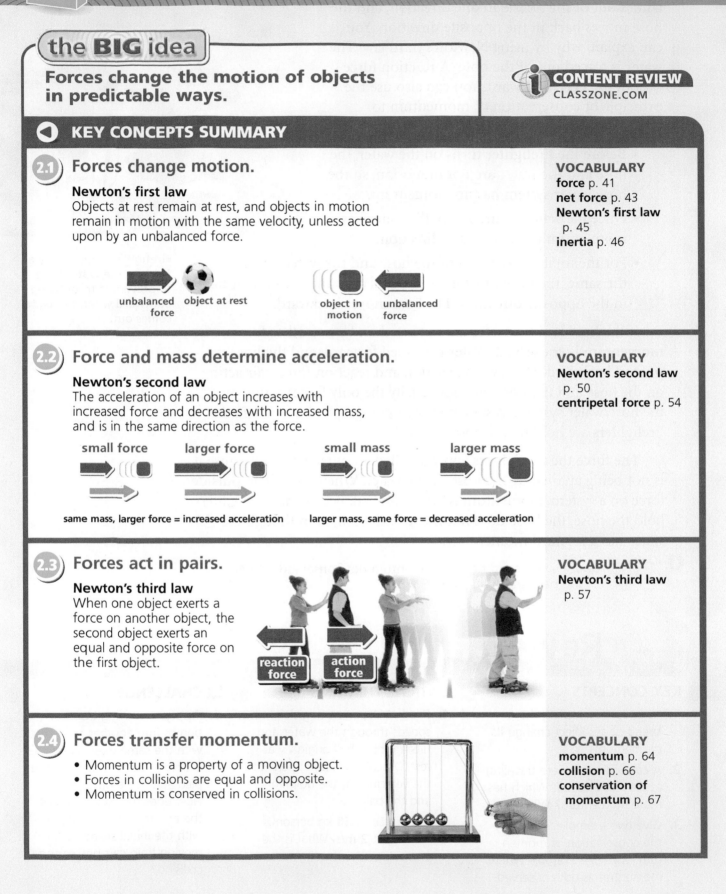

Reviewing Vocabulary

Copy and complete the chart below. If the left column is blank, give the correct term. If the right column is blank, give an example from real life.

Term	Example from Real Life
1. acceleration	
2. centripetal force	
3.	The pull of a handle on a wagon
4. inertia	
5. mass	
6. net force	
7. Newton's first law	
8. Newton's second law	
9.	When you're walking, you push backward on the ground, and the ground pushes you forward with equal force.
10. momentum	

Reviewing Key Concepts

Multiple Choice *Choose the letter of the best answer.*

11. Newton's second law states that to increase acceleration, you
- **a.** increase force
- **b.** decrease force
- **c.** increase mass
- **d.** increase inertia

12. What units are used to measure force?
- **a.** kilograms
- **b.** meters
- **c.** newtons
- **d.** seconds

13. A wagon is pulled down a hill with a constant velocity. All the forces on the wagon are
- **a.** balanced
- **b.** unbalanced
- **c.** increasing
- **d.** decreasing

14. An action force and its reaction force are
- **a.** equal in size and direction
- **b.** equal in size and opposite in direction
- **c.** different in size but in the same direction
- **d.** different in size and in direction

15. John pulls a box with a force of 4 N, and Jason pulls the box from the opposite side with a force of 3 N. Ignore friction. Which of the following statements is true?
- **a.** The box moves toward John.
- **b.** The box moves toward Jason.
- **c.** The box does not move.
- **d.** There is not enough information to determine if the box moves.

16. A more massive marble collides with a less massive one that is not moving. The total momentum after the collision is equal to
- **a.** zero
- **b.** the original momentum of the more massive marble
- **c.** the original momentum of the less massive marble
- **d.** twice the original momentum of the more massive marble

Short Answer *Write a short answer to each question.*

17. List the following objects in order, from the object with the least inertia to the object with the most inertia: feather, large rock, pencil, book. Explain your reasoning.

18. During a race, you double your velocity. How does that change your momentum?

19. Explain how an object can have forces acting on it but not be accelerating.

20. A sea scallop moves by shooting jets of water out of its shell. Explain how this works.

Thinking Critically

Use the information in the photographs below to answer the next four questions.

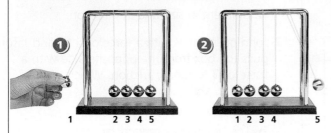

The photographs above show a toy called Newton's Cradle. In the first picture (1), ball 1 is lifted and is being held in place.

21. Are the forces on ball 1 balanced? How do you know?

22. Draw a diagram showing the forces acting on ball 2. Are these forces balanced?

In the second picture (2), ball 1 has been let go.

23. Ball 1 swung down, hit ball 2, and stopped. Use Newton's laws to explain why ball 1 stopped.

24. Use the principle of conservation of momentum to explain why ball 5 swung into the air.

Copy the chart below. Write what will happen to the object in each case.

Cause	Effect
25. Balanced forces act on an object.	
26. Unbalanced forces act on an object.	
27. No force acts on an object.	

28. INFER A baseball is three times more massive than a tennis ball. If the baseball and the tennis ball are accelerating equally, what can you determine about the net force on each?

Using Math Skills in Science

Complete the following calculations.

29. What force should Lori apply to a 5 kg box to give it an acceleration of 2 m/s²?

30. If a 10 N force accelerates an object 5 m/s², how massive is the object?

31. Ravi applies a force of 5 N to a wagon with a mass of 10 kg. What is the wagon's acceleration?

32. Use the information in the photograph on the right to calculate the momentum of the shopping cart.

velocity = 0.5 m/s

mass = 40 kg

the **BIG** idea

33. PREDICT Look again at the tug of war pictured on pages 38–39. Describe what information you need to know to predict the outcome of the game. How would you use that information and Newton's laws to make your prediction?

34. WRITE Pick an activity you enjoy, such as running or riding a scooter, and describe how Newton's laws apply to that activity.

35. SYNTHESIZE Think of a question you have about Newton's laws that is still unanswered. What information do you need in order to answer the question? How might you find the information?

UNIT PROJECTS

If you need to do an experiment for your unit project, gather the materials. Be sure to allow enough time to observe results before the project is due.

Analyzing Data

To test Newton's second law, Jodie accelerates blocks of ice across a smooth, flat surface. The table shows her results. (For this experiment, you can ignore the effects of friction.)

Accelerating Blocks of Ice							
Mass (kg)	1.0	1.5	2.0	2.5	3.0	3.5	4.0
Acceleration (m/s²)	4.0	2.7	2.0	1.6	1.3	1.1	1.0

Study the data table and then answer the questions that follow.

1. The data show that as mass becomes greater, acceleration
   a. increases
   b. decreases
   c. stays the same
   d. cannot be predicted

2. From the data, you can tell that Jodie was applying a force of
   a. 1 N
   b. 2 N
   c. 3 N
   d. 4 N

3. If Jodie applied less force to the ice blocks, the accelerations would be
   a. greater
   b. less
   c. the same
   d. inconsistent

4. If Jodie applied a force of 6 N to the 2 kg block of ice, the acceleration would be
   a. 2 m/s^2
   b. 4 m/s^2
   c. 3 m/s^2
   d. 5 m/s^2

5. The average mass of the ice blocks she pushed was
   a. 1.5 kg
   b. 2.5 kg
   c. 3 kg
   d. 4 kg

6. If Jodie used a 3.25 kg block in her experiment, the force would accelerate the block somewhere between
   a. 1.0 and 1.1 m/s^2
   b. 1.1 and 1.3 m/s^2
   c. 1.3 and 1.6 m/s^2
   d. 1.6 and 2.0 m/s^2

Extended Response

Answer the two questions in detail. Include some of the terms shown in the word box. Underline each term you use in your answer.

Newton's second law	velocity
mass	inertia
gravity	balanced forces
centripetal force	unbalanced forces

7. Tracy ties a ball to a string and starts to swing the ball around her head. What forces are acting on the ball? What happens if the string breaks?

8. Luis is trying to pull a wagon loaded with rocks. What can he do to increase the wagon's acceleration?

CHAPTER 3

Gravity, Friction, and Pressure

the BIG idea

Newton's laws apply to all forces.

Key Concepts

SECTION 3.1
Gravity is a force exerted by masses.
Learn about gravity, weight, and orbits.

SECTION 3.2
Friction is a force that opposes motion.
Learn about friction and air resistance.

SECTION 3.3
Pressure depends on force and area.
Learn about pressure and how forces act on objects in fluids.

SECTION 3.4
Fluids can exert a force on objects.
Learn how fluids apply forces to objects and how forces are transmitted through fluids.

Internet Preview

CLASSZONE.COM

Chapter 3 online resources: Content Review, Simulation, two Visualizations, three Resource Centers, Math Tutorial, Test Practice

What forces are acting on this snowboarder? What forces are acting on the snow?

Let It Slide

Make a ramp using a board and some books. Slide an object down the ramp. Change the surface of the ramp using various materials such as sandpaper.

Observe and Think What effects did different surfaces have on the motion of the object? What may have caused these effects?

Under Pressure

Take two never-opened plastic soft-drink bottles. Open and reseal one of them. Squeeze each bottle.

Observe and Think How did the fluid inside each bottle react to your force? What may have caused the difference in the way the bottles felt?

Internet Activity: Gravity

Go to **ClassZone.com** to explore gravity. Learn more about the force of gravity and its effect on you, objects on Earth, and orbits of planets and satellites. Explore how gravity determines weight, and find out how your weight would be different on other planets.

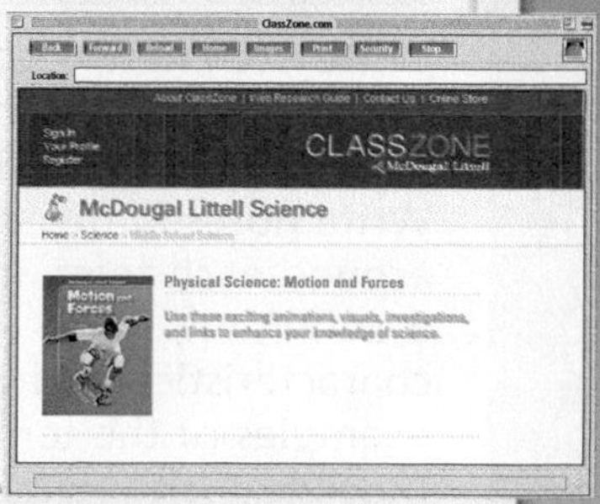

Observe and Think What would you weigh on Mars? What would you weigh on Neptune?

NSTA
scilinks.org
SCiLINKS

Pressure **Code: MDL006**

Getting Ready to Learn

◀ CONCEPT REVIEW

- The motion of an object will not change unless acted upon by an unbalanced force.
- The acceleration of an object depends on force and mass.
- For every action force there is an equal and opposite reaction.

◀ VOCABULARY REVIEW

force p. 41

Newton's first law p. 45

Newton's second law p. 50

Newton's third law p. 57

density *See Glossary.*

ⓘ CONTENT REVIEW
CLASSZONE.COM
Review concepts and vocabulary.

▶ TAKING NOTES

SUPPORTING MAIN IDEAS

Make a chart to show main ideas and the information that supports them. Copy the main ideas. Below each main idea, add supporting information, such as reasons, explanations, and examples.

VOCABULARY STRATEGY

Write each new vocabulary term in the center of a **four square** diagram. Write notes in the squares around each term. Include a definition, some characteristics, and some examples of the term. If possible, write some things that are not examples of the term.

See the Note-Taking Handbook on pages R45–R51.

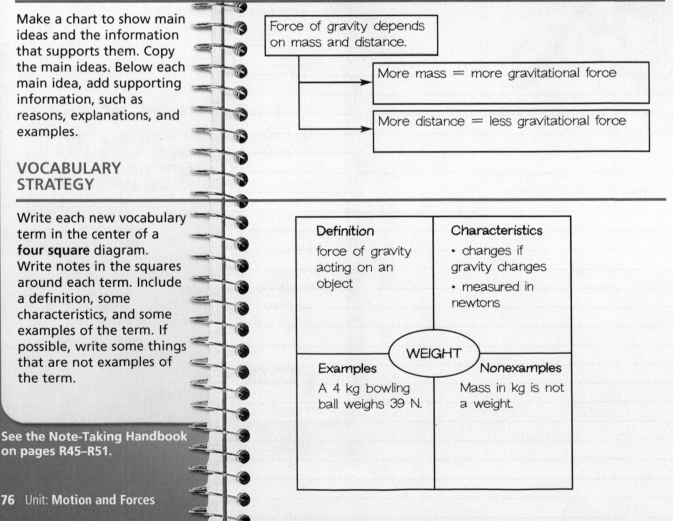

SCIENCE NOTEBOOK

Force of gravity depends on mass and distance.

→ More mass = more gravitational force

→ More distance = less gravitational force

Definition	Characteristics
force of gravity acting on an object	• changes if gravity changes • measured in newtons

WEIGHT

Examples	Nonexamples
A 4 kg bowling ball weighs 39 N.	Mass in kg is not a weight.

3.1
Gravity is a force exerted by masses.

BEFORE, you learned

- Every action force has an equal and opposite reaction force
- Newton's laws are used to describe the motions of objects
- Mass is the amount of matter an object contains

NOW, you will learn

- How mass and distance affect gravity
- What keeps objects in orbit

VOCABULARY

gravity p. 77
weight p. 79
orbit p. 80

EXPLORE Downward Acceleration

How do the accelerations of two falling objects compare?

PROCEDURE

1. Make a prediction: Which ball will fall faster?

2. Drop both balls from the same height at the same time.

3. Observe the balls as they hit the ground.

WHAT DO YOU THINK?

- Were the results what you had expected?
- How did the times it took the two balls to hit the ground compare?

MATERIALS
- golf ball
- Ping-Pong ball

Masses attract each other.

VOCABULARY
Create a four square diagram for *gravity* in your notebook.

When you drop any object—such as a pen, a book, or a football—it falls to the ground. As the object falls, it moves faster and faster. The fact that the object accelerates means there must be a force acting on it. The downward pull on the object is due to gravity. **Gravity** is the force that objects exert on each other because of their masses. You are familiar with the force of gravity between Earth and objects on Earth.

Gravity is present not only between objects and Earth, however. Gravity is considered a universal force because it acts between any two masses anywhere in the universe. For example, there is a gravitational pull between the Sun and the Moon. Even small masses attract each other. The force of gravity between dust and gas particles in space helped form the solar system.

 Why is gravity considered a universal force?

The Force of Gravity

SUPPORTING MAIN IDEAS
Support the main ideas about the force of gravity with details and examples.

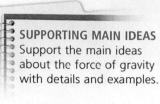

If there is a force between all masses, why are you not pulled toward your desk by the desk's gravity when you walk away from it? Remember that the net force on you determines how your motion changes. The force of gravity between you and the desk is extremely small compared with other forces constantly acting on you, such as friction, the force from your muscles, Earth's gravity, and the gravitational pull from many other objects. The strength of the gravitational force between two objects depends on two factors, mass and distance.

The Mass of the Objects The more mass two objects have, the greater the force of gravity the masses exert on each other. If one of the masses is doubled, the force of gravity between the objects is doubled.

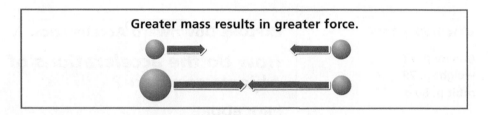

Greater mass results in greater force.

The Distance Between the Objects As distance between the objects increases, the force of gravity decreases. If the distance is doubled, the force of gravity is one-fourth as strong as before.

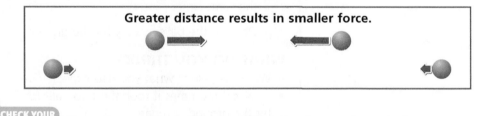

Greater distance results in smaller force.

CHECK YOUR READING How do mass and distance affect the force of gravity?

Gravity on Earth

The force of gravity acts on both masses equally, even though the effects on both masses may be very different. Earth's gravity exerts a downward pull on a dropped coin. Remember that every action force has an equal and opposite reaction force. The coin exerts an equal upward force on Earth. Because the coin has an extremely small mass compared with Earth, the coin can be easily accelerated. Earth's acceleration due to the force of the coin is far too small to notice because of Earth's large mass.

The acceleration due to Earth's gravity is called g and is equal to 9.8 m/s² at Earth's surface. You can calculate the force of gravity on an object using the object's mass and this acceleration. The formula that expresses Newton's second law is $F = ma$. If you use g as the acceleration, the formula for calculating the force due to gravity on a mass close to Earth's surface becomes $F = mg$.

Acceleration Due to Gravity

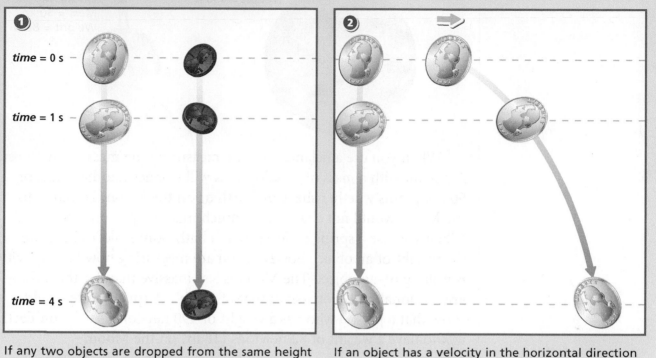

If any two objects are dropped from the same height in a vacuum, they fall at the same rate even if they have different masses.

If an object has a velocity in the horizontal direction when it falls, the horizontal velocity does not change its downward acceleration.

In a vacuum—that is, where there is no air—all falling objects have the same acceleration.

❶ The quarter falls at the same rate as the penny when they are dropped together. Because the quarter has more mass, gravity exerts more force on it. But greater mass also means more inertia, so the greater force does not produce a larger acceleration. Objects with different masses fall with the same acceleration.

❷ A coin that is dropped falls at the same rate as one that is thrown forward. Horizontal velocity does not affect acceleration due to gravity. Because gravity is directed downward, it changes only the downward velocity of the coin, not its forward velocity.

VISUALIZATION
CLASSZONE.COM

Explore how objects fall at the same rate in a vacuum.

CHECK YOUR READING Compare the times it takes two objects with different masses to fall from the same height.

Weight and Mass

While weight and mass are related, they are not the same properties. Mass is a measure of how much matter an object contains. **Weight** is the force of gravity on an object. Mass is a property that an object has no matter where it is located. Weight, on the other hand, depends on the force of gravity acting on that object.

On Earth
Mass = 50 kg
Weight = 490 N

On the Moon
Mass = 50 kg
Weight = 82 N

When you use a balance, you are measuring the mass of an object. A person with a mass of 50 kilograms will balance another mass of 50 kilograms whether she is on Earth or on the Moon. Traveling to the Moon would not change how much matter a person is made of. When you use a spring scale, such as a bathroom scale, to measure the weight of an object, however, you are measuring how hard gravity is pulling on an object. The Moon is less massive than Earth, and its gravitational pull is one-sixth that of Earth's. A spring scale would show that a person who has a weight of 490 newtons (110 lb) on Earth would have a weight of 82 newtons (18 lb) on the Moon.

Gravity keeps objects in orbit.

READING TIP

An ellipse is shaped as shown below. A circle is a special type of ellipse.

Sir Isaac Newton hypothesized that the force that pulls objects to the ground—gravity—also pulls the Moon in its orbit around Earth. An **orbit** is the elliptical path one body, such as the Moon, follows around another body, such as Earth, due to the influence of gravity. The centripetal force keeping one object in orbit around another object is due to the gravitational pull between the two objects. In the case of the Moon's orbit, the centripetal force is the gravitational pull between the Moon and Earth. Similarly, Earth is pulled around the Sun by the gravitational force between Earth and the Sun.

You can think of an object orbiting Earth as an object that is falling around Earth rather than falling to the ground. Consider what happens to the ball in the illustration on page 81. A dropped ball will fall about five meters during the first second it falls. Throwing the ball straight ahead will not change that falling time. What happens as you throw faster and faster?

Earth is curved. This fact is noticeable only over very long distances. For every 8000 meters you travel, Earth curves downward about 5 meters. If you could throw a ball at 8000 meters per second, it would fall to Earth in such a way that its path would curve the same amount that Earth curves. Since the ball would fall along the curve of Earth, the ball would never actually land on the ground. The ball would be in orbit.

Orbits

An object in orbit, like an object falling to the ground, is pulled toward Earth's center. If the object moves far enough forward as it falls, it orbits around Earth instead of hitting the ground.

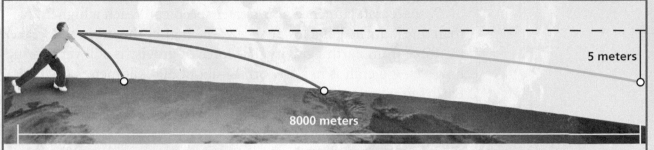

5 meters

8000 meters

If a ball is thrown straight ahead from a 5-meter height, it will drop 5 meters in the first second it falls. At low speeds, the ball will hit the ground after 1 second.

If the ball is going fast enough, the curvature of Earth becomes important. While the ball still drops 5 meters in the first second, it must fall farther than 5 meters to hit the ground.

If the ball is going fast enough to travel 8000 meters forward as it drops downward 5 meters, it follows the curvature of Earth. The ball will fall around Earth, not into it.

A ball thrown horizontally at 8000 m/s will not hit Earth during its fall. Gravity acts as a centripetal force, continually pulling the ball toward Earth's center. The ball circles Earth in an orbit.

Real-World Application
A satellite is launched upward until it is above Earth's atmosphere. The engine then gives the satellite a horizontal speed great enough to keep it in orbit.

➡ = force

➡ = velocity

READING VISUALS Compare the direction of the velocity with the direction of the force for an object in a circular orbit.

Spacecraft in Orbit

The minimum speed needed to send an object into orbit is approximately 8000 meters per second. At this speed, the path of a falling object matches the curve of Earth's surface. If you launch a spacecraft or a satellite at a slower speed, it will eventually fall to the ground.

A spacecraft launched at a greater speed can reach a higher orbit than one launched at a lower speed. The higher the orbit, the weaker the force from Earth's gravity. The force of gravity is still very strong, however. If a craft is in a low orbit—about 300 kilometers (190 mi)—Earth's gravitational pull is about 91 percent of what it is at Earth's surface. The extra distance makes a difference in the force of only about 9 percent.

If a spacecraft is launched with a speed of 11,000 meters per second or more, it is moving too fast to go into an orbit. Instead, the spacecraft will ultimately escape the pull of Earth's gravity altogether. The speed that a spacecraft needs to escape the gravitational pull of an object such as a planet or a star is called the escape velocity. A spacecraft that escapes Earth's gravity will go into orbit around the Sun unless it is also going fast enough to escape the Sun's gravity.

CHECK YOUR READING Did any facts in the text above surprise you? If so, which surprised you and why?

INVESTIGATE Gravity

How does gravity affect falling objects?

PROCEDURE

1. Carefully use the pencil to punch a hole that is the width of the pencil in the side of the cup, about one-third of the way up from the bottom.

2. Holding your finger over the hole, fill the cup three-fourths full of water.

3. Hold the cup above the dishpan. Predict what will happen if you remove your finger from the hole. Remove your finger and observe what happens.

4. With your finger over the hole, refill the cup to the same level as in step 2. Predict how the water will move if you hold the cup 50 cm above the dishpan and drop the cup and its contents straight down into the pan.

5. Drop the cup and observe what happens to the water while the cup is falling.

WHAT DO YOU THINK?

- What happened to the water in step 3? in step 5?
- How did gravity affect the water when you dropped the cup?

CHALLENGE Why did the water behave differently the second time?

SKILL FOCUS
Predicting

MATERIALS
- pencil
- paper cup
- water
- dishpan

TIME
15 minutes

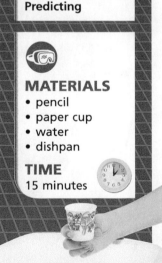

People in Orbit

When an elevator you are riding in accelerates downward, you may feel lighter for a short time. If you were standing on a scale during the downward acceleration, the scale would show that you weighed less than usual. Your mass would not have changed, nor would the pull of gravity. What would cause the apparent weight loss?

When the elevator is still, the entire force of your weight presses against the scale. When the elevator accelerates downward, you are not pressing as hard on the scale, because the scale is also moving downward. Since the scale measures how hard you are pushing on it, you appear to weigh less. If you and the scale were in free fall—a fall due entirely to gravity—the scale would fall as fast as you did. You would not press against the scale at all, so you would appear to be weightless.

Astronaut Mae Jemison is shown here working in a microgravity environment.

A spacecraft in orbit is in free fall. Gravity is acting on the astronauts and on the ship—without gravity, there could be no orbit. However, the ship and the astronauts are falling around Earth at the same rate. While astronauts are in orbit, their weight does not press against the floor of the spacecraft. The result is an environment, called a microgravity environment, in which objects behave as if there were no gravity. People and objects simply float as if they were weightless.

CHECK YOUR READING Why do astronauts float when they are in orbit?

3.1 Review

KEY CONCEPTS

1. What effect would increasing the mass of two objects have on the gravitational attraction between them?

2. What effect would decreasing the distance between objects have on their gravitational attraction to each other?

3. How does gravity keep the Moon in orbit around Earth?

CRITICAL THINKING

4. **Compare** How does the size of the force exerted by Earth's gravity on a car compare with the size of the force the car exerts on Earth?

5. **Apply** What would be the effect on the mass and the weight of an object if the object were taken to a planet with twice the gravity of Earth?

⬤ CHALLENGE

6. **Synthesize** Precision measurements of the acceleration due to gravity show that the acceleration is slightly different in different locations on Earth. Explain why the force of gravity is not exactly the same everywhere on Earth's surface. **Hint:** Think about the details of Earth's surface.

Bending Light

You know that gravity can pull objects toward each other, but did you know that gravity can also affect light? Very extreme sources of gravity cause the normally straight path of a light beam to bend.

Going in Circles

Although Earth is massive, the effects of its gravity on light are not noticeable. However, scientists can model what a familiar scene might look like with an extreme source of gravity nearby. The image to the left shows how the light from the Seattle Space Needle could be bent almost into circles if an extremely small yet extremely massive object, such as a black hole, were in front of it.

Seeing Behind Galaxies

How do we know that gravity can bend light? Astronomers, who study space, have seen the phenomenon in action. If a very bright but distant object is behind a very massive one, such as a large galaxy, the mass of the galaxy bends the light coming from the distant object. This effect, called gravitational lensing, can produce multiple images of the bright object along a ring around the massive galaxy. Astronomers have observed gravitational lensing in their images.

Facts About Bending Light

- Gravitational lensing was predicted by Albert Einstein in the early 1900s, but the first example was not observed until 1979.

- The masses of distant galaxies can be found by observing their effect on light.

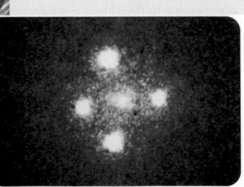

Seeing Quadruple

This gravitational lens is called the Einstein Cross. The four bright objects that ring the central galaxy are all images of the same very bright yet very distant object that is located 20 times farther away than the central galaxy.

EXPLORE

1. **INFER** Why are you unable to notice the gravitational bending of light by an object such as a large rock?

2. **CHALLENGE** Look at the photographs in the Resource Center. Find the multiple images of the distant objects and the more massive object bending the light from them.

RESOURCE CENTER
CLASSZONE.COM

Find out more information about gravitational lenses.

3.2 Friction is a force that opposes motion.

◀ BEFORE, you learned	▶ NOW, you will learn
• Gravity is the attractive force masses exert on each other • Gravity increases with greater mass and decreases with greater distance • Gravity is the centripetal force keeping objects in orbit	• How friction affects motion • About factors that affect friction • About air resistance

VOCABULARY

friction p. 85
fluid p. 88
air resistance p. 89

THINK ABOUT

What forces help you to walk?

As a person walks, she exerts a backward force on the ground. A reaction force moves her forward. But some surfaces are harder to walk on than others. Ice, for example, is harder to walk on than a dry surface because ice is slippery. How can different surfaces affect your ability to walk?

Friction occurs when surfaces slide against each other.

SUPPORTING MAIN IDEAS
Take notes about friction, including details and examples.

Have you ever pushed a heavy box across the floor? You probably noticed that it is easier to push the box over some surfaces than over others. You must apply a certain amount of force to the box to keep it moving. The force that acts against your pushing force is called friction. **Friction** is a force that resists the motion between two surfaces in contact.

When you try to slide two surfaces across each other, the force of friction resists the sliding motion. If there were no friction, the box would move as soon as you applied any force to it. Although friction can make some tasks more difficult, most activities, including walking, would be impossible without it. Friction between your feet and the ground is what provides the action and reaction forces that enable you to walk.

Forces and Surfaces

RESOURCE CENTER
CLASSZONE.COM

Learn more about friction, forces, and surfaces.

REMINDER

Remember that balanced forces on an object do not change the object's motion.

If you look down from a great height, such as from the window of an airplane, a flat field appears to be smooth. If you were to walk in the field, however, you would see that the ground has many bumps and holes. In the same way, a flat surface such as a piece of plastic may look and feel smooth. However, if you look at the plastic through a strong microscope, you see that it has tiny bumps and ridges. Friction depends on how these bumps and ridges on one surface interact with and stick to the bumps and ridges on other surfaces. There are several factors that determine the friction between two surfaces.

Types of Surfaces Friction between two surfaces depends on the materials that make up the surfaces. Different combinations of surfaces produce different frictional forces. A rubber hockey puck sliding across ice has a smaller frictional force on it than the same puck sliding across a wooden floor. The friction between rubber and ice is less than the friction between rubber and wood.

Motion of the Surfaces You need a larger force to start something moving than you do to keep something moving. If you have ever tried to push a heavy chair, you may have noticed that you had to push harder and harder until the chair suddenly accelerated forward.

As you apply a force to push a chair or any other object that is not moving, the frictional force keeping it from sliding increases so the forces stay balanced. However, the frictional force has a limit to how

Friction and Motion

Before Object Moves

applied force

friction

When an object is standing still, there is a maximum force needed to overcome friction and start it moving. Any force less than this will be exactly balanced by the force of friction, and the object will not move.

While Object Moves

acceleration

applied force

friction

Once the object is moving, the frictional force remains constant. This constant force is less than the maximum force needed to start the object moving.

large it can be. When your force is greater than this limit, the forces on the chair are no longer balanced, and the chair moves. The frictional force remains at a new lower level once the chair is moving.

Force Pressing the Surfaces Together The harder two surfaces are pushed together, the more difficult it is for the surfaces to slide over each other. When an object is placed on a surface, the weight of the object presses on that surface. The surface exerts an equal and opposite reaction force on the object. This reaction force is one of the factors that determines how much friction there is.

If you push a chair across the floor, there will be a certain amount of friction between the chair and the floor. Increasing the weight of the chair increases the force pushing the surfaces together. The force of friction between the chair and the floor is greater when a person is sitting in it than when the chair was empty.

Friction depends on the total force pressing the surfaces together, not on how much area this force acts over. Consider a rectangular cardboard box. It can rest with its smaller or larger side on the floor. The box will have the same force from friction regardless of which side sits on the floor. The larger side has more area in contact with the floor than the smaller side, but the weight of the box is more spread out on the larger side.

○ **CHECK YOUR READING** What factors influence frictional force? Give two examples.

Friction and Weight

Less Weight

weight

applied force

friction

The force of friction depends on the total force pushing the surfaces together. Here the weight of the chair is the force pressing the surfaces together.

More Weight

weight

applied force

friction

The weight of the chair increases when someone sits in it. The force of friction is now greater than when the chair was empty.

Friction and Heat

Friction between surfaces produces heat. You feel heat produced by friction when you rub your hands together. As you rub, friction causes the individual molecules on the surface of your hands to move faster. As the individual molecules in an object move faster, the temperature of the object increases. The increased speed of the molecules on the surface of your hands produces the warmth that you feel.

The heat produced by friction can be intense. The friction that results from striking a match against a rough surface produces enough heat to ignite the flammable substance on the head of the match. In some machines, such as a car engine, too much heat from friction can cause serious damage. Substances such as oil are often used to reduce friction between moving parts in machines. Without motor oil, a car's engine parts would overheat and stop working.

Friction produces sparks between a match head and a rough surface. The heat from friction eventually lights the match.

Motion through fluids produces friction.

As you have seen, two objects falling in a vacuum fall with the same acceleration. Objects falling through air, however, have different accelerations. This difference occurs because air is a fluid. A **fluid** is a substance that can flow easily. Gases and liquids are fluids.

INVESTIGATE Friction in Air

How does the shape of an object affect how it falls?

DESIGN —YOUR OWN— EXPERIMENT

Write a hypothesis that explains how shape affects the speed of falling objects. Design an experiment that tests your hypothesis.

PROCEDURE

1. Figure out how you can use the three sheets of paper to test your hypothesis. Remember to control all other variables, including the mass of the paper.

2. Write up your procedure.

3. Conduct your experiment.

WHAT DO YOU THINK?

- What were the results of your experiment?
- Did the results support your hypothesis? Explain your answer.
- Write a statement that summarizes your findings.

CHALLENGE What other variable might affect falling time? How could you test it?

SKILL FOCUS
Designing experiments

MATERIALS
3 identical sheets of paper

TIME
30 minutes

When an object moves through a fluid, it pushes the molecules of the fluid out of the way. At the same time, the molecules of the fluid exert an equal and opposite force on the object that slows it down. This force resisting motion through a fluid is a type of friction that is often called drag. Friction in fluids depends on the shape of the moving object. Objects can be designed either to increase or reduce the friction caused by a fluid. Airplane designs, for example, improve as engineers find ways to reduce drag.

The friction due to air is often called **air resistance.** Air resistance differs from the friction between solid surfaces. Air resistance depends on surface area and the speed of an object in the following ways:

- An object with a larger surface area comes into contact with more molecules as it moves than an object with a smaller surface area. This increases the air resistance.

- The faster an object moves through air, the more molecules it comes into contact with in a given amount of time. As the speed of the object increases, air resistance increases.

When a skydiver jumps out of a plane, gravity causes the skydiver to accelerate toward the ground. As the skydiver falls, his body pushes against the air. The air pushes back—with the force of air resistance. As the skydiver's speed increases, his air resistance increases. Eventually, air resistance balances gravity, and the skydiver reaches terminal velocity, which is the final, maximum velocity of a falling object. When the skydiver opens his parachute, air resistance increases still further, and he reaches a new, slower terminal velocity that enables him to land safely.

When the force of air resistance equals the force from gravity, a skydiver falls at a constant speed.

CHECK YOUR READING How do speed and surface area affect air resistance?

3.2 Review

KEY CONCEPTS

1. How does friction affect forward motion? Give an example.

2. Describe two ways to change the frictional force between two solid surfaces.

3. How does air resistance affect the velocity of a falling object?

CRITICAL THINKING

4. **Infer** What two sources of friction do you have to overcome when you are walking?

5. **Synthesize** If you push a chair across the floor at a constant velocity, how does the force of friction compare with the force you exert? Explain.

CHALLENGE

6. **Synthesize** If you push a book against a wall hard enough, it will not slide down even though gravity is pulling it. Use what you know about friction and Newton's laws of motion to explain why the book does not fall.

MATH in SCIENCE

MATH TUTORIAL
CLASSZONE.COM

Click on Math Tutorial for more help with creating a line graph.

Smoke jumpers parachute into burning forests in order to contain the flames.

Smoke Jumpers in Action

Scientists often use graphs as a way to present data. Sometimes information is easier to understand when it is presented in graphic form.

Example

Smoke jumpers are firefighters who parachute down into a forest that is on fire. Suppose you measured how the velocity of a smoke jumper changed as he was free-falling, and recorded the following data:

Time (s)	0	2	4	6	8	10	12	14	16	18
Velocity (m/s)	0	18	29	33	35	36	36	36	36	36

Follow these steps to make a line graph of the data in the table.

(1) For both variables, decide the scale that each box on your graph will represent and what range you will show for each variable. For the above time data you might choose a range of 0 to 18 s, with each interval representing 2 s. For velocity, a range of 0 to 40 m/s with intervals of 5 m/s each is reasonable.

(2) Determine the dependent and independent variables. In this example, the velocity depends on the falling time, so velocity is the dependent variable.

(3) Plot the independent variable along the horizontal axis, or x-axis. Plot the dependent variable along the vertical axis, or y-axis. Connect the points with a smooth line.

ANSWER

Use the data below to answer the following questions.

Suppose a smoke jumper varied the mass of his equipment over 5 jumps, and you measured his different terminal velocities as follows:

Extra Mass (kg)	0	5	10	15	20
Terminal Velocity (m/s)	36	37	38	39	40

1. Identify the independent and dependent variables.

2. Choose the scales and intervals you would use to graph the data. **Hint:** Your velocity range does not have to start at 0 m/s.

3. Plot your graph.

CHALLENGE How do different scales give different impressions of the data? Try comparing several different scales for the same data.

3.3

KEY CONCEPT

Pressure depends on force and area.

◀ **BEFORE, you learned**

- Frictional forces oppose motion when surfaces resist sliding
- Frictional force depends on the surface types and the total force pushing them together
- Air resistance is a type of friction on objects moving through air

▶ **NOW, you will learn**

- How pressure is determined
- How forces act on objects in fluids
- How pressure changes in fluids

VOCABULARY

pressure p. 91
pascal p. 92

EXPLORE Pressure

How does surface area affect pressure?

PROCEDURE

① Place the pencil flat on the Styrofoam board. Balance the book on top of the pencil. After 5 seconds, remove the book and the pencil. Observe the Styrofoam.

② Balance the book on top of the pencil in an upright position as shown. After 5 seconds, remove the book and the pencil. Observe the Styrofoam.

WHAT DO YOU THINK?

- How did the effect on the Styrofoam change from step 1 to step 2?
- What do you think accounts for any differences you noted?

MATERIALS

- sharpened pencil
- Styrofoam board
- book

Pressure describes how a force is spread over an area.

VOCABULARY
Create a four square diagram for *pressure* in your notebook.

Pressure is a measure of how much force is acting on a certain area. In other words, pressure describes how concentrated a force is. When a cat lies down on your lap, all the force of the cat's weight is spread out over a large area of your lap. If the cat stands up, however, all the force from the cat's weight is concentrated into its paws. The pressure the cat exerts on you increases when the cat stands up in your lap.

While the increased pressure may make you feel as if there is more force on you, the force is actually the same. The cat's weight is simply pressing on a smaller area. How you feel a force when it is pressing on you depends on both the force and the area over which it is applied.

Chapter 3: **Gravity, Friction, and Pressure** 91

One way to increase pressure is to increase force. If you press a wall with your finger, the harder you press, the more pressure you put on the wall. But you can also increase the pressure by decreasing the area. When you push a thumbtack into a wall, you apply a force to the thumbtack. The small area of the sharp point of the thumbtack produces a much larger pressure on the wall than the area of your finger does. The greater pressure from the thumbtack can pierce the wall, while the pressure from your finger alone cannot.

The following formula shows exactly how pressure depends on force and area:

$$\text{Pressure} = \frac{\text{Force}}{\text{Area}} \qquad P = \frac{F}{A}$$

In this formula, P is the pressure, F is the force in newtons, and A is the area over which the force is exerted, measured in square meters (m^2). The unit for pressure is the **pascal** (Pa). One pascal is the pressure exerted by one newton (1 N) of force on an area of one square meter (1 m^2). That is, one pascal is equivalent to one N/m^2.

Sometimes knowing pressure is more useful than knowing force. For example, many surfaces will break or crack if the pressure on them is too great. A person with snowshoes can walk on top of snow, while a person in hiking boots will sink into the snow.

READING TIP

Notice that when a unit, such as pascal or newton, is named for a person, the unit is not capitalized but its abbreviation is.

COMPARE How does the pressure from her snowshoes compare to the pressure from her boots?

Calculating Pressure

▶ **Sample Problem**

A winter hiker weighing 500 N is wearing snowshoes that cover an area of 0.2 m^2. What pressure does the hiker exert on the snow?

What do you know?	Area = 0.2 m^2, Force = 500 N
What do you want to find out?	Pressure
Write the formula:	$P = \dfrac{F}{A}$
Substitute into the formula:	$P = \dfrac{500 \text{ N}}{0.2 \text{ m}^2}$
Calculate and simplify:	$P = 2500 \dfrac{\text{N}}{\text{m}^2} = 2500 \text{ N/m}^2$
Check that your units agree:	Unit is N/m^2. Unit of pressure is Pa, which is also N/m^2. Units agree.
Answer:	$P = 2500$ Pa

▶ **Practice the Math**

1. If a winter hiker weighing 500 N is wearing boots that have an area of 0.075 m^2, how much pressure is exerted on the snow?

2. A pressure of 2000 Pa is exerted on a surface with an area of 20 m^2. What is the total force exerted on the surface?

Pressure acts in all directions in fluids.

Fluids are made of loosely connected particles that are too small to see. These particles are in constant, rapid motion. The motion is random, which means particles are equally likely to move in any direction. Particles collide with—or crash into—one another and into the walls of a container holding the fluid. The particles also collide with any objects in the fluid.

As particles collide with an object in the fluid, they apply a constant force to the surfaces of the object. This force produces a pressure against the surfaces that the particles come in contact with. A fluid contains many particles, each moving in a different direction, and the force from each particle can be exerted in any direction. Therefore, the pressure exerted by the fluid acts on an object from all directions.

The diver in the picture below experiences a constant pressure from the particles—or molecules—in the water. Water molecules are constantly hitting her body from all directions. The collisions on all parts of her body produce a net force on the surface of her body.

CHECK YOUR READING How does understanding particle motion help you understand fluid pressure?

SIMULATION
CLASSZONE.COM

Explore how a fluid produces pressure.

Pressure in Fluids

Randomly moving water molecules collide with a diver. The net force from the many collisions produces the pressure on the diver.

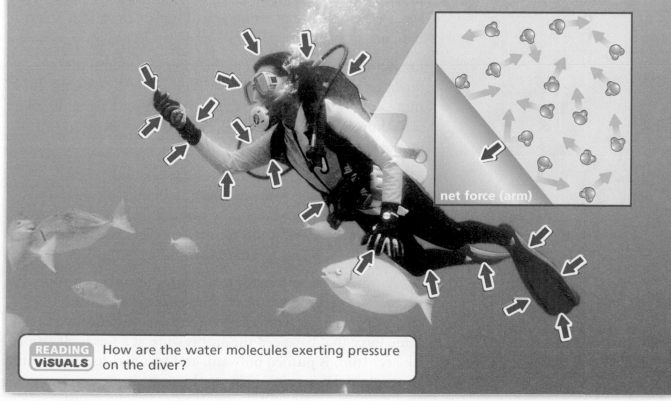

net force (arm)

READING VISUALS How are the water molecules exerting pressure on the diver?

Pressure in fluids depends on depth.

The pressure that a fluid exerts depends on the density and the depth of the fluid. Imagine that you have a tall cylinder sitting on the palm of your hand. As you fill the cylinder with water, the force of the water's weight exerts more and more pressure on your hand. The force of the water's weight increases as you put in more water.

Suppose you had two identical cylinders of water sitting on your hand. The cylinders would push with twice the weight of a single cylinder, but the force would be spread over twice the area. Therefore, the pressure would still be the same. The pressure does not depend on the total volume of the fluid, only on the depth and density.

Pressure in Air

Although you do not notice the weight of air, air exerts pressure on you at all times. At sea level, air exerts a pressure on you equal to about 100,000 pascals. This pressure is called atmospheric pressure and is referred to as one atmosphere. At this pressure, every square centimeter of your body experiences a force of ten newtons (2.2 lb). You do not notice it pushing your body inward, however, because the materials in your body provide an equal outward pressure that balances the air pressure.

Changing Elevation Air has weight. The more air there is above you, the greater the weight of that air. As you climb a mountain, the column of air above you is shorter and weighs less, so the pressure of air on you at higher elevations is less than one atmosphere.

Changing Density The air at the top of a column presses down on the air below it. The farther down the column, the more weight there is above to press downward. Air at lower elevations is more compressed, and therefore denser, than air at higher elevations.

Effects on Pressure Pressure is exerted by individual molecules colliding with an object. In denser air, there are more molecules—and therefore more collisions. An increase in the number of collisions results in an increase in the force, and therefore pressure, exerted by the air.

As you travel up a mountain, the air pressure on you decreases. For a short time, the pressure on the inside surface of your eardrum may continue to push out with the same force that balanced the air pressure at a lower elevation. The eardrum is pushed outward, and you may feel pain until your internal pressure adjusts to the new air pressure.

decreasing pressure

A person at an altitude of 2000 meters experiences approximately 20 percent less atmospheric pressure than a person at sea level.

Pressure in Water

Unlike air molecules, water molecules are already very close together. The density of water does not change very much with depth. However, the deeper you go underwater, the more water there is above you. The weight of that water above you produces the water pressure acting on your body. Just as air pressure increases at lower elevations, water pressure increases with greater water depth.

Water exerts more pressure on you than air does because water has a greater density than air. Therefore, the change in weight of the column of water above you as you dive is greater for each meter that you descend than it is in air. There is a greater difference in pressure if you dive ten meters farther down in the ocean than if you walked ten meters down a mountain. In fact, ten meters of water above you applies about as much pressure on you as the entire atmosphere does.

If you were to dive 1000 meters (3300 ft) below the surface of the ocean, the pressure would be nearly 100 times greater than pressure from the atmosphere. The force of this pressure would collapse your lungs unless you were protected by special deep-sea diving equipment. As scientists explore the ocean to greater depths, new underwater vehicles are designed that can withstand the increase in water pressure. Some whales, however, can dive to a depth of 1000 meters without being injured. As these whales dive to great depths, their lungs are almost completely collapsed by the pressure. However, the whales have adapted to the collapse—they store most of their oxygen intake in their muscles and blood instead of within their lungs.

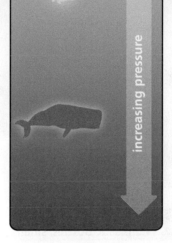

increasing pressure

A deep-diving whale at 1000 meters below the surface experiences about 34 times more pressure than a turtle diving to a depth of 20 meters (65 ft).

CHECK YOUR READING Why is water pressure greater than air pressure?

3.3 Review

KEY CONCEPTS

1. How is pressure related to force and surface area?

2. Describe the way in which a fluid exerts pressure on an object immersed in it.

3. How does changing elevation affect air pressure? How does changing depth affect water pressure?

CRITICAL THINKING

4. **Calculate** If a board with an area of 3 m² has a 12 N force exerted on it, what is the pressure on the board?

5. **Infer** What might cause a balloon blown up at a low altitude to burst if it is taken to a higher altitude?

CHALLENGE

6. **Synthesize** During cold winters, ice can form on small lakes and ponds. Many people enjoy skating on the ice. Occasionally, a person skates on thin ice and breaks through it. Why do rescue workers lie flat on the ice instead of walking upright when reaching out to help rescue a skater?

CHAPTER INVESTIGATION

Pressure in Fluids

OVERVIEW AND PURPOSE When you put your hand under a faucet, you experience water pressure. Underwater explorers also experience water pressure. In this investigation you will
- change the depth and volume of a column of water
- determine what factors affect pressure

▶ Problem

What factors affect water pressure?

▶ Hypothesize

Write two hypotheses to explain what you expect to happen to the water pressure as you change the depth and volume of the water column. Your hypotheses (one for depth, one for volume) should take the form of "If . . . , then . . . , because . . ." statements.

▶ Procedure

1. Create a data table like the one shown on the sample notebook page.

2. Using a nail, poke a hole in the side of each bottle 4 cm from the bottom of the bottle.

3. Set up the materials as shown on the left. Put a ruler in the small bottle so that the lower numbers are at the bottom.

4. Put your finger over the hole so no water will squirt out. Add or remove water (by lifting your finger off the hole) so that the water level is exactly at the 12 cm mark.

step 4

step 3

5. Release your finger from the hole, while your partner reads the exact mark where the water hits the meter stick. Cover the hole immediately after your partner reads the distance the water squirted. Record the distance on the line for this depth in your table.

MATERIALS
- nail
- 2 plastic bottles, small and large, with tops cut off
- ruler
- plastic container
- meter stick
- coffee can
- water

6 Add or remove water so that the water level is now exactly at the 11 cm mark. Repeat step 5.

7 Continue adding, removing, and squirting water at each whole centimeter mark until no more water squirts from the bottle.

8 Repeat steps 4–7 two more times for a total of three trials.

9 Repeat steps 4–8 using the large bottle.

▶ Observe and Analyze

1. **RECORD OBSERVATIONS** Be sure that your data table is complete.

2. **GRAPH** Construct a graph showing distance versus depth. Draw two curves, one for the small bottle and one for the large bottle. Use different colors for the two curves.

3. **IDENTIFY VARIABLES AND CONSTANTS** List the variables and constants for the experiment using the small bottle and the experiment using the large bottle.

4. **ANALYZE** Is the depth greater when the bottle is more full or more empty? When did the water squirt farther, when the bottle was more full or more empty?

5. **ANALYZE** Did the water squirt farther when you used the small or the large bottle?

▶ Conclude

Write It Up

1. **INTERPRET** Answer the question posed in the problem.

2. **ANALYZE** Examine your graph and compare your results with your hypotheses. Do your results support your hypotheses?

3. **INFER** How does depth affect pressure? How does volume affect pressure?

4. **IDENTIFY LIMITS** What possible limitations or errors did you experience or could you have experienced with this investigation?

5. **APPLY** Dams store water for irrigation, home use, and hydroelectric power. Explain why dams must be constructed so that they are much thicker at the bottom than at the top.

6. **APPLY** Have you ever dived to the bottom of a swimming pool to pick up a coin? Describe what you felt as you swam toward the bottom.

▶ INVESTIGATE Further

CHALLENGE Repeat the investigation using a liquid with a density that is quite different from water. Measure the distance the liquid travels, and graph the new data in a different color. Is there a difference? Why do you think there is or is not a difference in pressure between liquids of different densities?

Pressure in Fluids

Problem What factors affect water pressure?

Hypothesize

Observe and Analyze

Table 1. Distance Water Squirted with Small Bottle

Depth of water small bottle (cm)	Trial 1	Trial 2	Trial 3	Average
12				
11				
10				

Table 2. Distance Water Squirted with Large Bottle

Depth of water large bottle (cm)	Trial 1	Trial 2	Trial 3	Average
12				
11				
10				

Conclude

3.4 Fluids can exert a force on objects.

◀ BEFORE, you learned	▶ NOW, you will learn
• Pressure depends on force and area • Pressure acts in all directions in fluids • Density is mass divided by volume	• How fluids apply forces to objects • How the motion of a fluid affects the pressure it exerts • How forces are transmitted through fluids

VOCABULARY

buoyant force p. 98
Bernoulli's principle p. 100
Pascal's principle p. 102

EXPLORE Forces in Liquid

How does water affect weight?

PROCEDURE

1. Tie a piece of string to the middle of the pencil. Tie 4 paper clips to each end of the pencil as shown.

2. Move the middle string along the pencil until the paper clips are balanced and the pencil hangs flat.

3. While keeping the pencil balanced, slowly lower the paper clips on one end of the pencil into the water. Observe what happens.

MATERIALS
• 3 pieces of string
• pencil
• 8 paper clips
• cup full of water

WHAT DO YOU THINK?
• How did the water affect the balance between the two sets of paper clips?
• Did the water exert a force on the paper clips? Explain.

Fluids can exert an upward force on objects.

If you drop an ice cube in air, it falls to the floor. If you drop the ice cube into water, it may sink a little at first, but the cube quickly rises upward until it floats. You know that gravity is pulling downward on the ice, even when it is in the water. If the ice cube is not sinking, there must be some force balancing gravity that is pushing upward on it.

The upward force on objects in a fluid is called **buoyant force,** or buoyancy. Buoyancy is why ice floats in water. Because of buoyant force, objects seem lighter in water. For example, it is easier to lift a heavy rock in water than on land because the buoyant force pushes upward on the rock, reducing the net force you need to lift it.

VOCABULARY
Create a four square diagram for *buoyant force.*

Buoyancy

The photograph on the right shows a balloon that has been pushed into a beaker of water. Remember that in a fluid, pressure increases with depth. This means that there is greater pressure acting on the bottom of the balloon than on the top of it. The pressure difference between the top and bottom of the balloon produces a net force that is pushing the balloon upward.

When you push a balloon underwater, the water level rises because the water and the balloon cannot be in the same place at the same time. The volume of the water has not changed, but some of the water has been displaced, or moved, by the balloon. The volume of the displaced water is equal to the volume of the balloon. The buoyant force on the balloon is equal to the weight of the displaced water. A deflated balloon would displace less water and would therefore have a smaller buoyant force on it.

net force

 CHECK YOUR READING Why does increasing the volume of an object increase the buoyant force on it when it is in a fluid?

Density and Buoyancy

Whether or not an object floats in a fluid depends on the densities of both the object and the fluid. Density is a measure of the amount of matter packed into a unit volume. The density of an object is equal to its mass divided by its volume, and is commonly measured in grams per cubic centimeter (g/cm^3).

If an object is less dense than the fluid it is in, the fluid the object displaces can weigh more than the object. A wooden ball that is pushed underwater, as in the beaker below and on the left, rises to the top and floats. An object rising in a liquid has a buoyant force acting upon it that is greater than its own weight. If an object is floating in a liquid, the buoyant force is balancing the weight.

READING TiP

Remember that both air and water are fluids, and water has a greater density than air. Therefore, water has a greater buoyant force.

If the object is more dense than the fluid it is in, the object weighs more than the fluid it displaces. A glass marble placed in the beaker on the far right sinks to the bottom because glass is denser than water. The weight of the water the marble displaces is less than the weight of the marble. A sinking object has a weight that is greater than the buoyant force on it.

weight · buoyant force · no net force

weight · buoyant force · net force

The motion of a fluid affects its pressure.

The motion of a fluid affects the amount of pressure it exerts. A faster-moving fluid exerts less pressure as it flows over the surface of an object than a slower moving fluid. For example, wind blowing over a chimney top decreases the pressure at the top of the chimney. The faster air has less pressure than the slower-moving air in the fireplace. The increased pressure difference more effectively pulls the smoke from a fire out of the fireplace and up the chimney.

Bernoulli's Principle

Bernoulli's principle, named after Daniel Bernoulli (buhr-NOO-lee), a Swiss mathematician who lived in the 1700s, describes the effects of fluid motion on pressure. In general, **Bernoulli's principle** says that an increase in the speed of the motion of a fluid decreases the pressure within the fluid. The faster a fluid moves, the less pressure it exerts on surfaces or openings it flows over.

CHECK YOUR READING What is the relationship between the speed of a fluid and the pressure that the fluid exerts?

INVESTIGATE Bernoulli's Principle

How does the speed of air affect air pressure?

PROCEDURE

1. Use the pen to mark off intervals of 1 cm along the length of one of the straws.

2. Put a drop of food coloring in the cup of water and stir it. Place the marked straw into the cup and hold it upright so that the water level in the straw is at one of the marks. The straw should not touch the bottom of the cup.

3. Position the second straw as shown. Blow across the open end of the marked straw. Observe the level of the water in the marked straw as you blow.

4. Blow harder and then softer. Observe the water level as you change the speed of the air.

WHAT DO YOU THINK?

- What happened to the water in the straw as you blew?
- How did the speed of the air relate to the changes you observed?

CHALLENGE What results would you expect if you blew over the top of a tube with a closed bottom instead of the straw? Explain.

SKILL FOCUS
Observing

MATERIALS
- pen
- ruler
- two clear straws
- clear plastic cup filled with water
- food coloring

TIME
15 minutes

Applying Bernoulli's Principle

Bernoulli's principle has many applications. One important application is used in airplanes. Airplane wings can be shaped to take advantage of Bernoulli's principle. Certain wing shapes cause the air flowing over the top of the wing to move faster than the air flowing under the wing. Such a design improves the lifting force on a flying airplane.

Many racecars, however, have a device on the rear of the car that has the reverse effect. The device is designed like an upside-down airplane wing. This shape increases the pressure on the top of the car. The car is pressed downward on the road, which increases friction between the tires and the road. With more friction, the car is less likely to skid as it goes around curves at high speeds.

A prairie-dog colony also shows Bernoulli's principle in action. The mounds that prairie dogs build over some entrances to their burrows help to keep the burrows well-ventilated.

1 Air closer to the ground tends to move at slower speeds than air higher up. The air over an entrance at ground level generally moves slower than the air over an entrance in a raised mound.

2 The increased speed of the air over a raised mound entrance decreases the pressure over that opening.

3 The greater air pressure over a ground-level entrance produces an unbalanced force that pushes air through the tunnels and out the higher mound entrance.

Bernoulli's Principle in Nature

Bernoulli's principle explains why having two entrances at different heights helps ventilate a prairie-dog burrow.

1 Air moves more slowly near the ground.

2 The air over the raised entrance moves faster and has less pressure than the slower-moving air near the ground.

3 The pressure difference between the two entrances moves air through the tunnel.

Forces can be transmitted through fluids.

Imagine you have a bottle full of water. You place the bottle cap on it, but you do not tighten the cap. You give the bottle a hard squeeze and the cap falls off. How was the force you put on the bottle transferred to the bottle cap?

Pascal's Principle

In the 1600s Blaise Pascal (pa-SKAL), a French scientist for whom the unit of measure called the pascal was named, experimented with fluids in containers. One of his key discoveries is called Pascal's principle. **Pascal's principle** states that when an outside pressure is applied at any point to a fluid in a container, that pressure is transmitted throughout the fluid with equal strength.

You can use Pascal's principle to transmit a force through a fluid. Some car jacks lift cars using Pascal's principle. These jacks contain liquids that transmit and increase the force that you apply.

1 The part of the jack that moves down and pushes on the liquid is called a piston. As you push down on the piston, you increase the pressure on the liquid.

2 The increase in pressure is equal to your applied force divided by the area of the downward-pushing piston. This increase in pressure is transmitted throughout the liquid.

Pascal's Principle

The pressure from the smaller piston is equal to the pressure pushing up the larger one. The large piston can exert more force because of its greater area.

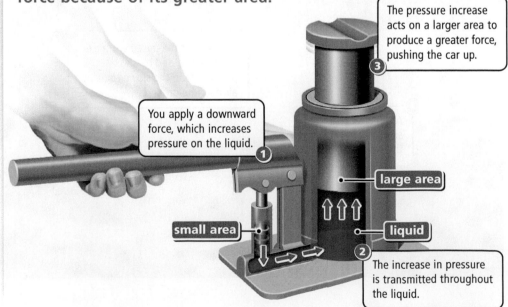

The pressure increase acts on a larger area to produce a greater force, pushing the car up. **3**

You apply a downward force, which increases pressure on the liquid. **1**

large area

small area

liquid

The increase in pressure is transmitted throughout the liquid. **2**

③ The increased pressure pushes upward on another piston, which raises the car. This piston has a large area compared with the first piston, so the upward force is greater than the downward force. A large enough area produces the force needed to lift a car. However, the larger piston does not move upward as far as the smaller one moved downward.

CHECK YOUR READING Describe how pressure is transmitted through a fluid.

Hydraulics

Machines that use liquids to transmit or increase a force are called hydraulic (hy-DRAW-lihk) machines. The advantage to using a liquid instead of a gas is that when you squeeze a liquid, its volume does not change much. The molecules in a liquid are so close together that it is hard to push the molecules any closer. Gas molecules, however, have a lot of space between them. If you apply pressure to a gas, you decrease its volume.

The hydraulic arm on the garbage truck lifts and empties trash cans.

Although hydraulic systems are used in large machines such as garbage trucks, research is being done on using hydraulics on a much smaller scale. Researchers are developing a storage chip similar to a computer chip that uses hydraulics rather than electronics. This chip uses pipes and pumps to move fluid into specific chambers on a rubber chip. Researchers hope that a hydraulic chip system will eventually allow scientists to use a single hand-held device to perform chemical experiments with over a thousand different liquids.

3.4 Review

KEY CONCEPTS

1. Why is there an upward force on objects in water?

2. How does changing the speed of a fluid affect its pressure?

3. If you push a cork into the neck of a bottle filled with air, what happens to the pressure inside the bottle?

CRITICAL THINKING

4. **Infer** Ebony is a dark wood that has a density of 1.2 g/cm³. Water has a density of 1.0 g/cm³. Will a block of ebony float in water? Explain.

5. **Analyze** When you use a spray bottle, you force air over a small tube inside the bottle. Explain why the liquid inside the bottle comes out.

○ CHALLENGE

6. **Synthesize** If you apply a force of 20 N downward on a car jack piston with an area of 2.5 cm², what force will be applied to the upward piston if it has an area of 400 cm²? Hint: Remember that pressure equals force divided by area.

the **BIG** idea

Newton's laws apply to all forces.

CONTENT REVIEW
CLASSZONE.COM

◀ KEY CONCEPTS SUMMARY

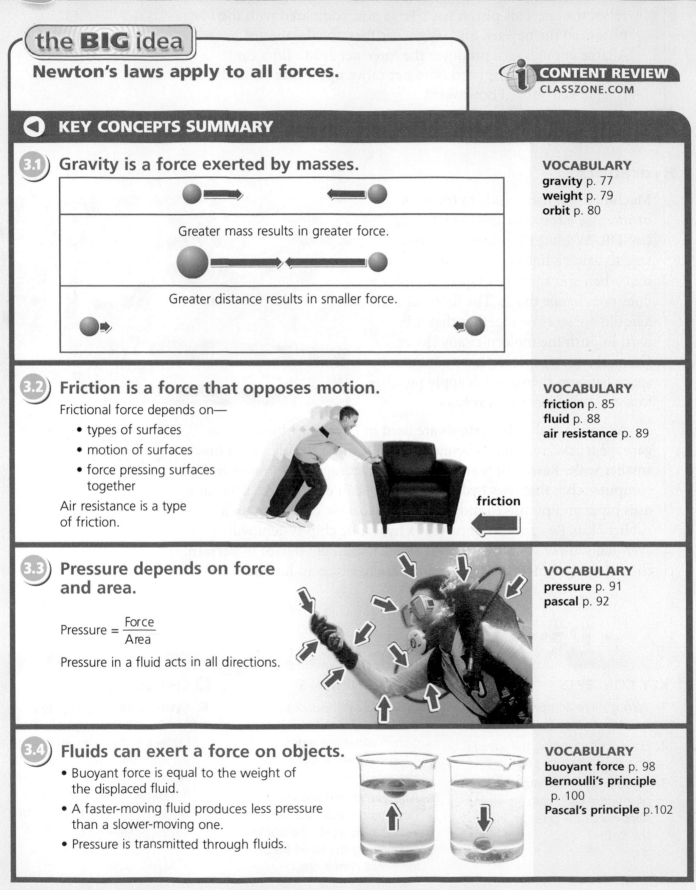

3.1 Gravity is a force exerted by masses.

Greater mass results in greater force.

Greater distance results in smaller force.

VOCABULARY
gravity p. 77
weight p. 79
orbit p. 80

3.2 Friction is a force that opposes motion.

Frictional force depends on—

- types of surfaces
- motion of surfaces
- force pressing surfaces together

Air resistance is a type of friction.

friction

VOCABULARY
friction p. 85
fluid p. 88
air resistance p. 89

3.3 Pressure depends on force and area.

$$\text{Pressure} = \frac{\text{Force}}{\text{Area}}$$

Pressure in a fluid acts in all directions.

VOCABULARY
pressure p. 91
pascal p. 92

3.4 Fluids can exert a force on objects.

- Buoyant force is equal to the weight of the displaced fluid.
- A faster-moving fluid produces less pressure than a slower-moving one.
- Pressure is transmitted through fluids.

VOCABULARY
buoyant force p. 98
Bernoulli's principle p. 100
Pascal's principle p.102

Reviewing Vocabulary

Write a sentence describing the relationship between each pair of terms.

1. gravity, weight

2. gravity, orbit

3. pressure, pascal

4. fluid, friction

5. density, buoyant force

6. fluid, Bernoulli's principle

Reviewing Key Concepts

Multiple Choice *Choose the letter of the best answer.*

7. Which force keeps Venus in orbit around the Sun?
   a. gravity   **c.** hydraulic
   b. friction   **d.** buoyancy

8. You and a classmate are one meter apart. If you move farther away, how does the gravitational force between you and your classmate change?
   a. It increases.
   b. It decreases.
   c. It stays the same.
   d. It disappears.

9. You kick a ball on a level sidewalk. It rolls to a stop because
   a. there is no force on the ball
   b. gravity slows the ball down
   c. air pressure is pushing down on the ball
   d. friction slows the ball down

10. You push a chair at a constant velocity using a force of 5 N to overcome friction. You stop to rest, then push again. To start the chair moving again, you must use a force that is
    a. greater than 5 N
    b. equal to 5 N
    c. greater than 0 N but less than 5 N
    d. 0 N

11. How could you place an empty bottle on a table so that it produces the greatest amount of pressure on the table?

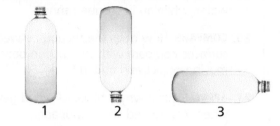

   a. position 1
   b. position 2
   c. position 3
   d. All positions produce the same pressure.

12. As you climb up a mountain, air pressure
    a. increases
    b. decreases
    c. stays the same
    d. changes unpredictably

13. If you squeeze a balloon in the middle, what happens to the air pressure inside the balloon?
    a. It increases only in the middle.
    b. It decreases only in the middle.
    c. It increases throughout.
    d. It decreases throughout.

Short Answer *Write a short answer to each question.*

14. How does the force of attraction between large masses compare with the force of attraction between small masses at the same distance?

15. Explain why a satellite in orbit around Earth does not crash into Earth.

16. You are pushing a dresser with drawers filled with clothing. What could you do to reduce the friction between the dresser and the floor?

17. Why is water pressure greater at a depth of 20 feet than it is at a depth of 10 feet?

18. If you blow over the top of a small strip of paper, the paper bends upward. Why?

19. **APPLY** Explain why an iron boat can float in water, while an iron cube cannot.

20. **COMPARE** How does the friction between solid surfaces compare with the friction between a moving object and a fluid?

21. **APPLY** Explain why a block of wood gets warm when it is rubbed with sandpaper.

22. **PREDICT** The Moon's orbit is gradually increasing. Each year the Moon is about 3.8 cm farther from Earth than the year before. How does this change affect the force of gravity between Earth and the Moon?

23. **APPLY** The Moon has one-sixth the gravity of Earth. Why would it be easier to launch spacecraft into orbit around the Moon than around Earth?

Use the photograph below to answer the next three questions.

24. **APPLY** A skydiver jumps out of a plane. After he reaches terminal velocity, he opens his parachute. Draw a sketch showing the forces of air resistance and gravity on the skydiver after the parachute opens. Use a longer arrow for a greater force.

25. **SYNTHESIZE** Air is a fluid, which produces a small buoyant force on the skydiver. How does this buoyant force change after he opens his parachute? Why?

26. **INFER** The Moon has no atmosphere. Would it be safe to skydive on the Moon? Why or why not?

27. **INFER** When oil and water are mixed together, the two substances separate and the oil floats to the top. How does the density of oil compare with the density of water?

28. **COMPARE** Three flasks are filled with colored water as shown below. How does the water pressure at the bottom of each flask compare with the water pressure at the bottom of the other two?

1   2   3

Using Math Skills in Science

Complete the following calculations.

29. How much force does a 10 kg marble exert on the ground?

30. A force of 50 N is applied on a piece of wood with an area of 0.5 m^2. What is the pressure on the wood?

the **BIG** idea

31. **ANALYZE** Look again at the picture on pages 74–75. What forces are acting on the snowboarder? on the snow? Use Newton's laws to explain how these forces enable the snowboarder to move down the hill.

32. **SYNTHESIZE** Choose two concepts discussed in this chapter, and describe how Newton's laws relate to those concepts.

UNIT PROJECTS

Check your schedule for your unit project. How are you doing? Be sure that you have placed data or notes from your research into your project folder.

Interpreting Diagrams

Study the diagram and then answer the questions that follow.

Bernoulli's principle states that an increase in the speed of the motion of a fluid decreases the pressure exerted by the fluid. The diagram below relates the movement of a curve ball in baseball to this principle. The ball is shown from above.

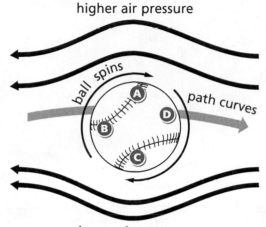

higher air pressure

ball spins

path curves

lower air pressure

1. To which of these properties does Bernoulli's principle apply?
  a. air pressure
  b. temperature
  c. air resistance
  d. density

2. Where is the air moving fastest in the diagram?
  a. region A
  b. region B
  c. region C
  d. region D

3. Because the ball is spinning, the air on one side is moving faster than on the other side. This causes the ball to curve due to the
  a. air molecules moving slowly and evenly around the ball
  b. forward motion of the ball
  c. difference in air pressure on the ball
  d. changing air temperature around the ball

4. If the baseball were spinning as it moved forward underwater, instead of through the air, how would the pressure of the fluid act on the ball?
  a. The water pressure would be the same on all sides.
  b. The water pressure would vary as air pressure does.
  c. The water pressure would be greatest on the side where air pressure was least.
  d. The water pressure would prevent the ball from spinning.

Extended Response

Answer the two questions below in detail. Include some of the terms from the word box. Underline each term you use in your answer.

acceleration	air resistance	density
fluid	friction	gravity
mass	pressure	velocity

5. If a feather and a bowling ball are dropped from the same height, will they fall at the same rate? Explain.

6. A balloon filled with helium or hot air can float in the atmosphere. A balloon filled with air from your lungs falls to the ground when it is released. Why do these balloons behave differently?

TIMELINES in Science

UNDERSTANDING FORCES

In ancient times, people thought that an object would not move unless it was pushed. Scientists came up with ingenious ways to explain how objects like arrows stayed in motion. Over time, they came to understand that all motion could be described by three basic laws. Modern achievements such as suspension bridges and space exploration are possible because of the experiments with motion and forces performed by scientists and philosophers over hundreds of years.

This timeline shows just a few of the many steps on the path toward understanding forces. Notice how scientists used the observations and ideas of previous thinkers as a springboard for developing new theories. The boxes below the timeline show how technology has led to new insights and to applications of those ideas.

350 B.C.
Aristotle Discusses Motion
The Greek philosopher Aristotle states that the natural condition of an object is to be at rest. A force is necessary to keep the object in motion. The greater the force, the faster the object moves.

EVENTS

400 B.C.   350 B.C.   300 B.C.

APPLICATIONS AND TECHNOLOGY

TECHNOLOGY
Catapulting into History
As early as 400 B.C., armies were using objects in motion to do work. Catapults, or machines for hurling stones and spears, were used as military weapons. Five hundred years later, the Roman army used catapults mounted on wheels. In the Middle Ages, young trees were sometimes bent back, loaded with an object, and then released like a large slingshot. Today catapult technology is used to launch airplanes from aircraft carriers. A piston powered by steam propels the plane along the deck of the aircraft carrier until it reaches takeoff speed.

A.D. 1121

Force Acting on Objects Described

Persian astronomer al-Khazini asserts that a force acts on all objects to pull them toward the center of Earth. This force varies, he says, depending on whether the object moves through air, water, or another medium. His careful notes and drawings illustrate these principles.

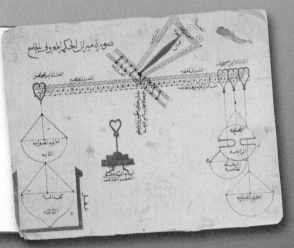

250 B.C.

Levers and Buoyancy Explained

The Greek inventor Archimedes uses a mathematical equation to explain how a small weight can balance a much larger weight near a lever's fulcrum. He also explains buoyancy, which provides a way of measuring volume.

1150

Perpetual-Motion Machine Described

Indian mathematician and physicist Bhaskara describes a wheel that uses closed containers of liquid to turn forever without stopping. If it worked, his idea would promise an unending source of power that does not rely on an external source.

| 250 B.C. | A.D. 1100 | 1150 | 1200 |

APPLICATION

The First Steam-Powered Engine

In the first century A.D., Hero of Alexandria, a Greek inventor, created the first known steam engine, called the aeolipile. It was a hollow ball with two cylinders jutting out in opposite directions. The ball was suspended above a kettle that was filled with water and placed over a fire. As the water boiled, steam caused the ball to spin. The Greeks never used this device for work. In 1690, Sir Isaac Newton formulated the principle of the aeolipile in scientific terms in his third law of motion. A steam engine designed for work was built in 1698. The aeolipile is the earliest version of steam-powered pumps, steam locomotives, jet engines, and rockets.

1638

*Objects Need No
Force to Keep Moving*

Italian astronomer Galileo
Galilei says that an object's
natural state is either in constant
motion or at rest. Having observed the
motion of objects on ramps, he concludes that an
object in motion will slow down or speed up only if
a force is exerted on it. He also claims that all objects
dropped near the surface of Earth fall with the same
acceleration due to the force of gravity.

1494

*Perpetual-Motion Machine
Impossible*

Italian painter and engineer
Leonardo da Vinci proves that it is
impossible to build a perpetual-
motion machine that works. He
states that the force of friction
keeps a wheel from turning forever
without more force being applied.

1687

*An Object's Motion Can
Be Predicted*

English scientist Sir Isaac
Newton publishes his three
laws of motion, which use
Galileo's ideas as a founda-
tion. He concludes that
Earth exerts a gravitational
force on objects on its surface and that Earth's gravity
keeps the Moon in orbit.

| 1500 | 1550 | 1600 | 1650 | 1700 | 1750 | 1800 |

APPLICATION

A New and Improved Steam Engine

Scottish scientist James Watt designed steam engines
that were much more efficient, and much smaller,
than older models. About 500 of Watt's engines
were in use by 1800. His pump engines drew
water out of coal mines, and his rotating
engines were used in factories and
cotton mills. Watt's steam engines
opened the way to the Industrial
Revolution. They were used in
major industries such as textile
manufacturing, railroad transportation, and mining. Watt's steam
technology also opened up new
areas of research in heat, kinetic
energy, and motion.

1919

Gravity Bends Light

A solar eclipse confirms German-American physicist Albert Einstein's modification of Newton's laws. Einstein's theory states that the path of a light beam will be affected by nearby massive objects. During the eclipse, the stars appear to shift slightly away from one another because their light has been bent by the Sun's gravity.

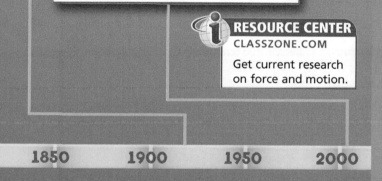

2001

Supercomputers Model Strong Force

Scientists have been using supercomputers to model the force that holds particles in the nucleus of an atom together. This force, called the strong force, cannot be measured directly in the same way that gravity and other forces can. Instead, computer models allow scientists to make predictions that are then compared with experimental results.

RESOURCE CENTER
CLASSZONE.COM

Get current research on force and motion.

1850   1900   1950   2000

TECHNOLOGY

Science Propels Exploration of Outer Space

An increased understanding of forces made space exploration possible. In 1926 American scientist Robert H. Goddard constructed and tested the first liquid-propelled rocket. A replica of Goddard's rocket can be seen at the National Air and Space Museum in Washington, D.C. In 1929 Goddard launched a rocket that carried the first scientific payload, a barometer and a camera.

Many later achievements—including the 1969 walk on the Moon—are a direct result of Goddard's trail-blazing space research.

SPOTLIGHT on CLAUDIA ALEXANDER

Claudia Alexander is a space plasma scientist at NASA's Jet Propulsion Laboratory (JPL) at the California Institute of Technology in Pasadena. She studies comets and other solid, icy bodies in the solar system.

Alexander was the seventh and final project manager of NASA's *Galileo* mission to Jupiter. *Galileo* was an unmanned spacecraft launched from the space shuttle *Atlantis* in 1989. By the end of the mission, *Galileo* had discovered evidence of water on three of Jupiter's moons. The spacecraft sent back spectacular photos from outer space. *Galileo* was programmed to crash into Jupiter at the end of its mission in 2003. Alexander reported that *Galileo* collected valuable data about the planet's environment up until the very end.

ACTIVITIES

Reliving History

Bhaskara's design for a perpetual-motion machine involved a wheel with containers of mercury around the rim. As the wheel turned, the mercury would move in such a way that the wheel would always be heavier on one side—and stay in motion. Now we know that this theory goes against the laws of physics. Observe a wheel, a pendulum, or a swing. Think about why it cannot stay in motion forever.

Writing About Science

Suppose you won a trip to outer space. Write a letter accepting or refusing the prize. Give your reasons.

Work and Energy

the **BIG** idea

Energy is transferred when a force moves an object.

Key Concepts

SECTION

4.1 Work is the use of force to move an object.
Learn about the relationship between force and work.

SECTION

4.2 Energy is transferred when work is done.
Learn how energy is related to work.

SECTION

4.3 Power is the rate at which work is done.
Learn to calculate power from work and energy.

Which takes more work, lifting a box or holding a box? Why?

Internet Preview

Bouncing Ball

Drop a large ball on a hard, flat floor. Let it bounce several times. Notice the height the ball reaches after each bounce.

Observe and Think
How did the height change? Why do you think this happens? Sketch the path of the ball through several bounces.

Power Climbing

Walk up a flight of stairs wearing a backpack. Run up the same flight of stairs wearing the backpack.

Observe and Think
Compare and contrast both trips up the stairs. Which one took greater effort? Did you apply the same force against gravity each time?

Internet Activity: Work

Go to **ClassZone.com** to simulate lifting weights of different masses. Determine how much work is done in lifting each weight by watching your progress on a work meter.

Observe and Think
Do you think more work will be done if the weights are lifted higher?

NSTA
scilinks.org

SciLINKS

Potential and Kinetic Energy **Code: MDL007**

Getting Ready to Learn

◀ CONCEPT REVIEW

- Forces change the motion of objects in predictable ways.
- Velocity is a measure of the speed and direction of an object.
- An unbalanced force produces acceleration.

◀ VOCABULARY REVIEW

velocity p. 22

force p. 41

See Glossary for definitions.

energy, mass

 **CONTENT REVIEW**
CLASSZONE.COM
Review concepts and vocabulary.

▶ TAKING NOTES

MAIN IDEA WEB

Write each new blue heading in a box. Then write notes in boxes around it that give important terms and details about that blue heading.

CHOOSE YOUR OWN STRATEGY

Take notes about new vocabulary terms using one or more of the strategies from earlier chapters—**description wheel, magnet words,** or **four square.** Feel free to mix and match the strategies or use a different strategy.

See the Note-Taking Handbook on pages R45–R51.

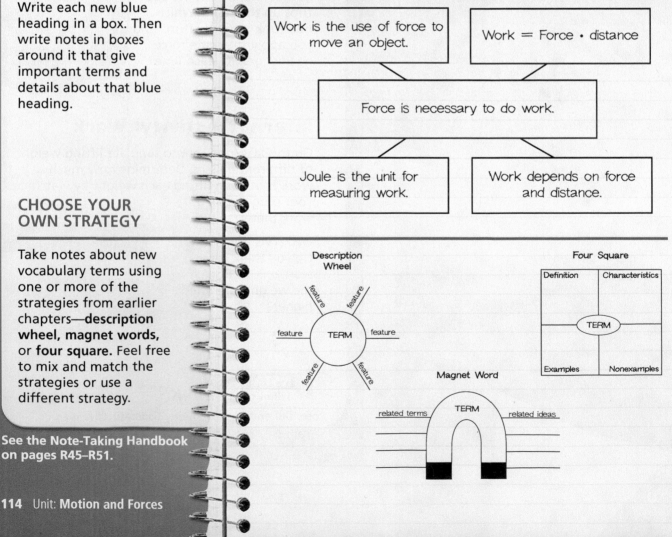

SCIENCE NOTEBOOK

Work is the use of force to move an object.

Work = Force · distance

Force is necessary to do work.

Joule is the unit for measuring work.

Work depends on force and distance.

Description Wheel

feature feature
feature TERM feature
feature feature

Magnet Word

related terms TERM related ideas

Four Square

Definition	Characteristics
TERM	
Examples	Nonexamples

KEY CONCEPT

4.1 Work is the use of force to move an object.

◁ BEFORE, you learned	▷ NOW, you will learn
• An unbalanced force produces acceleration	• How force and work are related
• Weight is measured in newtons	• How moving objects do work

VOCABULARY

work p. 115
joule p. 117

EXPLORE Work

How do you work?

PROCEDURE

MATERIALS
book

(1) Lift a book from the floor to your desktop. Try to move the book at a constant speed.

(2) Now lift the book again, but stop about halfway up and hold the book still for about 30 seconds. Then continue lifting the book to the desktop.

WHAT DO YOU THINK?

• Do you think you did more work the first time you lifted the book or the second time you lifted the book?
• What do you think *work* means?

Force is necessary to do work.

VOCABULARY
You might want to make a description wheel diagram in your notebook for *work*.

What comes to mind when you think of work? Most people say they are working when they do anything that requires a physical or mental effort. But in physical science, **work** is the use of force to move an object some distance. In scientific terms, you do work only when you exert a force on an object and move it. According to this definition of work, reading this page is not doing work. Turning the page, however, would be work because you are lifting the page.

Solving a math problem in your head is not doing work. Writing the answer is work because you are moving the pencil across the paper. If you want to do work, you have to use force to move something.

CHECK YOUR READING How does the scientific definition of work differ from the familiar definition?

Force, Motion, and Work

Work is done only when an object that is being pushed or pulled actually moves. If you lift a book, you exert a force and do work. What if you simply hold the book out in front of you? No matter how tired your muscles may become from holding the book still, you are not doing work unless you move the book.

The work done by a force is related to the size of the force and the distance over which the force is applied. How much work does it take to push a grocery cart down an aisle? The answer depends on how hard you push the cart and the length of the aisle. If you use the same amount of force, you do more work pushing a cart down a long aisle than a short aisle.

Work is done only by the part of the applied force that acts in the same direction as the motion of an object. Suppose you need to pull a heavy suitcase on wheels. You pull the handle up at an angle as you pull the suitcase forward. Only the part of the force pulling the suitcase forward is doing work. The force with which you pull upward on the handle is not doing work because the suitcase is not moving upward—unless you are going uphill.

CHECK YOUR READING Give two examples of when you are applying a force but not doing work.

Work

Work is done by force that acts in the same direction as the motion of an object.

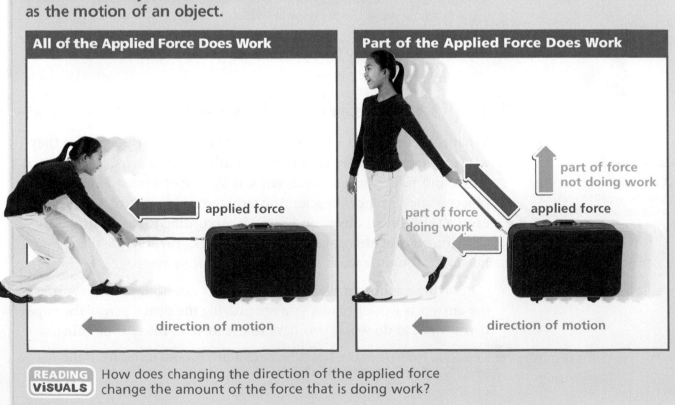

All of the Applied Force Does Work

applied force

direction of motion

Part of the Applied Force Does Work

part of force not doing work

part of force doing work

applied force

direction of motion

READING VISUALS How does changing the direction of the applied force change the amount of the force that is doing work?

Calculating Work

Work is a measure of how much force is applied over a certain distance. You can calculate the work a force does if you know the size of the force applied to an object and the distance over which the force acts. The distance involved is the distance the object moved in the direction of that force. The calculation for work is shown in the following formula:

$$\textbf{Work} = \textbf{Force} \cdot \textbf{distance}$$
$$\textbf{W} = \textbf{Fd}$$

You read in previous chapters that you can measure force in newtons. You also know that you can measure distance in meters. When you multiply a force in newtons times a distance in meters, the product is a measurement called the newton-meter (N·m), or the **joule** (jool).

The joule (J) is the standard unit used to measure work. One joule of work is done when a force of one newton moves an object one meter. To get an idea of how much a joule of work is, lift an apple (which weighs about one newton) from your foot to your waist (about one meter).

Use the formula for work to solve the problem below.

This man is doing work when he applies force to lift his body.

Calculating Work

▶ Sample Problem

How much work is done if a person lifts a barbell weighing 450 N to a height of 2 m?

What do you know?	force needed to lift = 450 N, distance = 2 m
What do you want to find out?	Work
Write the formula:	$W = Fd$
Substitute into the formula:	$W = 450$ N · 2 m
Calculate and simplify:	$W = 900$ N·m
Check that your units agree:	Unit is newton-meter (N·m). Unit of work is joule, which is N·m. Units agree.
Answer:	$W = 900$ J

▶ Practice the Math

1. If you push a cart with a force of 70 N for 2 m, how much work is done?
2. If you did 200 J of work pushing a box with a force of 40 N, how far did you push the box?

▼ **REMINDER**

You know that $W = Fd$. You can manipulate the formula to find force or distance.
$d = \dfrac{W}{F}$ and $F = \dfrac{W}{d}$

Objects that are moving can do work.

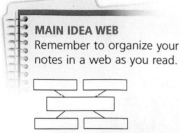

MAIN IDEA WEB
Remember to organize your notes in a web as you read.

You do work when you pick up your books, hit a baseball, swim a lap, or tap a keyboard. These examples show that you do work on objects, but objects can also do work.

For example, in a bowling alley, the bowling balls do work on the pins they hit. Outdoors, the moving air particles in a gust of wind do work that lifts a leaf off the ground. Moving water, such as the water in a river, also does work. If the windblown leaf lands in the water, it might be carried downstream by the current. As the leaf travels downstream, it might go over the edge of a waterfall. In that case, the gravitational force of Earth would pull the leaf and water down.

You can say that an object or person does work on an object, or that the force the object or person is exerting does work. For example, you could say that Earth (an object) does work on the falling water, or that gravity (a force) does work on the water.

INVESTIGATE Work

How much work does it take?
PROCEDURE

1. Have a partner help you measure how high your shoulders are from the ground. Record the distance in meters. Round to the nearest tenth of a meter.

2. Attach the notebook to the spring scale. Then slowly lift the notebook to your shoulder to see how much force you are exerting. Record the amount in newtons.

3. Calculate the work you did while lifting one notebook. Use this information to estimate how much work you do every day when you pick up all your notebooks to take them to school. (**Hint:** Work equals force times distance.)

WHAT DO YOU THINK?

- Approximately how much work does it take to pick up your notebook?

- How would the amount of work you do change if you were shorter? taller?

- How much work are you doing on the notebook if you have stopped to talk to a friend?

CHALLENGE If you pick up a notebook 10 times a day during the school year, how much work do you do on the notebook in one year? (Assume that there are 180 school days in a year.)

SKILL FOCUS
Measuring

MATERIALS
- meter stick
- spiral notebook
- spring scale

TIME
20 minutes

APPLY How could you increase the work done by this water wheel?

Throughout history, people have taken advantage of the capability of objects in motion to do work. Many early cultures built machines such as water wheels to use the force exerted by falling water, and windmills to use the force exerted by moving air. In a water wheel like the one in the photograph, gravity does work on the water. As the water falls, it also can do work on any object that is put in its path. Falling water can turn a water wheel or the turbine of an electric generator.

The water wheel shown above uses the work done by water to turn gears that run a mill and grind grain. In the same way, windmills take advantage of the force of moving air particles. The wind causes the sails of a windmill to turn. The turning sails do work to run machinery or an irrigation system.

CHECK YOUR READING Describe how a water wheel does work.

4.1 Review

KEY CONCEPTS

1. If you push very hard on an object but it does not move, have you done work? Explain.

2. What two factors do you need to know to calculate how much work was done in any situation?

3. Was work done on a book that fell from a desk to the floor? If so, what force was involved?

CRITICAL THINKING

4. **Synthesize** Work is done on a ball when a soccer player kicks it. Is the player still doing work on the ball as it rolls across the ground? Explain.

5. **Calculate** Tina lifted a box 0.5 m. The box weighed 25 N. How much work did Tina do on the box?

CHALLENGE

6. **Analyze** Ben and Andy each pushed an empty grocery cart. Ben used twice the force, but they both did the same amount of work. Explain.

MATH TUTORIAL
CLASSZONE.COM
Click on Math Tutorial for more help with finding the mean.

Eliminating Extreme Values

A value that is far from most others in a set of data is called an outlier. Outliers make it difficult to find a value that might be considered average. Extremely high or extremely low values can throw off the mean. That is why the highest and lowest figures are ignored in some situations.

Example

The data set below shows the work an escalator does to move 8 people of different weights 5 meters. The work was calculated by multiplying the force needed to move each person by a distance of 5 meters.

| 4850 J | 1600 J | 3400 J | 2750 J |
| 2950 J | 1750 J | 3350 J | 3800 J |

The mean amount of work done is 3056 J.

(1) To calculate an adjusted mean, begin by identifying a high outlier in the data set.

High outlier: 4850

(2) Discard this value and find the new mean.

1600 J + 3400 J + 2750 J + 2950 J + 1750 J + 3350 J + 3800 J
= 19,600 J

$$\text{Mean} = \frac{19,600 \text{ J}}{7} = 2800 \text{ J}$$

ANSWER The mean amount of work done for this new data set is 2800 J.

Answer the following questions.

1. After ignoring the high outlier in the data set, does this new mean show a more typical level of work for the data set? Why or why not?

2. Do you think the lowest value in the data set is an outlier? Remove it and calculate the new average. How did this affect the results?

3. Suppose the heaviest person in the original data set were replaced by a person weighing the same as the lightest person. What would be the new mean for the data set?

CHALLENGE The median of a data set is the middle value when the values are written in numerical order. Find the median of the adjusted data set (without the high outlier). Compare it with the original and adjusted means. Why do you think it is closer to one than the other?

4.2 Energy is transferred when work is done.

BEFORE, you learned

- Work is the use of force to move an object
- Work can be calculated

NOW, you will learn

- How work and energy are related
- How to calculate mechanical, kinetic, and potential energy
- What the conservation of energy means

VOCABULARY

potential energy p. 122
kinetic energy p. 122
mechanical energy p. 125
conservation of energy p. 126

THINK ABOUT

How is energy transferred?

School carnivals sometimes include dunk tanks. The goal is to hit a target with a ball, causing a person sitting over a tank of water to fall into the water. You do work on the ball as you throw with your arm. If your aim is good, the ball does work on the target. How do you transfer your energy to the ball?

Work transfers energy.

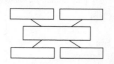

MAIN IDEA WEB
Remember to add boxes to your main idea web as you read.

When you change the position and speed of the ball in the carnival game, you transfer energy to the ball. Energy is the ability of a person or an object to do work or to cause a change. When you do work on an object, some of your energy is transferred to the object. You can think of work as the transfer of energy. In fact, both work and energy are measured in the same unit, the joule.

The man in the photograph above converts one form of energy into another form when he uses his muscles to toss the ball. You can think of the man and the ball as a system, or a group of objects that affect one another. Energy can be transferred from the man to the ball, but the total amount of energy in the system does not change.

CHECK YOUR READING How are work and energy related?

Work changes potential and kinetic energy.

When you throw a ball, you transfer energy to it and it moves. By doing work on the ball, you can give it **kinetic energy** (kuh-NEHT-ihk), which is the energy of motion. Any moving object has some kinetic energy. The faster an object moves, the more kinetic energy it has.

When you do work to lift a ball from the ground, you give the ball a different type of energy, called potential energy. **Potential energy** is stored energy, or the energy an object has due to its position or its shape. The ball's position in your hand above the ground means that it has the potential to fall to the ground. The higher you lift the ball, the more work you do, and the more potential energy the ball has.

You can also give some objects potential energy by changing their shape. For example, if you are holding a spring, you can do work on the spring by squeezing it. After you do the work, the spring has potential energy because it is compressed. This type of potential energy is called elastic potential energy. Just as position gives the spring the potential to fall, compression gives the spring the potential to expand.

READING TiP

The word *potential* comes from the Latin word *potentia*, which means "power." The word *kinetic* comes from the Greek word *kinetos,* which means "moving."

Potential and Kinetic Energy

Potential Energy

The boy has potential energy based on his position because gravity will pull him back down.

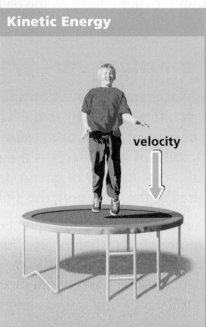

Kinetic Energy

velocity

As the boy falls, his potential energy changes into kinetic energy, and he moves faster.

Potential Energy

The trampoline has potential energy because it is stretched.

Calculating Gravitational Potential Energy

Potential energy caused by gravity is called gravitational potential energy. Scientists must take gravitational potential energy into account when launching a spacecraft. Designers of roller coasters must make sure that roller-coaster cars have enough potential energy at the top of a hill to reach the top of the next hill. You can use the following formula to calculate the gravitational potential energy of an object:

Gravitational Potential Energy = mass · gravitational acceleration · height
$$GPE = mgh$$

Recall that g is the acceleration due to Earth's gravity. It is equal to 9.8 m/s^2 at Earth's surface.

The diver in the photograph below has given herself gravitational potential energy by climbing to the diving board. If you know her mass and the height of the board, you can calculate her potential energy.

Calculating Potential Energy

Sample Problem

What is the gravitational potential energy of a girl who has a mass of 40 kg and is standing on the edge of a diving board that is 5 m above the water?

What do you know?	mass = 40 kg, gravitational acceleration = 9.8 m/s^2, height = 5 m
What do you want to find out?	Gravitational Potential Energy
Write the formula:	GPE = mgh
Substitute into the formula:	GPE = 40 kg · 9.8 m/s^2 · 5 m
Calculate and simplify:	GPE = 1960 kg m^2/s^2
Check that your units agree:	kg m^2/s^2 = kg · m/s^2 · m = N·m = J
	Unit of energy is J. Units agree.
Answer:	GPE = 1960 J

> **REMINDER**
>
> A newton (N) is a kg · m/s^2, and a joule (J) is a N·m.

Practice the Math

1. An apple with a mass of 0.1 kg is attached to a branch of an apple tree 4 m from the ground. How much gravitational potential energy does the apple have?
2. If you lift a 2 kg box of toys to the top shelf of a closet, which is 3 m high, how much gravitational potential energy will the box of toys have?

The formula for gravitational potential energy is similar to the formula for work $(W = Fd)$. The formula for GPE also has a force (mg) multiplied by a distance (h). To understand why mg is a force, remember two things: force equals mass times acceleration, and g is the acceleration due to Earth's gravity.

Calculating Kinetic Energy

The girl on the swing at left has kinetic energy. To find out how much kinetic energy she has at the bottom of the swing's arc, you must know her mass and her velocity. Kinetic energy can be calculated using the following formula:

$$\text{Kinetic Energy} = \frac{\text{mass} \cdot \text{velocity}^2}{2}$$

$$KE = \frac{1}{2}\, mv^2$$

Notice that velocity is squared while mass is not. Increasing the velocity of an object has a greater effect on the object's kinetic energy than increasing the mass of the object. If you double the mass of an object, you double its kinetic energy. Because velocity is squared, if you double the object's velocity, its kinetic energy is four times greater.

Calculating Kinetic Energy

Sample Problem

What is the kinetic energy of a girl who has a mass of 40 kg and a velocity of 3 m/s?

What do you know? mass = 40 kg, velocity = 3 m/s

What do you want to find out? Kinetic Energy

Write the formula: $KE = \frac{1}{2} mv^2$

Substitute into the formula: $KE = \frac{1}{2} \cdot 40 \text{ kg} \cdot (3 \text{ m/s})^2$

Calculate and simplify: $KE = \frac{1}{2} \cdot 40 \text{ kg} \cdot \frac{9 \text{ m}^2}{s^2}$

$$= \frac{360 \text{ kg} \cdot \text{m}^2}{2 \text{ s}^2}$$

$$= 180 \text{ kg} \cdot \text{m}^2/\text{s}^2$$

Check that your units agree: $\frac{\text{kg} \cdot \text{m}^2}{s^2} = \frac{\text{kg} \cdot \text{m}}{s^2} \cdot \text{m} = \text{N} \cdot \text{m} = \text{J}$

Unit of energy is J. Units agree.

Answer: KE = 180 J

Practice the Math

1. A grasshopper with a mass of 0.002 kg jumps up at a speed of 15 m/s. What is the kinetic energy of the grasshopper?

2. A truck with a mass of 6000 kg is traveling north on a highway at a speed of 17 m/s. A car with a mass of 2000 kg is traveling south on the same highway at a speed of 30 m/s. Which vehicle has more kinetic energy?

Calculating Mechanical Energy

Mechanical energy is the energy possessed by an object due to its motion or position—in other words, it is the object's combined potential energy and kinetic energy. A thrown baseball has mechanical energy as a result of both its motion (kinetic energy) and its position above the ground (gravitational potential energy). Any object that has mechanical energy can do work on another object.

Once you calculate an object's kinetic and potential energy, you can add the two values together to find the object's mechanical energy.

Mechanical Energy = Potential Energy + Kinetic Energy

$$ME = PE + KE$$

For example, a skateboarder has a potential energy of 200 joules due to his position at the top of a hill and a kinetic energy of 100 joules due to his motion. His total mechanical energy is 300 joules.

CHECK YOUR READING How is mechanical energy related to kinetic and potential energy?

VOCABULARY
Use a vocabulary strategy to help you remember *mechanical energy.*

INVESTIGATE Mechanical Energy

How does mechanical energy change?

PROCEDURE

1. Find and record the mass of the ball.

2. Build a ramp with the board and books. Measure and record the height of the ramp. You will place the ball at the top of the ramp, so calculate the ball's potential energy at the top of the ramp using mass and height.

3. Mark a line on the floor with tape 30 cm from the bottom of the ramp.

4. Place the ball at the top of the ramp and release it without pushing. Time how long the ball takes to travel from the end of the ramp to the tape.

5. Calculate the ball's speed using the time you measured in step 4. Use this speed to calculate the ball's kinetic energy after it rolled down the ramp.

WHAT DO YOU THINK?

- At the top of the ramp, how much potential energy did the ball have? kinetic energy? mechanical energy?

- Compare the ball's mechanical energy at the top of the ramp with its mechanical energy at the bottom of the ramp. Are they the same? Why or why not?

CHALLENGE Other than gravity, what forces could have affected the movement of the ball?

SKILL FOCUS
Analyzing data

MATERIALS
- ball
- balance
- board
- books
- ruler
- tape
- stopwatch
- calculator

TIME
20 minutes

The total amount of energy is constant.

You know that energy is transferred when work is done. No matter how energy is transferred or transformed, all of the energy is still present somewhere in one form or another. This is known as the **law of conservation of energy.** As long as you account for all the different forms of energy involved in any process, you will find that the total amount of energy never changes.

Conserving Mechanical Energy

Look at the photograph of the in-line skater on page 127. As she rolls down the ramp, the amounts of kinetic energy and potential energy change. However, the total—or the mechanical energy—stays the same. In this example, energy lost to friction is ignored.

1 At the top of the ramp, the skater has potential energy because gravity can pull her downward. She has no velocity; therefore, she has no kinetic energy.

2 As the skater rolls down the ramp, her potential energy decreases because the elevation decreases. Her kinetic energy increases because her velocity increases. The potential energy lost as the skater gets closer to the ground is converted into kinetic energy. Halfway down the ramp, half of her potential energy has been converted to kinetic energy.

3 At the bottom of the ramp, all of the skater's energy is kinetic. Gravity cannot pull her down any farther, so she has no more gravitational potential energy. Her mechanical energy—the total of her potential and kinetic energy—stays the same throughout.

Losing Mechanical Energy

A pendulum is an object that is suspended from a fixed support so that it swings freely back and forth under the influence of gravity. As a pendulum swings, its potential energy is converted into kinetic energy and then back to potential energy in a continuous cycle. Ideally, the potential energy at the top of each swing would be the same as it was the previous time. However, the height of the pendulum's swing actually decreases slightly each time, until finally the pendulum stops altogether.

In most energy transformations, some of the energy is transformed into heat. In the case of the pendulum, there is friction between the string and the support, as well as air resistance from the air around the pendulum. The mechanical energy is used to do work against friction and air resistance. This process transforms the mechanical energy into heat. The mechanical energy has not been destroyed; it has simply changed form and been transferred from the pendulum.

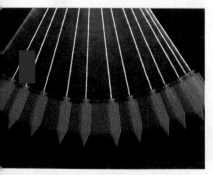

APPLY Energy must occasionally be added to a pendulum to keep it swinging. What keeps a grandfather clock's pendulum swinging regularly?

Conserving Mechanical Energy

The potential energy and kinetic energy in a system or process may vary, but the total energy remains unchanged.

① Top of Ramp

At the top of the ramp, the skater's mechanical energy is equal to her potential energy because she has no velocity.

100% PE

② Halfway Down Ramp

As the skater goes down the ramp, she loses height but gains speed. The potential energy she loses is equal to the kinetic energy she gains.

50% PE | 50% KE

③ Bottom of Ramp

As the skater speeds along the bottom of the ramp, all of the potential energy has changed to kinetic energy. Her mechanical energy remains unchanged.

100% KE

Fabiola da Silva is a professional in-line skater who was born in Brazil but now lives in California.

READING VISUALS How do the skater's kinetic and potential energy change as she skates up and down the ramp? (Assume she won't lose any energy to friction.)

Forms of Energy

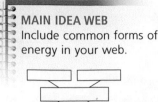

MAIN IDEA WEB
Include common forms of energy in your web.

As you have seen, mechanical energy is a combination of kinetic energy and potential energy. Other common forms of energy are discussed below. Each of these forms of energy is also a combination of kinetic energy and potential energy. Chemical energy, for example, is potential energy when it is stored in bonds.

Thermal energy is the energy an object has due to the motion of its molecules. The faster the molecules in an object move, the more thermal energy the object has.

Chemical energy is the energy stored in chemical bonds that hold chemical compounds together. If a molecule's bonds are broken or rearranged, energy is released or absorbed. Chemical energy is used to light up fireworks displays. It is also stored in food and in matches.

Nuclear energy is the potential energy stored in the nucleus of an atom. In a nuclear reaction, a tiny portion of an atom's mass is turned into energy. The source of the Sun's energy is nuclear energy. Nuclear energy can be used to run power plants that provide electricity.

Electromagnetic energy is the energy associated with electrical and magnetic interactions. Energy that is transferred by electric charges or current is often called electrical energy. Another type of electromagnetic energy is radiant energy, the energy carried by light, infrared waves, and x-rays.

It is possible to transfer, or convert, one energy form into one or more other forms. For example, when you rub your hands together on a cold day, you convert mechanical energy to thermal energy. Your body converts chemical energy stored in food to thermal and mechanical energy (muscle movement).

4.2 Review

KEY CONCEPTS

1. Explain the relationship between work and energy.

2. How are potential energy and kinetic energy related to mechanical energy?

3. When one form of energy changes into one or more other forms of energy, what happens to the total amount of energy?

CRITICAL THINKING

4. **Infer** Debra used 250 J of energy to roll a bowling ball. When the ball arrived at the end of the lane, it had only 200 J of energy. What happened to the other 50 J?

5. **Calculate** A satellite falling to Earth has a kinetic energy of 182.2 billion J and a potential energy of 1.6 billion J. What is its mechanical energy?

○ CHALLENGE

6. **Apply** At what point in its motion is the kinetic energy of the end of a pendulum greatest? At what point is its potential energy greatest? When its kinetic energy is half its greatest value, how much potential energy did it gain?

How Do They Do It?

Some women in Kenya and other African countries walk many miles every day carrying heavy loads on their heads without an increase in their heart rate. Most have done it since they were children. Scientists have studied African women to learn how they do this.

KENYA

▶ Variables

In scientific research, variables must be chosen and tested. Variables are usually compared with a control group—that is, a group for whom all potential variables are held constant. Scientists first asked several Kenyan women to walk on a treadmill. The scientists measured the women's heart rate and how much oxygen they used while carrying different weights on their heads. They found that the women could carry as much as 20 percent of their own body weight without using extra oxygen or increasing their heart rate.

The same scientists asked subjects in a control group in the United States to walk on a treadmill. The people in this group wore helmets lined with different amounts of lead. Even the lightest load caused their heart rate and oxygen consumption to increase.

If you were studying the way these African women carry loads, what variables would you choose to isolate? What control group would you use? Here are some variables and controls to consider:

- carrying the load on the head compared with carrying it on the back
- weight of the load
- women compared with men
- African women compared with other women
- method of walking

▶ Isolate the Variables

On Your Own Design an experiment that could test one of the variables without interference from other variables. Can each variable be tested independently?

As a Group Discuss each variable and see if the group agrees that it can be tested independently. Can you eliminate any of the variables based on information on this page?

CHALLENGE How would you measure the amount of energy used for the variable you chose?

Women in many countries, like this woman from Abidjan, Ivory Coast, balance heavy loads as they walk.

4.3 Power is the rate at which work is done.

BEFORE, you learned

- Mechanical energy is a combination of kinetic energy and potential energy
- Mechanical energy can be calculated
- Work transfers energy

NOW, you will learn

- How power is related to work and time
- How power is related to energy and time
- About common uses of power

VOCABULARY

power p. 130
watt p. 131
horsepower p. 132

EXPLORE Power

How does time affect work?

PROCEDURE

1. Place the cups side by side. Put all of the marbles in one cup.
2. Place each marble, one by one, into the other cup. Time how long it takes to do this.
3. Set the timer for half that amount of time. Then repeat step 2 in that time.

WHAT DO YOU THINK?

- Did you do more work the first time or the second time? Why?
- What differences did you notice between the two tries?

MATERIALS

- 2 plastic cups
- 10 marbles
- stopwatch

Power can be calculated from work and time.

VOCABULARY
Use a vocabulary strategy to help you remember the meaning of *power*.

If you lift a book one meter, you do the same amount of work whether you lift the book quickly or slowly. However, when you lift the book quickly, you increase your **power**—the rate at which you do work. A cook increases his power when he beats eggs rapidly instead of stirring them slowly. A runner increases her power when she breaks into a sprint to reach the finish line.

The word *power* has different common meanings. It is used to mean a source of energy, as in a power plant, or strength, as in a powerful engine. When you talk about a powerful swimmer, for example, you would probably say that the swimmer is very strong or very fast. If you use the scientific definition of power, you would instead say that a powerful swimmer is one who does the work of moving herself through the water in a short time.

Each of the swimmers shown in the photograph above is doing work—that is, she is using a certain force to move a certain distance. It takes time to cover that distance. The power a swimmer uses depends on the force, the distance, and the time it takes to cover that distance. The more force the swimmer uses, the more power she has. Also, the faster she goes, the more power she has because she is covering the same distance in a shorter time. Swimmers often increase their speed toward the end of a race, which increases their power, making it possible for them to reach the end of the pool in less time.

CHECK YOUR READING Summarize in your own words the difference between work and power.

Calculating Power from Work

You know that a given amount of work can be done by a slow-moving swimmer over a long period of time or by a fast-moving swimmer in a short time. Likewise, a given amount of work can be done by a low-powered motor over a long period of time or by a high-powered motor in a short time.

Because power is a measurement of how much work is done in a given time, power can be calculated based on work and time. To find power, divide the amount of work by the time it takes to do the work.

$$\text{Power} = \frac{\text{Work}}{\text{time}} \qquad P = \frac{W}{t}$$

READING TIP

W (in italicized type) is the letter that represents the variable *Work*. W, not italicized, is the abbreviation for watt.

Remember that work is measured in joules. Power is often measured in joules of work per second. The unit of measurement for power is the **watt** (W). One watt is equal to one joule of work done in one second. If an object does a large amount of work, its power is usually measured in units of 1000 watts, or kilowatts.

Calculating Power from Work

▶ **Sample Problem**

An Antarctic explorer uses 6000 J of work to pull his sled for 60 s. What power does he need?

What do you know?	Work = 6000 J, time = 60 s
What do you want to find out?	Power
Write the formula:	$P = \dfrac{W}{t}$
Substitute into the formula:	$P = \dfrac{6000\ J}{60\ s}$
Calculate and simplify:	P = 100 J/s = 100 W
Check that your units agree:	$\dfrac{J}{s} = W$
	Unit of power is W. Units agree.
Answer:	P = 100 W

▶ **Practice the Math**

1. If a conveyor belt uses 10 J to move a piece of candy a distance of 3 m in 20 s, what is the conveyor belt's power?

2. An elevator uses a force of 1710 N to lift 3 people up 1 floor. Each floor is 4 m high. The elevator takes 8 s to lift the 3 people up 2 floors. What is the elevator's power?

Horsepower

Both the horse and the tractor use power to pull objects around a farm.

James Watt, the Scottish engineer for whom the watt is named, improved the power of the steam engine in the mid-1700s. Watt also developed a unit of measurement for power called the horsepower.

Horsepower is based on what it sounds like—the amount of work a horse can do in a minute. In Watt's time, people used horses to do many different types of work. For example, horses were used on farms to pull plows and wagons.

Watt wanted to explain to people how powerful his steam engine was compared with horses. After observing several horses doing work, Watt concluded that an average horse could move 150 pounds a distance of 220 feet in 1 minute. Watt called this amount of power 1 horsepower. A single horsepower is equal to 745 watts. Therefore, a horsepower is a much larger unit of measurement than a watt.

Today horsepower is used primarily in connection with engines and motors. For example, you may see a car advertised as having a 150-horsepower engine. The power of a motorboat, lawn mower, tractor, or motorcycle engine is also referred to as horsepower.

How much power do you have?

PROCEDURE

① Measure a length of 5 meters on the floor. Mark the beginning and the end of the 5 meters with masking tape.

② Attach the object to the spring scale with a piece of string. Slowly pull the object across the floor using a steady amount of force. Record the force and the time it takes you to pull the object.

WHAT DO YOU THINK?

• How much power did you use to pull the object 5 meters?

• How do you think you could increase the power you used? decrease the power?

CHALLENGE How quickly would you have to drag the object along the floor to produce 40 watts of power?

SKILL FOCUS
Measuring

MATERIALS
• meter stick
• masking tape
• 100 g object
• spring scale
• string
• stopwatch

TIME
15 minutes

Power can be calculated from energy and time.

Sometimes you may know that energy is being transferred, but you cannot directly measure the work done by the forces involved. For example, you know that a television uses power. But there is no way to measure all the work every part of the television does in terms of forces and distance. Because work measures the transfer of energy, you can also think of power as the amount of energy transferred over a period of time.

Calculating Power from Energy

When you turn on a television, it starts using energy. Each second the television is on, a certain amount of electrical energy is transferred from a local power plant to your television. If you measure how much energy your television uses during a given time period, you can find out how much power it needs by using the following formula:

$$\text{Power} = \frac{\text{Energy}}{\text{time}} \qquad P = \frac{E}{t}$$

This formula should look familiar to you because it is very similar to the formula used to calculate power from work.

The photograph shows Hong Kong, China, at night. Every second, the city uses more than 4 billion joules of electrical energy!

You can think about power as any kind of transfer of energy in a certain amount of time. It is useful to think of power in this way if you cannot directly figure out the work used to transfer the energy. Power calculated from transferred energy is also measured in joules per second, or watts.

You have probably heard the term *watt* used in connection with light bulbs. A 60-watt light bulb requires 60 joules of energy every second to shine at its rated brightness.

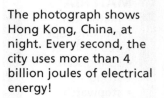 CHECK YOUR READING In what situations is it useful to think of power as the transfer of energy in a certain amount of time?

Calculating Power from Energy

▶ Sample Problem

A light bulb used 600 J of energy in 6 s. What is the power of the light bulb?

REMINDER

Remember that energy and work are both measured in joules.

What do you know?	Energy = 600 J, time = 6 s
What do you want to find out?	Power
Write the formula:	$P = \dfrac{E}{t}$
Substitute into the formula:	$P = \dfrac{600 \text{ J}}{6 \text{ s}}$
Calculate and simplify:	$P = 100$ J/s
Check that your units agree:	Unit is J/s. Unit for power is W, which is also J/s. Units agree.
Answer:	$P = 100$ W

▶ Practice the Math

1. A laptop computer uses 100 J every 2 seconds. How much power is needed to run the computer?
2. The power needed to pump blood through your body is about 1.1 W. How much energy does your body use when pumping blood for 10 seconds?

Everyday Power

Many appliances in your home rely on electricity for energy. Each appliance requires a certain number of joules per second, the power it needs to run properly. An electric hair dryer uses energy. For example, a 600-watt hair dryer needs 600 joules per second. The wattage of the hair dryer indicates how much energy per second it needs to operate.

The dryer works by speeding up the evaporation of water on the surface of hair. It needs only two main parts to do this: a heating coil and a fan turned by a motor.

➊ When the hair dryer is plugged into an outlet and the switch is turned on, electrical energy moves electrons in the wires, creating a current.

➋ This current runs an electric motor that turns the fan blades. Air is drawn into the hair dryer through small holes in the casing. The turning fan blades push the air over the coil.

➌ The current also makes the heating coil become hot.

➍ The fan pushes heated air out of the dryer.

Most hair dryers have high and low settings. At the high power setting, the temperature is increased, more air is pushed through the dryer, and the dryer does its work faster. Some dryers have safety switches that shut off the motor when the temperature rises to a level that could burn your scalp. Insulation keeps the outside of the dryer from becoming hot to the touch.

Many other appliances, from air conditioners to washing machines to blenders, need electrical energy to do their work. Take a look around you at all the appliances that help you during a typical day.

4.3 Review

KEY CONCEPTS

1. How is power related to work?
2. Name two units used for power, and give examples of when each unit might be used.
3. What do you need to know to calculate how much energy a light bulb uses?

CRITICAL THINKING

4. **Apply** Discuss different ways in which a swimmer can increase her power.
5. **Calculate** Which takes more power: using 15 N to lift a ball 2 m in 5 seconds or using 100 N to push a box 2 m in 1 minute?

◯ CHALLENGE

6. **Analyze** A friend tells you that you can calculate power by using a different formula from the one given in this book. The formula your friend gives you is as follows:
   Power = force · speed
   Do you think this is a valid formula for power? Explain.

CHAPTER INVESTIGATION

Work and Power

OVERVIEW AND PURPOSE People in wheelchairs cannot use steps leading up to a building's entrance. Sometimes there is a machine that can lift a person and wheelchair straight up to the entrance level. At other times, there is a ramp leading to the entrance. Which method takes more power?

▶ Problem

Write It Up

How does a ramp affect the amount of energy, work, and power used to lift an object?

▶ Hypothesize

Write It Up

Write a hypothesis to explain how the potential energy, the amount of work done, and the power required to lift an object straight up compare with the same quantities when the object is moved up a ramp. Your hypothesis should take the form of an "If . . . , then . . . , because . . ." statement.

MATERIALS
- board
- chair
- meter stick
- string
- small wheeled object
- spring scale
- stopwatch

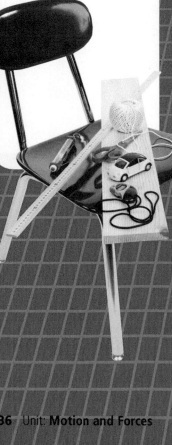

▶ Procedure

1. Make a data table like the one shown.

2. Lean the board up against the chair seat to create a ramp.

3. Measure and record the vertical distance from the floor to the top of the ramp. Also measure and record the length of the ramp.

4. Tie the string around the wheeled object. Make a loop so that you can hook the string onto the spring scale. Measure and record the weight of the object in newtons.

5. Lift the object straight up to the top of the ramp without using the ramp, as pictured.

6 On the spring scale, read and record the newtons of force needed to lift the object. Time how long it takes to lift the object from the floor to the top of the ramp. Conduct three trials and average your results. Record your measurements in the data table.

7 Drag the object from the bottom of the ramp to the top of the ramp with the spring scale, and record the newtons of force that were needed to move the object and the time it took. Conduct three trials and average your results.

▶ Observe and Analyze   Write It Up

1. **RECORD OBSERVATIONS** Draw the setup of the procedure. Be sure your data table is complete.

2. **IDENTIFY VARIABLES AND CONSTANTS** List the variables and constants in your notebook.

3. **CALCULATE**
   Potential Energy Convert centimeters to meters. Then calculate the gravitational potential energy (GPE) of the object at the top of the ramp. (Recall that weight equals mass times gravitational acceleration.)

   $$\text{Gravitational Potential Energy} = \text{weight} \cdot \text{height}$$

   Work Calculate the work done, first when the object was lifted and then when it was pulled. Use the appropriate distance.

   $$\text{Work} = \text{Force} \cdot \text{distance}$$

   Power Calculate the power involved in both situations.

   $$\text{Power} = \frac{\text{Work}}{\text{time}}$$

▶ Conclude   Write It Up

1. **COMPARE** How did the distance through which the object moved when it was pulled up the ramp differ from the distance when it was lifted straight up? How did the amount of force required differ in the two situations?

2. **COMPARE** How does your calculated value for potential energy compare with the values you obtained for work done?

3. **INTERPRET** Answer the question posed in the problem.

4. **ANALYZE** Compare your results with your hypothesis. Did your results support your hypothesis?

5. **IDENTIFY LIMITS** What possible limitations or sources of error could you have experienced?

6. **APPLY** A road going up a hill usually winds back and forth instead of heading straight to the top. How does this affect the work a car does to get to the top? How does it affect the power involved?

▶ INVESTIGATE Further

CHALLENGE Design a way to use potential energy to move the car up the ramp. What materials can you use? Think about the materials in terms of potential energy—that is, how high they are from the ground or how stretched or compressed they are.

Work and Power

Problem How does the amount of energy, work, and power used to lift an object?

Hypothesize

Observe and Analyze

Measured length of ramp = _____ cm

Height object is being lifted = _____ cm

Measured weight of the object = _____ N

Table 1. Measurements for Lifting the Object with and Without the Ramp

	Trial No.	Force (N)	Time (s)
Straight up	1		
	2		
	3		
	Average		
Ramp	1		

4 Chapter Review

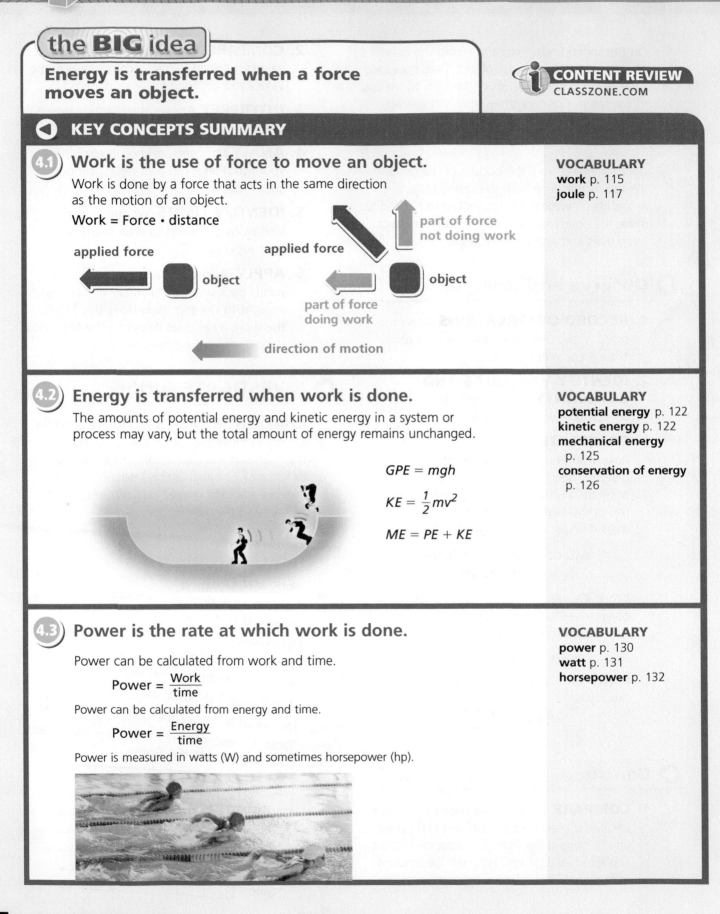

the BIG idea

Energy is transferred when a force moves an object.

CONTENT REVIEW
CLASSZONE.COM

◀ KEY CONCEPTS SUMMARY

4.1 Work is the use of force to move an object.

Work is done by a force that acts in the same direction as the motion of an object.

Work = Force · distance

applied force

object

part of force not doing work

applied force

object

part of force doing work

direction of motion

VOCABULARY
work p. 115
joule p. 117

4.2 Energy is transferred when work is done.

The amounts of potential energy and kinetic energy in a system or process may vary, but the total amount of energy remains unchanged.

$$GPE = mgh$$

$$KE = \frac{1}{2}mv^2$$

$$ME = PE + KE$$

VOCABULARY
potential energy p. 122
kinetic energy p. 122
mechanical energy
  p. 125
conservation of energy
  p. 126

4.3 Power is the rate at which work is done.

Power can be calculated from work and time.

$$Power = \frac{Work}{time}$$

Power can be calculated from energy and time.

$$Power = \frac{Energy}{time}$$

Power is measured in watts (W) and sometimes horsepower (hp).

VOCABULARY
power p. 130
watt p. 131
horsepower p. 132

Reviewing Vocabulary

Make a four square diagram for each of the terms listed below. Write the term in the center. Define it in one square. Write characteristics, examples, and formulas (if appropriate) in the other squares. A sample is shown below.

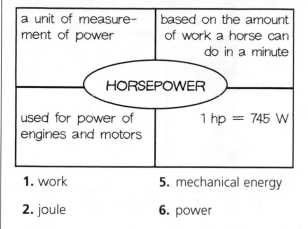

a unit of measure-ment of power	based on the amount of work a horse can do in a minute
HORSEPOWER	
used for power of engines and motors	1 hp = 745 W

1. work
2. joule
3. potential energy
4. kinetic energy
5. mechanical energy
6. power
7. watt

Reviewing Key Concepts

Multiple Choice *Choose the letter of the best answer.*

8. Work can be calculated from
   a. force and speed
   b. force and distance
   c. energy and time
   d. energy and distance

9. If you balance a book on your head, you are not doing work on the book because
   a. doing work requires moving an object
   b. you are not applying any force to the book
   c. the book is doing work on you
   d. the book has potential energy

10. Energy that an object has because of its position or shape is called
    a. potential energy   c. thermal energy
    b. kinetic energy   d. chemical energy

11. Suppose you are pushing a child on a swing. During what space of time are you doing work on the swing?
    a. while you hold it back before letting go
    b. while your hands are in contact with the swing and pushing forward
    c. after you let go of the swing and it continues to move forward
    d. all the time the swing is in motion

12. A falling ball has a potential energy of 5 J and a kinetic energy of 10 J. What is the ball's mechanical energy?
    a. 5 J   c. 15 J
    b. 10 J   d. 50 J

13. The unit that measures one joule of work done in one second is called a
    a. meter   c. newton-meter
    b. watt   d. newton

14. By increasing the speed at which you do work, you increase your
    a. force   c. energy
    b. work   d. power

15. A ball kicked into the air will have the greatest gravitational potential energy
    a. as it is being kicked
    b. as it starts rising
    c. at its highest point
    d. as it hits the ground

Short Answer *Answer each of the following questions in a sentence or two.*

16. How can you tell if a force you exert is doing work?

17. How does a water wheel do work?

18. State the law of conservation of energy. How does it affect the total amount of energy in any process?

19. Explain why a swing will not stay in motion forever after you have given it a push. What happens to its mechanical energy?

20. What are two ways to calculate power?

21. Why did James Watt invent a unit of measurement based on the work of horses?

22. SYNTHESIZE A weightlifter holds a barbell above his head. How do the barbell's potential energy, kinetic energy, and mechanical energy change as it is lifted and then lowered to the ground?

23. SYNTHESIZE What happens when you wind up a toy car and release it? Describe the events in terms of energy.

Use the photograph below to answer the next three questions.

24. APPLY When the boy first pushes on the chair, the chair does not move due to friction. Is the boy doing work? Why or why not?

25. ANALYZE For the first two seconds, the boy pushes the chair slowly at a steady speed. After that, he pushes the chair at a faster speed. How does his power change if he is using the same force at both speeds? How does his work change?

26. SYNTHESIZE As the boy pushes the chair, he does work. However, when he stops pushing, the chair stops moving and does not have any additional kinetic or potential energy. What happened to the energy he transferred by doing work on the chair?

27. APPLY A bouncing ball has mechanical energy. Each bounce, however, reaches a lower height than the last. Describe what happens to the mechanical, potential, and kinetic energy of the ball as it bounces several times.

28. CONNECT When you do work, you transfer energy. Where does the energy you transfer come from?

Complete the following calculations.

29. Use the information in the photograph below to calculate the work the person does in lifting the box.

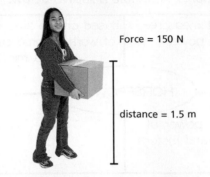

Force = 150 N

distance = 1.5 m

30. If you did 225 J of work to pull a wagon with a force of 25 N, how far did you pull it?

31. A kite with a mass of 0.05 kg is caught on the roof of a house. The house is 10 m high. What is the kite's gravitational potential energy? (Recall that $g = 9.8$ m/s^2.)

32. A baseball with a mass of 0.15 kg leaves a pitcher's hand traveling 40 m/s toward the batter. What is the baseball's kinetic energy?

33. Suppose it takes 150 J of force to push a cart 10 m in 60 s. Calculate the power.

34. If an electric hair dryer uses 1200 W, how much energy does it need to run for 2 s?

the BIG idea

35. SYNTHESIZE Look back at the photograph of the person lifting a box on pages 112–113. Describe the picture in terms of work, potential energy, kinetic energy, and power.

36. WRITE Think of an activity that involves work. Write a paragraph explaining how the work is transferring energy and where the transferred energy goes.

UNIT PROJECTS

If you need to create graphs or other visuals for your project, be sure you have grid paper, poster board, markers, or other supplies.

Understanding Experiments

Read the following description of an experiment. Then answer the questions that follow.

James Prescott Joule is well known for a paddle-wheel experiment he conducted in the mid-1800s. He placed a paddle wheel in a bucket of water. Then he set up two weights on either side of the bucket. As the weights fell, they turned the paddle wheel. Joule recorded the temperature of the water before and after the paddle wheel began turning. He found that the water temperature increased as the paddle wheel turned.

Based on this experiment, Joule concluded that the falling weights released mechanical energy, which was converted into heat by the turning wheel. He was convinced that whenever mechanical force is exerted, heat is produced.

1. Which principle did Joule demonstrate with this experiment?

   a. When energy is converted from one form to another, some energy is lost.

   b. The amount of momentum in a system does not change as long as there are no outside forces acting on the system.

   c. One form of energy can be converted into another form of energy.

   d. When one object exerts a force on another object, the second object exerts an equal and opposite force on the first object.

2. Which form of energy was released by the weights in Joule's experiment?

   a. electrical   **c.** nuclear

   b. mechanical   **d.** heat

3. Which form of energy was produced in the water?

   a. chemical   **c.** nuclear

   b. electrical   **d.** heat

4. Based on Joule's finding that movement causes temperature changes in water, which of the following would be a logical prediction?

   a. Water held in a container should increase in temperature.

   b. Water at the base of a waterfall should be warmer than water at the top.

   c. Water with strong waves should be colder than calm water.

   d. Water should increase in temperature with depth.

Extended Response

Answer the two questions below in detail. Include some of the terms from the word box. Underline each term you use in your answer.

potential energy	conservation of energy	force
kinetic energy	power	work

5. A sledder has the greatest potential energy at the top of a hill. She has the least amount of potential energy at the bottom of a hill. She has the greatest kinetic energy when she moves the fastest. Where on the hill does the sledder move the fastest? State the relationship between kinetic energy and potential energy in this situation.

6. Andre and Jon are moving boxes of books from the floor to a shelf in the school library. Each box weighs 15 lb. Andre lifts 5 boxes in one minute. Jon lifts 5 boxes in 30 seconds. Which person does more work? Which person applies more force? Which person has the greater power? Explain your answers.

5 Machines

the **BIG** idea

Machines help people do work by changing the force applied to an object.

Balls move through this sculpture. What do you think keeps the balls in motion?

Key Concepts

SECTION

5.1 Machines help people do work.
Learn about machines and how they are used to do work.

SECTION

5.2 Six simple machines have many uses.
Learn about levers and inclined planes and the other simple machines that are related to them.

SECTION

5.3 Modern technology uses compound machines.
Learn how scientists are using nanotechnology and robots to create new ways for machines to do work.

Internet Preview

CLASSZONE.COM

Chapter 5 online resources: Content Review, Simulation, four Resource Centers, Math Tutorial, Test Practice

EXPLORE (the BIG idea)

Changing Direction

Observe how a window blind works. Notice how you use a downward force to pull the blind up. Look around you for other examples.

Observe and Think Why does changing the direction of a force make work easier?

Shut the Door!

Find a door that swings freely on its hinges. Stand on the side where you can push the door to close it. Open the door. Push the door closed several times, placing your hand closer to or farther from the hinge each time.

Observe and Think Which hand placement made it easiest to shut the door? Why do you think that is so?

Internet Activity: Machines

Go to **ClassZone.com** to learn more about the simple machines in everyday objects. Select an item and think about how it moves and does its job. Then test your knowledge of simple machines.

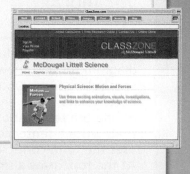

Observe and Think What other objects contain simple machines?

NSTA
scilinks.org
SCiLINKS

Simple Machines **Code: MDL008**

Getting Ready to Learn

◀ CONCEPT REVIEW

- Work is done when a force moves an object over a distance.
- Energy can be converted from one form to another.
- Energy is transferred when work is done.

◀ VOCABULARY REVIEW

work p. 115
mechanical energy p. 125
power p. 130

See Glossary for definitions.

energy, technology

CONTENT REVIEW
CLASSZONE.COM

Review concepts and vocabulary.

▶ TAKING NOTES

CHOOSE YOUR OWN STRATEGY

Take notes using one or more of the strategies from earlier chapters—**outline, combination notes, supporting main ideas,** and **main idea web.** Feel free to mix and match the strategies, or use an entirely different note-taking strategy.

VOCABULARY STRATEGY

Draw a **word triangle** diagram for each new vocabulary term. On the bottom line, write and define the term. Above that, write a sentence that uses the term correctly. At the top, draw a small picture to show what the term looks like.

See the Note-Taking Handbook on pages R45–R51.

SCIENCE NOTEBOOK

Outline

I. Main idea
  A. Supporting idea
    1. Detail
    2. Detail
  B. Supporting idea

Combination Notes

Supporting Main Ideas

Main Idea Web

The ramp in front of our school is an inclined plane.

inclined plane—a simple machine that is a sloping surface

5.1

Machines help people do work.

◀ **BEFORE**, you learned

- Work is done when a force is exerted over a distance
- Some work can be converted to heat or sound energy

▶ **NOW**, you will learn

- How machines help you do work
- How to calculate a machine's efficiency

VOCABULARY

machine p. 145
mechanical advantage p. 147
efficiency p. 150

EXPLORE Machines

How do machines help you work?

PROCEDURE

① Look at one of the machines closely. Carefully operate the machine and notice how each part moves.

② Sketch a diagram of the machine. Try to show all of the working parts. Add arrows and labels to show the direction of motion for each part.

WHAT DO YOU THINK?

- What is the function of the machine?
- How many moving parts does it have?
- How do the parts work together?
- How does this machine make work easier?

MATERIALS
various small machines

Machines change the way force is applied.

For thousands of years, humans have been improving their lives with technology. Technology is the use of knowledge to create products or tools that make life easier. The simplest machine is an example of technology.

A **machine** is any device that helps people do work. A machine does not decrease the amount of work that is done. Instead, a machine changes the way in which work is done. Recall that work is the use of force to move an object. If, for example, you have to lift a heavy box, you can use a ramp to make the work easier. Moving the box up a ramp—which is a machine—helps you do the work by reducing the force you need to lift the box.

VOCABULARY
Make a word triangle diagram in your notebook for *machine*.

If machines do not reduce the amount of work required, how do they help people do work? Machines make work easier by changing

- the size of the force needed to do the work and the distance over which the force is applied
- the direction in which the force is exerted

Machines can be powered by different types of energy. Electronic machines, such as computers, use electrical energy. Mechanical machines, such as a rake, use mechanical energy. Often this mechanical energy is supplied by the person who is using the machine.

Changing Size and Distance

Some machines help you do work by changing the size of the force needed. Have you ever tried to open a door by turning the doorknob's shaft instead of the handle? This is not easy to do. It takes less force to turn the handle of the doorknob than it does to turn the shaft. Turning the handle makes opening the door easier, even though you must turn it through a greater distance.

If a machine—such as a doorknob attached to a shaft—allows you to exert less force, you must apply that force over a greater distance. The total amount of work remains the same whether it is done with a machine or not. You can think of this in terms of the formula for calculating work—work is force times distance. Because a machine does not decrease the amount of work to be done, less force must mean greater distance.

A doorknob allows you to apply a smaller force over a greater distance. Some machines allow you to apply a greater input force over a shorter distance. Look at the boy using a rake, which is a machine. The boy moves his hands a short distance to move the end of the rake a large distance, allowing him to rake up more leaves.

Input force is the force exerted on a machine. Output force is the force that a machine exerts on an object. The boy in the photograph is exerting an input force on the rake. As a result, the rake exerts an output force on the leaves. The work the boy puts into the rake is the same as the work he gets out of the rake. However, the force he applies is greater than the force the rake can apply to the leaves. The output force is less than the input force, but it acts over a longer distance.

A rake is a machine that changes a large force over a short distance to a smaller force over a larger distance.

input force

output force

CHECK YOUR READING How can a rake help you do work? Use the word *force* in your answer.

Changing Direction

Machines also can help you work by changing the direction of a force. Think of raising a flag on a flagpole. You pull down on the rope, and the flag moves up. The rope system is a machine that changes the direction in which you exert your force. The rope system does not change the size of the force, however. The force pulling the flag upward is equal to your downward pull.

A shovel is a machine that can help you dig a hole. Once you have the shovel in the ground, you push down on the handle to lift the dirt up. You can use some of the weight of your body as part of your input force. That would not be possible if you were lifting the dirt by using only your hands. A shovel also changes the size of the force you apply, so you need less force to lift the dirt.

Mechanical Advantage of a Machine

When machines help you work, there is an advantage—or benefit—to using them. The number of times a machine multiplies the input force is called the machine's **mechanical advantage** (MA). To find a machine's mechanical advantage, divide the output force by the input force.

APPLY How does the rope system help the man raise the flag?

$$\text{Mechanical Advantage} = \frac{\textbf{Output Force}}{\textbf{Input Force}}$$

For machines that allow you to apply less force over a greater distance—such as a doorknob—the output force is greater than the input force. Therefore, the mechanical advantage of this type of machine is greater than 1. For example, if the input force is 10 newtons and the output force is 40 newtons, the mechanical advantage is 40 N divided by 10 N, or 4.

For machines that allow you to apply greater force over a shorter distance—such as a rake—the output force is less than the input force. In this case, the mechanical advantage is less than 1. If the input force is 10 newtons and the output force is 5 newtons, the mechanical advantage is 0.5. However, such a machine allows you to move an object a greater distance.

Sometimes changing the direction of the force is more useful than decreasing the force or the distance. For machines that change only the direction of a force—such as the rope system on a flagpole—the input force and output force are the same. Therefore, the mechanical advantage of the machine is 1.

Work transfers energy.

NOTE-TAKING STRATEGY
Remember to organize your notes in a chart or web as you read.

Machines transfer energy to objects on which they do work. Every time you open a door, the doorknob is transferring mechanical energy to the shaft. A machine that lifts an object gives it potential energy. A machine that causes an object to start moving, such as a baseball bat hitting a ball, gives the object kinetic energy.

Energy

When you lift an object, you transfer energy to it in the form of gravitational potential energy—that is, potential energy caused by gravity. The higher you lift an object, the more work you must do and the more energy you give to the object. This is also true if a machine lifts an object. The gravitational potential energy of an object depends on its height above Earth's surface, and it equals the work required to lift the object to that height.

Recall that gravitational potential energy is the product of an object's mass, gravitational acceleration, and height *(GPE = mgh)*. In the diagram on page 149, the climber wants to reach the top of the hill. The higher she climbs, the greater her potential energy. This energy comes from the work the climber does. The potential energy she gains equals the amount of work she does.

Work

As you have seen, when you use a machine to do work, there is always an exchange, or tradeoff, between the force you use to do the work and the distance over which you apply that force. You apply less force over a longer distance or greater force over a shorter distance.

To reach the top of the hill, the climber must do work. Because she needs to increase her potential energy by a certain amount, she must do the same amount of work to reach the top of the hill whether she climbs a steep slope or a gentle slope.

The sloping surface of the hill acts like a ramp, which is a simple machine called an inclined plane. You know that machines make work easier by changing the size or direction of a force. How does this machine make the climber's work easier?

As the climber goes up the hill, she is doing work against gravity.

❶ One side of the hill is a very steep slope—almost straight up. If the climber takes the steep slope, she climbs a shorter distance, but she must use more force.

❷ Another side of the hill is a long, gentle slope. Here the climber travels a greater distance but uses much less effort.

If the climber uses the steep slope, she must lift almost her entire weight. The inclined plane allows her to exert her input force over a longer distance; therefore, she can use just enough force to overcome the net force pulling her down the inclined plane. This force is less than her weight. In many cases, it is easier for people to use less force over a longer distance than it is for them to use more force over a shorter distance.

Energy and Work

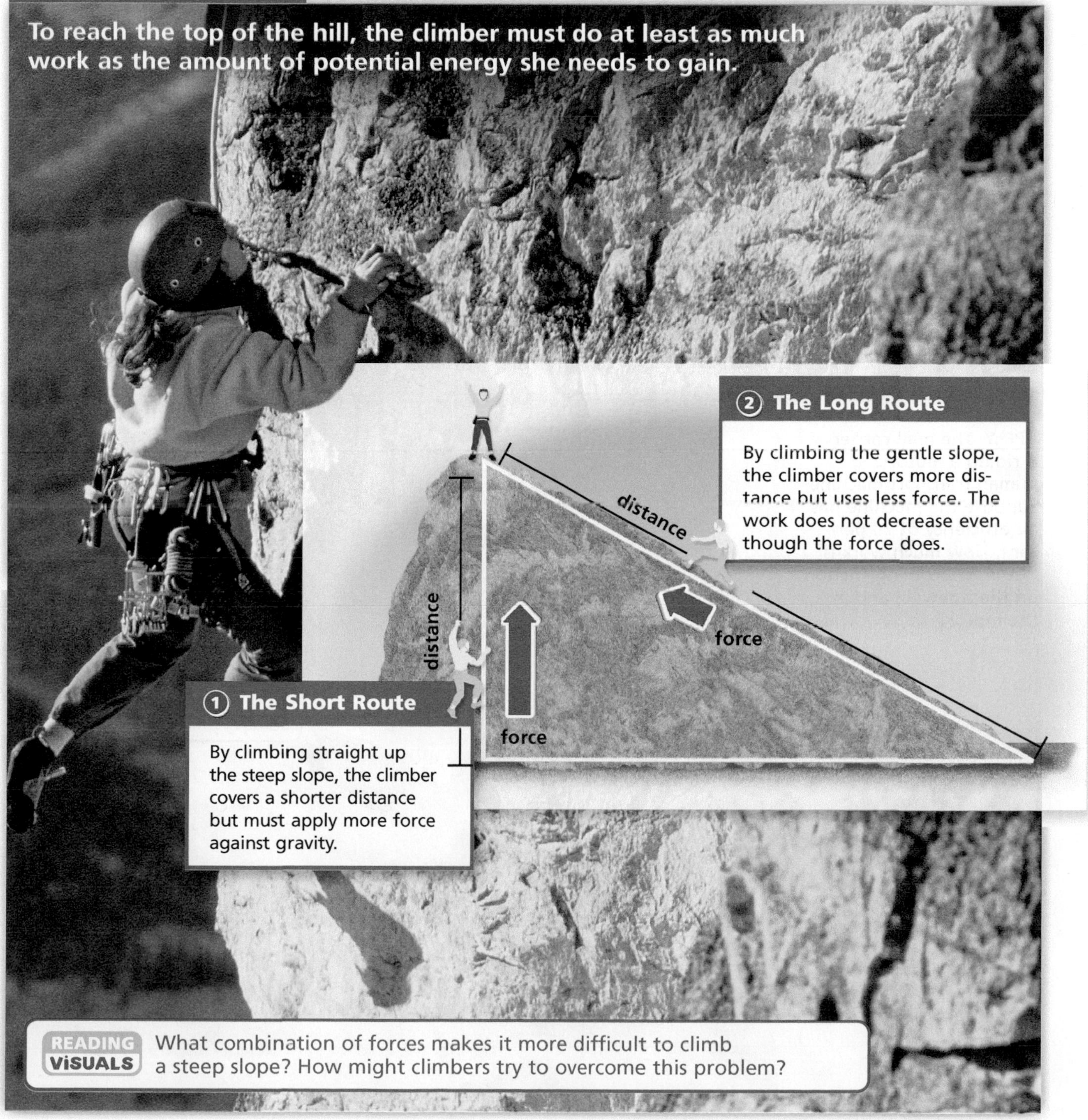

To reach the top of the hill, the climber must do at least as much work as the amount of potential energy she needs to gain.

② The Long Route

By climbing the gentle slope, the climber covers more distance but uses less force. The work does not decrease even though the force does.

distance

force

distance

① The Short Route

By climbing straight up the steep slope, the climber covers a shorter distance but must apply more force against gravity.

force

READING VISUALS What combination of forces makes it more difficult to climb a steep slope? How might climbers try to overcome this problem?

Output work is always less than input work.

The work you do on a machine is called the input work, and the work the machine does in turn is called the output work. A machine's **efficiency** is the ratio of its output work to the input work. An ideal machine would be 100 percent efficient. All of the input work would be converted to output work. Actual machines lose some input work to friction.

You can calculate the efficiency of a machine by dividing the machine's output work by its input work and multiplying that number by 100.

$$\text{Efficiency (\%)} = \frac{\text{Output work}}{\text{Input work}} \cdot 100$$

Recall that work is measured in joules. Suppose you do 600 J of work in using a rope system to lift a box. The work done on the box is 540 J. You would calculate the efficiency of the rope system as follows:

$$\text{Efficiency} = \frac{540\ \text{J}}{600\ \text{J}} \cdot 100 = 90\%$$

CHECK YOUR READING What is a machine's efficiency? How does it affect the amount of work a machine can do?

APPLY The mail carrier is riding a motorized human transport machine. Suppose the machine has an efficiency of 70 percent. How much work is lost in overcoming friction on the sidewalk and in the motor?

Input work

Work lost

Output work

Efficiency
The work you put into a machine will always be greater than the work done by the machine. Some input work is always lost in overcoming friction.

Efficiency and Energy

You know that work transfers energy and that machines make work easier. The more mechanical energy is lost in the transfer to other forms of energy, the less efficient the machine. Machines lose some energy in the form of heat due to friction. The more moving parts a machine has, the more energy it loses to friction because the parts rub together. Machines can lose energy to other processes as well.

For example, a car engine has an efficiency of only about 25 percent. It loses much of the energy supplied by its fuel to heat from combustion. By comparison, a typical electric motor has more than an 80 percent efficiency. That means the motor converts more than 80 percent of the input energy into mechanical energy, or motion.

Many appliances come with energy guides that can help a buyer compare the energy efficiency of different models. A washing machine with the highest energy rating may not always save the most energy, however, because users may have to run those machines more often.

INVESTIGATE Efficiency

What is the efficiency of a ramp?

PROCEDURE

1. Build a ramp as shown. Measure the vertical height of the ramp and the length of the ramp in centimeters. Convert these distances to meters and record.

2. Attach the block to the spring scale and measure the force in newtons needed to lift the block straight up. Record this force as the output force. Multiply the output force by the height of the ramp in meters to get the output work. Record the output work.

3. Use the spring scale to pull the block up the ramp with a constant force. Record the force measured on the spring scale as the input force. Multiply the input force by the length of the ramp in meters to get the input work. Record the input work.

4. Use the input work and output work from steps 2 and 3 to calculate the efficiency of the ramp. Record your results.

WHAT DO YOU THINK?

- How did your input work compare with your output work?
- What could you do to increase the efficiency of the ramp?

CHALLENGE Would adding sandpaper on the surface of the ramp increase or decrease the efficiency of the ramp? Why? Test your hypothesis.

SKILL FOCUS
Analyzing data

MATERIALS
- board
- books
- meter stick
- wooden block with eye hook
- spring scale
for Challenge:
- sandpaper

TIME
20 minutes

Proper maintenance can help keep a bicycle running as efficiently as possible.

Increasing Efficiency

Because all machines lose input work to friction, one way to improve the efficiency of a machine is by reducing friction. Oil is used to reduce friction between the moving parts of car engines. The use of oil makes engines more efficient.

Another machine that loses input work is a bicycle. Bicycles lose energy to friction and to air resistance. Friction losses result from the meeting of the gears, from the action of the chain on the sprocket, and from the tires changing shape against the pavement. A bicycle with poorly greased parts or other signs of poor maintenance requires more force to move. For a mountain bike that has had little maintenance, as much as 15 percent of the total work may be lost to friction. A well-maintained Olympic track bike, on the other hand, might lose only 0.5 percent.

CHECK YOUR READING What is a common way to increase a machine's efficiency?

5.1 Review

KEY CONCEPTS

1. In what ways can a machine change a force?

2. How is a machine's efficiency calculated?

3. Why is a machine's actual output work always less than its input work?

CRITICAL THINKING

4. **Apply** How would the input force needed to push a wheelchair up a ramp change if you increased the height of the ramp but not its length?

5. **Compare** What is the difference between mechanical advantage and efficiency?

● CHALLENGE

6. **Apply** Draw and label a diagram to show how to pull down on a rope to raise a load of construction materials.

MATH TUTORIAL
CLASSZONE.COM

Click on Math Tutorial
for more help with
percents and fractions.

How Efficient Are Machines?

A hammer is used to pound in nails. It can also be used to pry nails out of wood. When used to pry nails, a hammer is a machine called a lever. Like all machines, the hammer is not 100 percent efficient.

Efficiency is the amount of work a machine does divided by the amount of work that is done on the machine. To calculate efficiency, you must first find the ratio of the machine's output work to the input work done on the machine. A ratio is the comparison of two numbers by means of division. You convert the ratio to a decimal by dividing. Then convert the decimal to a percent.

Example

A person is doing 1000 joules of work on a hammer to pry up a nail. The hammer does 925 joules of work on the nail to pull it out of the wood.

(1) Find the ratio of output work to input work.

$$\frac{\text{Output work}}{\text{Input work}} = \frac{925 \text{ J}}{1000 \text{ J}} = 0.925$$

(2) To convert the decimal to a percent, multiply 0.925 by 100 and add a percent sign.

$$0.925 \cdot 100 = 92.5\%$$

ANSWER The efficiency of the hammer is 92.5 percent. This means that the hammer loses 7.5 percent of the input work to friction and other products.

Answer the following questions.

1. A construction worker does 1000 J of work in pulling down on a rope to lift a weight tied to the other end. If the output work of the rope system is 550 J, what is the ratio of output work to input work? What is the efficiency of the rope system?

2. If a machine takes in 20,000 J and puts out 5000 J, what is its efficiency?

3. You do 6000 J of work to pull a sled up a ramp. After you reach the top, you discover that the sled had 3600 J of work done on it. What is the efficiency of the ramp?

CHALLENGE If you put 7000 J of work into a machine with an efficiency of 50 percent, how much work will you get out?

No machine, no matter how large or small, is 100 percent efficient. Some of the input energy is lost to sound, heat, or other products.

5.2 Six simple machines have many uses.

BEFORE, you learned

- Machines help you work by changing the size or direction of a force
- The number of times a machine multiplies the input force is the machine's mechanical advantage

NOW, you will learn

- How six simple machines change the size or direction of a force
- How to calculate mechanical advantage

VOCABULARY

simple machine p. 154
lever p. 155
fulcrum p. 155
wheel and axle p. 156
pulley p. 156
inclined plane p. 158
wedge p. 158
screw p. 159

EXPLORE Changing Forces

How can you change a force?

PROCEDURE

1. Lay one pencil on a flat surface. Place the other pencil on top of the first pencil and perpendicular to it, as shown. Place the book on one end of the top pencil.

2. Push down on the free end of the top pencil to raise the book.

3. Change the position of the bottom pencil so that it is closer to the book and repeat step 2. Then move the bottom pencil closer to the end of the pencil you are pushing on and repeat step 2.

MATERIALS

- 2 pencils
- small book

WHAT DO YOU THINK?

- How did changing the position of the bottom pencil affect how much force you needed to lift the book?
- At which position is it easiest to lift the book? most difficult?

There are six simple machines.

NOTE-TAKING STRATEGY
As you read, remember to take notes about the main ideas and supporting details.

You have read about how a ramp and a shovel can help you do work. A ramp is a type of inclined plane, and a shovel is a type of lever. An inclined plane and a lever are both simple machines. **Simple machines** are the six machines on which all other mechanical machines are based. In addition to the inclined plane and the lever, simple machines include the wheel and axle, pulley, wedge, and screw. As you will see, the wheel and axle and pulley are related to the lever, and the wedge and screw are related to the inclined plane. You will read about each of the six simple machines in detail in this section.

Lever

A **lever** is a solid bar that rotates, or turns, around a fixed point. The bar can be straight or curved. The fixed point is called the **fulcrum.** A lever can multiply the input force. It can also change the direction of the input force. If you apply a force downward on one end of a lever, the other end can lift a load.

The way in which a lever changes an input force depends on the positions of the fulcrum, the input force, and the output force in relation to one another. Levers with different arrangements have different uses. Sometimes a greater output force is needed, such as when you want to pry up a bottle cap. At other times you use a greater input force on one end to get a higher speed at the other end, such as when you swing a baseball bat. The three different arrangements, sometimes called the three classes of levers, are shown in the diagram below.

CHECK YOUR READING What two parts are needed to make a lever?

Levers

Levers can be classified according to where the fulcrum is.

First-Class Lever

The fulcrum is located between the input force and the output force. Use this type of lever to change the direction and size of a force.

input force ⬇ output force ⬆

fulcrum

Second-Class Lever

The output force is located between the input force and the fulcrum. Use this type of lever if you need a greater output force.

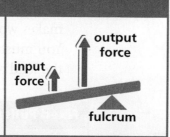

output force ⬆

input force ⬆

fulcrum

Third-Class Lever

The input force is located between the output force and the fulcrum. Use this type of lever to reduce the distance over which you apply the input force or increase the speed of the end of the lever.

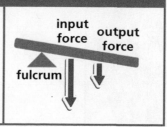

input force   output force

fulcrum ⬇

Wheel and Axle

A **wheel and axle** is a simple machine made of a wheel attached to a shaft, or axle. The wheels of most means of transportation—such as a bicycle and a car—are attached to an axle. The wheel and axle act like a rotating collection of levers. The axle at the wheel's center is like a fulcrum. Other examples of wheels and axles are screwdrivers, steering wheels, doorknobs, and electric fans.

Depending on your purpose for using a wheel and axle, you might apply a force to turn the wheel or the axle. If you turn the wheel, your input force is transferred to the axle. Because the axle is smaller than the wheel, the output force acts over a shorter distance than the input force. A driver applies less force to a steering wheel to get a greater turning force from the axle, or steering column. This makes it easier to steer the car.

If, instead, you turn the axle, your force is transferred to the wheel. Because the wheel is larger than the axle, the force acts over a longer distance. A car also contains this use of a wheel and axle. The engine turns the drive axles, which turn the wheels.

CHECK YOUR READING Compare the results of putting force on the axle with putting force on the wheel.

Pulley

A **pulley** is a wheel with a grooved rim and a rope or cable that rides in the groove. As you pull on the rope, the wheel turns.

A pulley that is attached to something that holds it steady is called a fixed pulley. An object attached to the rope on one side of the wheel rises as you pull down on the rope on the other side of the wheel. The fixed pulley makes work easier by changing the direction of the force. You must apply enough force to overcome the weight of the load and any friction in the pulley system.

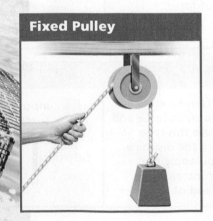

Fixed Pulley

A fixed pulley allows you to take advantage of the downward pull of your weight to move a load upward. It does not, however, reduce the force you need to lift the load. Also, the distance you pull the rope through is the same distance that the object is lifted. To lift a load two meters using a fixed pulley, you must pull down two meters of rope.

In a movable pulley setup, one end of the rope is fixed, but the wheel can move. The load is attached to the wheel. The person pulling the rope provides the output force that lifts the load. A single movable pulley does not change the direction of the force. Instead, it multiplies the force. Because the load is supported by two sections of rope, you need only half the force you would use with a fixed pulley to lift it. However, you must pull the rope through twice the distance.

CHECK YOUR READING How does a single fixed pulley differ from a single movable pulley?

Movable Pulley

A combination of fixed and movable pulleys is a pulley system called a block and tackle. A block and tackle is used to haul and lift very heavy objects. By combining fixed and movable pulleys, you can use more rope sections to support the weight of an object. This reduces the force you need to lift the object. The mechanical advantage of a single pulley can never be greater than 2. If engineers need a pulley system with a mechanical advantage greater than 2, they often use a block-and-tackle system.

INVESTIGATE Pulleys

What is the mechanical advantage of a pulley system?

PROCEDURE

1. Hang the mass on the spring scale to find its weight in newtons. Record this weight as your output force.

2. Tie the top of one pulley to the ring stand.

3. Attach the mass to the second pulley.

4. Attach one end of the second pulley's rope to the bottom of the first pulley. Then thread the free end of the rope through the second pulley. Loop the rope up and over the first pulley, as shown.

5. Attach the spring scale to the free end of the rope. Pull down to lift the mass. Record the force you used as your input force. Calculate the mechanical advantage of this pulley system.
   Hint: The mechanical advantage can be calculated by dividing the output force by the input force.

WHAT DO YOU THINK?

- How did your input force compare with your output force?
- What caused the results you observed?

CHALLENGE Explain what the mechanical advantage would be for a pulley system that includes another movable pulley.

SKILL FOCUS
Inferring

MATERIALS
- 100 g mass
- spring scale
- 2 pulleys with rope
- ring stand

TIME
20 minutes

Inclined Plane

Recall that it is difficult to lift a heavy object straight up because you must apply a force great enough to overcome the downward pull of the force of gravity. For this reason people often use ramps. A ramp is an **inclined plane,** a simple machine that is a sloping surface. The photograph at the left shows the interior of the Guggenheim Museum in New York City. The levels of the art museum are actually one continuous inclined plane.

Inclined Plane

Inclined planes make the work of raising an object easier because they support part of the weight of the object while it is being moved from one level to another. The surface of an inclined plane applies a reaction force on the object resting on it. This extra force on the object helps to act against gravity. If you are pushing an object up a ramp, you have to push with only enough force to overcome the smaller net force that pulls the object down parallel to the incline.

The less steep an inclined plane is, the less force you need to push or pull an object on the plane. This is because a less steep plane supports more of an object's weight than a steeper plane. However, the less steep an inclined plane is, the farther you must go to reach a certain height. While you use less force, you must apply that force over a greater distance.

CHECK YOUR READING How do inclined planes help people do work? Your answer should mention force.

Wedge

Wedge

A **wedge** is a simple machine that has a thick end and a thin end. Wedges are used to cut, split, or pierce objects—or to hold objects together. A wedge is a type of inclined plane, but inclined planes are stationary, while wedges often move to do work.

Some wedges are single, movable inclined planes, such as a doorstop, a chisel, or an ice scraper. Another kind of wedge is made of two back-to-back inclined planes. Examples include the blade of an axe or a knife. In the photograph at the left, a sculptor is using a chisel to shape stone. The sculptor applies an input force on the chisel by tapping its thicker end with a mallet. That force pushes the thinner end of the chisel into the stone. As a result, the sides of the thinner end exert an output force that separates the stone.

The angle of the cutting edge determines how easily a wedge can cut through an object. Thin wedges have small angles and need less input force to cut than do thick wedges with large angles. That is why a sharp knife blade cuts more easily than a dull one.

You also can think of a wedge that cuts objects in terms of how it changes the pressure on a surface. The thin edges of a wedge provide a smaller surface area for the input force to act on. This greater pressure makes it easier to break through the surface of an object. A sharp knife can cut through an apple skin, and a sharp chisel can apply enough pressure to chip stone.

A doorstop is a wedge that is used to hold objects together. To do its job, a doorstop is pressed tip-first under a door. As the doorstop is moved into position, it lifts the door slightly and applies a force to the bottom of the door. In return, the door applies pressure to the doorstop and causes the doorstop to press against the floor with enough force to keep the doorstop—and the door—from moving.

Screw

A **screw** is an inclined plane wrapped around a cylinder or cone to form a spiral. A screw is a simple machine that can be used to raise and lower weights as well as to fasten objects. Examples of screws include drills, jar lids, screw clamps, and nuts and bolts. The spiraling inclined plane that sticks out from the body of the screw forms the threads of the screw.

In the photograph at right, a person is using a screwdriver, which is a wheel and axle, to drive a screw into a piece of wood. Each turn of the screwdriver pushes the screw farther into the wood. As the screw is turned, the threads act like wedges, exerting an output force on the wood. If the threads are very close together, the force must be applied over a greater distance—that is, the screw must be turned many times—but less force is needed.

The advantage of using a screw instead of a nail to hold things together is the large amount of friction that keeps the screw from turning and becoming loose. Think of pulling a nail out of a piece of wood compared with pulling a screw from the same piece of wood. The nail can be pulled straight out. The screw must be turned through a greater distance to remove it from the wood.

Notice that the interior of the Guggenheim Museum shown on page 158 is not only an inclined plane. It is also an example of a screw. The inclined plane is wrapped around the museum's atrium, which is an open area in the center.

Screw

CHECK YOUR READING Explain how a screw moves deeper into the wood as it is turned.

The mechanical advantage of a machine can be calculated.

Recall that the number of times a machine multiplies the input force is the machine's mechanical advantage. You can calculate a machine's mechanical advantage using this formula:

$$\text{Mechanical Advantage} = \frac{\text{Output Force}}{\text{Input Force}}$$

$$MA = \frac{F_{out}}{F_{in}}$$

This formula works for all machines, regardless of whether they are simple machines or more complicated machines.

If a machine decreases the force you use to do work, the distance over which you have to apply that force increases. It is possible to use this idea to calculate the mechanical advantage of a simple machine without knowing what the input and output forces are. To make this calculation, however, you must assume that your machine is not losing any work to friction. In other words, you must assume that your machine is 100 percent efficient. The mechanical advantage that you calculate when making this assumption is called the ideal mechanical advantage.

READING TIP

Scientists often consider the way in which an object will behave under ideal conditions, such as when there is no friction.

Inclined Plane You can calculate the ideal mechanical advantage of an inclined plane by dividing its length by its height.

$$\text{Ideal Mechanical Advantage} = \frac{\text{length of incline}}{\text{height of incline}}$$

$$IMA = \frac{l}{h}$$

Be sure to use the length of the incline in your calculation, as shown in the diagram, and not the length of the base. If the mover in the photograph on page 160 increased the length of the ramp, he would increase the ramp's mechanical advantage. However, he would also increase the distance over which he had to carry the box.

Wheel and Axle To calculate the ideal mechanical advantage of a wheel and axle, use the following formula:

$$\text{Ideal Mechanical Advantage} = \frac{\text{Radius of input}}{\text{Radius of output}}$$

$$IMA = \frac{R_{in}}{R_{out}}$$

The Ferris wheel below is a giant wheel and axle. A motor applies an input force to the Ferris wheel's axle, which turns the wheel. In this example, the input force is applied to the axle, so the radius of the axle is the input radius in the formula above. The output force is applied by the wheel, so the radius of the wheel is the output radius.

For a Ferris wheel, the input force is greater than the output force. The axle turns through a shorter distance than the wheel does. The ideal mechanical advantage of this type of wheel and axle is less than 1.

Sometimes, as with a steering wheel, the input force is applied to turn the wheel instead of the axle. Then the input radius is the wheel's radius, and the output radius is the axle's radius. In this case, the input force on the wheel is less than the output force applied by the axle. The ideal mechanical advantage of this type of wheel and axle is greater than 1.

SIMULATION
CLASSZONE.COM

Explore the mechanical advantage of an inclined plane.

▼ REMINDER

The radius is the distance from the center of the wheel or axle to any point on its circumference.

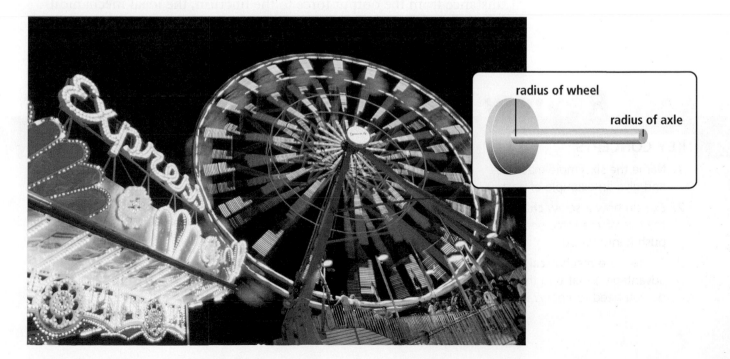

radius of wheel

radius of axle

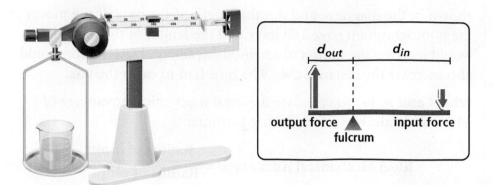

Lever The beam balance above is a lever. The beam is the solid bar that turns on a fixed point, or fulcrum. The fulcrum is the beam's balance point. When you slide the weight across the beam, you are changing the distance between the input force and the fulcrum. The mechanical advantage depends on the distances of the input force and output force from the fulcrum. The output force is applied to balance the beaker.

To calculate the ideal mechanical advantage of a lever, use the following formula:

$$\text{Ideal Mechanical Advantage} = \frac{\text{distance from input force to fulcrum}}{\text{distance from output force to fulcrum}}$$

$$IMA = \frac{d_{in}}{d_{out}}$$

This formula applies to all three arrangements of levers. If the distance from the input force to the fulcrum is greater than the distance from the output force to the fulcrum, the ideal mechanical advantage is greater than 1. The beam balance is an example of this type of lever.

5.2 Review

KEY CONCEPTS

1. Name the six simple machines and give an example of each.

2. Explain how a screw changes the size of the force needed to push it into wood.

3. To calculate mechanical advantage, what two things do you need to know?

CRITICAL THINKING

4. **Synthesize** How is a pulley similar to a wheel and axle?

5. **Calculate** What is the ideal mechanical advantage of a wheel with a diameter of 30 cm fixed to an axle with a diameter of 4 cm if the axle is turned?

CHALLENGE

6. **Infer** How can you increase a wedge's mechanical advantage? Draw a diagram to show your idea.

A Running Machine

Marlon Shirley, who lives in California, lost his left foot due to an accident at the age of five. He is a champion sprinter who achieved his running records while using a prosthesis (prahs-THEE-sihs), or a device used to replace a body part. Like his right leg and foot, his prosthesis is a combination of simple machines that convert the energy from muscles in his body to move him forward. The mechanical system is designed to match the forces of his right leg.

Legs as Levers

Compare Marlon Shirley's prosthesis with his right leg. Both have rods—one made of bone and the other of metal—that provide a strong frame. These rods act as levers. At the knee and ankle, movable joints act as fulcrums for these levers to transfer energy between the runner's body and the ground.

How Does It Work?

1. As the foot—real or artificial—strikes the ground, the leg stops moving forward and downward and absorbs the energy of the change in motion. The joints in the ankle and knee act as fulcrums as the levers transfer the energy to the muscle in the upper leg. This muscle acts like a spring to store the energy.

2. When the runner begins the next step, the energy is transferred back into the leg from the upper leg muscle. The levers in the leg convert the energy into forward motion of the runner's body.

The people who design prosthetic legs study the natural motion of a runner to learn exactly how energy is distributed and converted to motion so that they can build an artificial leg that works well with the real leg.

EXPLORE

1. **VISUALIZE** Run across a room, paying close attention to the position of one of your ankles and knees as you move. Determine where the fulcrum is in the lever formed by your lower leg.
2. **CHALLENGE** Use the library or the Internet to learn more about mechanical legs used in building robots that walk. How do the leg motions of these robots resemble your walking motions? How are they different?

RESOURCE CENTER
CLASSZONE.COM
Find out more about
artificial limbs.

Other parts of the human body can act like simple machines. For example, teeth work like wedges.

5.3 Modern technology uses compound machines.

◀ BEFORE, you learned	▶ NOW, you will learn
• Simple machines change the size or direction of a force • All machines have an ideal and an actual mechanical advantage	• How simple machines can be combined • How scientists have developed extremely small machines • How robots are used

VOCABULARY

compound machine p. 164

nanotechnology p. 167

robot p. 169

THINK ABOUT

How does a tow truck do work?

When a car is wrecked or disabled, the owner might call a towing service. The service sends a tow truck to take the car to be repaired. Tow trucks usually are equipped with a mechanism for freeing stuck vehicles and towing, or pulling, them. Look at the tow truck in the photograph at the right. What simple machines do you recognize?

Compound machines are combinations of simple machines.

Like the tow truck pictured above, many of the more complex devices that you see or use every day are combinations of simple machines. For example, a pair of scissors is a combination of two levers. The cutting edges of those levers are wedges. A fishing rod is a lever with the fishing line wound around a wheel and axle, the reel. A machine that is made of two or more simple machines is called a **compound machine.**

In a very complex compound machine, such as a car, the simple machines may not be obvious at first. However, if you look carefully at a compound machine, you should be able to identify forms of levers, pulleys, and wheels and axles.

VOCABULARY
Remember to write a definition for *compound machine* in a word triangle.

CHECK YOUR READING How are simple machines related to compound machines?

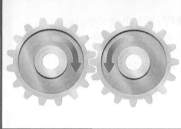

The gears in the photograph and diagram are spur gears, the most common type of gear.

Gears

Gears

Gears are based on the wheel and axle. Gears have teeth on the edge of the wheel that allow one gear to turn another. A set of gears forms a compound machine in which one wheel and axle is linked to another.

Two linked gears that are the same size and have the same number of teeth will turn at the same speed. They will move in opposite directions. In order to make them move in the same direction, a third gear must be added between them. The gear that turns another gear applies the input force; the gear that is turned exerts the output force. A difference in speed between two gears—caused by a difference in size and the distance each turns through—produces a change in force.

CHECK YOUR READING How do gears form a compound machine?

Mechanical Advantage of Compound Machines

The mechanical advantage of any compound machine is equal to the product of the mechanical advantages of all the simple machines that make up the compound machine. For example, the ideal mechanical advantage of a pair of scissors would be the product of the ideal mechanical advantages of its two levers and two wedges.

The mechanical advantage of a pair of gears with different diameters can be found by counting the teeth on the gears. The mechanical advantage is the ratio of the number of teeth on the output gear to the number of teeth on the input gear. If there are more than two gears, count only the number of teeth on the first and last gears in the system. This ratio is the mechanical advantage of the whole gear system.

Compound machines typically must overcome more friction than simple machines because they tend to have many moving parts. Scissors, for example, have a lower efficiency than one lever because there is friction at the point where the two levers are connected. There is also friction between the blades of the scissors as they close.

APPLY What simple machines do you see in this Jaws of Life cutting tool?

Modern technology creates new uses for machines.

Sophisticated modern machinery is often based on or contains simple machines. Consider Jaws of Life tools, which are used to help rescue people who have been in accidents. These cutters, spreaders, and rams are powered by hydraulics, the use of fluids to transmit force. When every second counts, these powerful machines can be used to pry open metal vehicles or collapsed concrete structures quickly and safely. The cutters are a compound machine made up of two levers—much like a pair of scissors. Their edges are wedges.

Contrast this equipment with a drill-like machine so small that it can be pushed easily through human arteries. Physicians attach the tiny drill to a thin, flexible rod and push the rod through a patient's artery to an area that is blocked. The tip rotates at extremely high speeds to break down the blockage. The tiny drill is a type of wheel and axle.

Microtechnology and Nanotechnology

Manufacturers make machines of all sizes by shaping and arranging pieces of metal, plastic, and other materials. Scientists have used technology to create very small machines through miniaturization—the making of smaller and smaller, or miniature, parts. Micromachines are too small to be seen by the naked eye but are visible under a microscope. There is a limit, however, to how far micromachines can be shrunk.

To develop even tinier machines, scientists needed a new approach. Scientists have used processes within the human body as their model. For example, inside the body a protein molecule carries materials back and forth within a cell on regular paths that are similar to little train tracks. The natural machines in the human body inspired scientists to develop machines that could be 1000 times smaller than the diameter of a human hair.

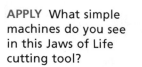

READING TiP

Micro-means "one-millionth." For example, a microsecond is one-millionth of a second. *Nano*-means "one-billionth." A nanosecond is one-billionth of a second.

Learn more about nanomachines.

These extremely tiny machines are products of **nanotechnology,** the science and technology of building electronic circuits and devices from single atoms and molecules. Scientists say that they create these machines, called nanomachines, from the bottom up. Instead of shaping already formed material—such as metal and plastic—they guide individual atoms of material to arrange themselves into the shapes needed for the machine parts.

Tools enable scientists to see and manipulate single molecules and atoms. The scanning tunneling microscope can create pictures of individual atoms. To manipulate atoms, special tools are needed to guide them into place. Moving and shaping such small units presents problems, however. Atoms tend to attach themselves to other atoms, and the tools themselves are also made of atoms. Thus it is difficult to pick up an atom and place it in another position using a tool because the atom might attach itself to the tool.

CHECK YOUR READING Compare the way in which nanomachines are constructed with the way in which larger machines are built.

Nanomachines are still mostly in the experimental stage. Scientists have many plans for nanotechnology, including protecting computers from hackers and performing operations inside the body. For example, a nanomachine could be injected into a person's bloodstream, where it could patrol and search out infections before they become serious problems. When the machine had completed its work, it could switch itself off and be passed out of the body. Similar nanomachines could carry anti-cancer drugs to specific cells in the body.

This microgear mechanism could be used in a micro-machine that includes microscopic sensors and tiny robots.

Nanotechnology could also be used to develop materials that repel water and dirt and make cleaning jobs easy. Nanoscale biosensors could be used to detect harmful substances in the environment. Another possible use for nanotechnology is in military uniforms that can change color— the perfect camouflage.

In the future, nanotechnology may change the way almost everything is designed and constructed. As with any new technology, it will be important to weigh both the potential risks and benefits.

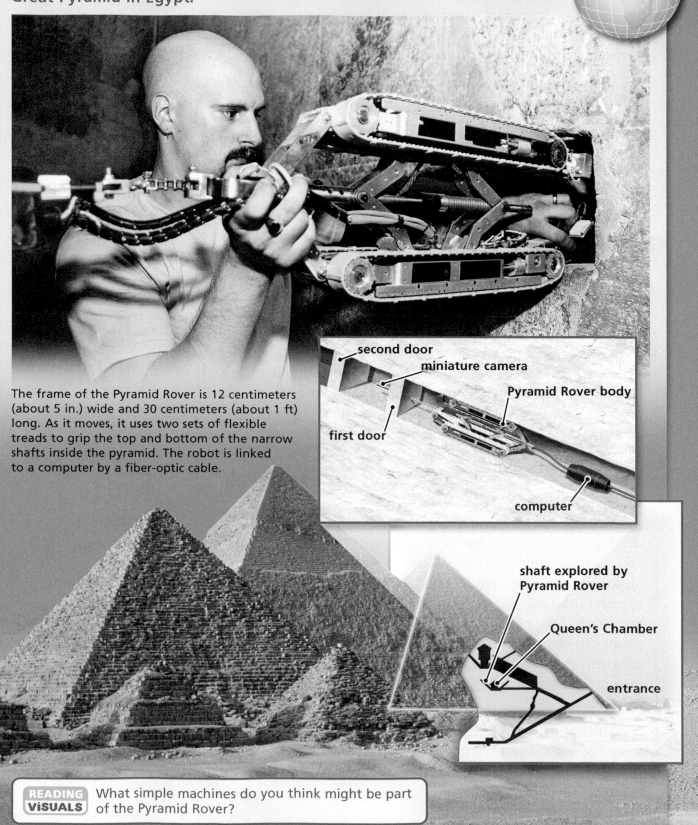

A Robot at Work

Scientists are using a robot to unlock the secrets of the Great Pyramid in Egypt.

EGYPT

The frame of the Pyramid Rover is 12 centimeters (about 5 in.) wide and 30 centimeters (about 1 ft) long. As it moves, it uses two sets of flexible treads to grip the top and bottom of the narrow shafts inside the pyramid. The robot is linked to a computer by a fiber-optic cable.

second door

miniature camera

Pyramid Rover body

first door

computer

shaft explored by Pyramid Rover

Queen's Chamber

entrance

READING VISUALS What simple machines do you think might be part of the Pyramid Rover?

Robots

Humans have always taken risks to do jobs in places that are dangerous or difficult to get to. More and more often, robots can be used to do these jobs. A **robot** is a machine that works automatically or by remote control. When many people hear the word *robot,* they think of a machine that looks or moves like a person. However, most robots do not resemble humans at all. That is because they are built to do things humans cannot do or to go places where it is difficult for humans to go.

RESOURCE CENTER
CLASSZONE.COM
Find out more about the Pyramid Rover and other robots.

The Pyramid Rover, shown on page 168, is an example of a robot developed to go where people cannot. After a camera revealed a door at the end of an eight-inch-square shaft inside the Great Pyramid, the Pyramid Rover was sent through the shaft to explore the area. While researchers remained in the Queen's Chamber in the center of the pyramid, the robot climbed the shaft until it came to a door. Using ultrasound equipment mounted on the robot, researchers determined that the door was three inches thick. The robot drilled a hole in the door for a tiny camera and a light to pass through. The camera then revealed another sealed door!

Many companies use robots to manufacture goods quickly and efficiently. Robots are widely used for jobs such as welding, painting, and assembling products. Robots do some repetitive work better than humans, because robots do not get tired or bored. Also, they do the task in exactly the same way each time. Robots are very important to the automobile and computer industries.

CHECK YOUR READING How are robots better than humans at some jobs?

5.3 Review

KEY CONCEPTS

1. How do you estimate the mechanical advantage of a compound machine?

2. What are some uses of nanotechnology? Can you think of other possible uses for nanomachines?

3. What are three types of jobs that robots can do?

CRITICAL THINKING

4. **Synthesize** What factors might limit how large or how small a machine can be?

5. **Infer** How do you think the size of a gear compared with other gears in the same system affects the speed of its rotation?

CHALLENGE

6. **Apply** Robots might be put to use replacing humans in firefighting and other dangerous jobs. Describe a job that is dangerous. Tell what a robot must be able to do and what dangers it must be able to withstand to accomplish the required tasks.

CHAPTER INVESTIGATION

Design a Machine

OVERVIEW AND PURPOSE

Although simple machines were developed thousands of years ago, they are still used today for a variety of purposes. Tasks such as cutting food with a knife, using a screwdriver to tighten a screw, and raising a flag on a flagpole all require simple machines. Activities such as riding a bicycle and raising a drawbridge make use of compound machines. In this investigation you will use what you have learned about simple and compound machines to
  • choose a machine to design
  • build your machine, test it, and calculate its mechanical advantage and efficiency

▶ Procedure

1. Make a data table like the one shown on page 171.

2. From among the three choices listed below, choose which problem you are going to solve.

Carnival Game You work for a company that builds carnival games. Your supervisor has asked you to build a game in which a simple machine moves a 500-gram object from the bottom of the game 1 meter up to the top. This simple machine can be powered only by the person operating the game.

Video Game Contest The marketing department of a video game company is holding a contest. Candidates are asked to submit a working model of a compound machine that will move a 500-gram object a distance of 1 meter. The winning design will be used in a new video game the company hopes to sell. This compound machine must include at least 2 simple machines.

Construction Company You work for a construction company. Your boss has asked you to design a machine for lifting. Your first step is to build a scale model. The model must be a compound machine with a mechanical advantage of 5 that can move a 500-gram object a distance of 1 meter. You also can use a 100-gram object in your design.

MATERIALS
• 500 g object
• 100 g object
• meter stick
• spring scale
• pulleys with rope
• board
• stick or pole

Brainstorm design ideas on paper. Think of different types of machines you might want to build. Choose one machine to build.

Build your machine. Use your machine to perform the task of moving a 500-gram object a distance of 1 meter.

If you chose the third problem, test your compound machine to determine if it has a mechanical advantage of 5. If not, modify your machine and retest it.

Record all measurements in your data table.

▶ Observe and Analyze Write It Up

1. **RECORD OBSERVATIONS** Make a sketch of your machine.

2. **CALCULATE** Use your data to calculate the mechanical advantage and efficiency of your machine. Use the formulas below.

$$\text{Mechanical Advantage} = \frac{\text{Output Force}}{\text{Input Force}}$$

$$\text{Efficiency (\%)} = \frac{\text{Output work}}{\text{Input work}} \cdot 100$$

3. **ANALYZE**

   Carnival Game Add arrows to the drawing of your machine to show the forces involved and the direction of those forces. If your goal was to move the ball from the top of the game to the bottom at a constant speed, how would your machine and diagram have to be changed?

   Video Game Contest Does your machine change the size of the force, the direction of the force, or both? If you used a pulley system (two or more pulleys working together), describe the advantages of using such a system.

   Construction Company Determine whether force or distance is changed by each simple machine in your compound machine. In what ways might you improve your machine to increase its efficiency?

▶ Conclude

Write It Up

1. **INFER** How might changing the arrangement of the parts in your machine affect the machine's mechanical advantage?

2. **IDENTIFY LIMITS** What was the hardest part about designing and constructing your machine?

3. **APPLY** If you needed to lift a large rock from a hole at a construction site, which type of simple machine would you use and why? Which type of compound machine would be useful?

▶ INVESTIGATE Further

CHALLENGE If you made a simple machine, how would you combine it with another simple machine to increase its mechanical advantage?

If you made a compound machine, redesign it to increase its efficiency or mechanical advantage. What made the difference and why?

Draw a plan for the new machine. Circle the parts that were changed. If you have time, build your new machine.

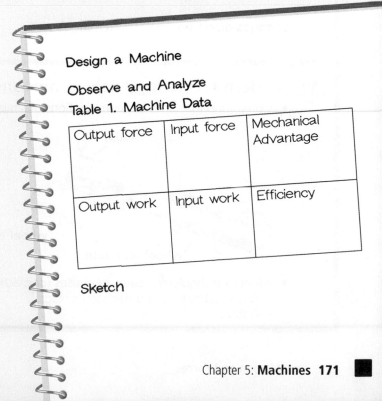

Design a Machine

Observe and Analyze

Table 1. Machine Data

Output force	Input force	Mechanical Advantage
Output work	Input work	Efficiency

Sketch

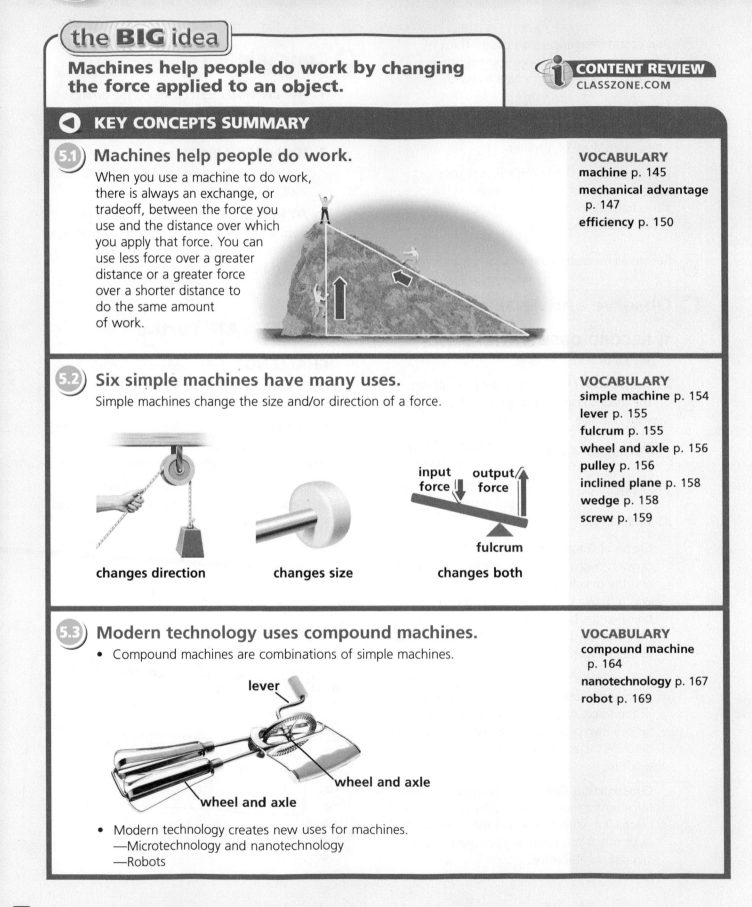

CONTENT REVIEW
CLASSZONE.COM

the BIG idea

Machines help people do work by changing the force applied to an object.

KEY CONCEPTS SUMMARY

5.1 Machines help people do work.

When you use a machine to do work, there is always an exchange, or tradeoff, between the force you use and the distance over which you apply that force. You can use less force over a greater distance or a greater force over a shorter distance to do the same amount of work.

VOCABULARY
machine p. 145
mechanical advantage p. 147
efficiency p. 150

5.2 Six simple machines have many uses.

Simple machines change the size and/or direction of a force.

input force   output force

fulcrum

changes direction   changes size   changes both

VOCABULARY
simple machine p. 154
lever p. 155
fulcrum p. 155
wheel and axle p. 156
pulley p. 156
inclined plane p. 158
wedge p. 158
screw p. 159

5.3 Modern technology uses compound machines.

• Compound machines are combinations of simple machines.

lever

wheel and axle

wheel and axle

• Modern technology creates new uses for machines.
—Microtechnology and nanotechnology
—Robots

VOCABULARY
compound machine p. 164
nanotechnology p. 167
robot p. 169

Reviewing Vocabulary

Write the name of the simple machine shown in each illustration. Give an example from real life for each one.

1.

2.

3.

4.

5.

6.

Copy the chart below, and write the definition for each term in your own words. Use the meaning of the term's root to help you.

Term	Root Meaning	Definition
7. machine	having power	
8. nanotechnology	one–billionth	
9. simple machine	basic	
10. efficiency	to accomplish	
11. compound machine	put together	
12. robot	work	
13. fulcrum	to support	

Reviewing Key Concepts

Multiple Choice *Choose the letter of the best answer.*

14. Machines help you work by
   a. decreasing the amount of work that must be done
   b. changing the size and/or direction of a force
   c. decreasing friction
   d. conserving energy

15. To calculate mechanical advantage, you need to know
   a. time and energy
   b. input force and output force
   c. distance and work
   d. size and direction of a force

16. A machine in which the input force is equal to the output force has a mechanical advantage of
   a. 0   **c.** 1
   b. between 0 and 1   **d.** more than 1

17. You can increase a machine's efficiency by
   a. increasing force   **c.** increasing distance
   b. reducing work   **d.** reducing friction

18. Levers turn around a
   a. fixed point called a fulcrum
   b. solid bar that rotates
   c. wheel attached to an axle
   d. sloping surface called an inclined plane

19. When you bite into an apple, your teeth act as what kind of simple machine?
   a. lever   **c.** wedge
   b. pulley   **d.** screw

Short Answer *Answer each of the following questions in a sentence or two.*

20. Describe the simple machines that make up scissors.

21. How do you calculate the mechanical advantage of a compound machine?

22. How did scientists use processes inside the human body as a model for making nanomachines?

23. SYNTHESIZE How is a screw related to an inclined plane?

24. INFER Which simple machine would you use to raise a very heavy load to the top of a building? Why?

25. APPLY If you reached the top of a hill by using a path that wound around the hill, would you do more work than someone who climbed a shorter path? Why or why not? Who would use more force?

26. APPLY You are using a board to pry a large rock out of the ground when the board suddenly breaks apart in the middle. You pick up half of the board and use it to continue prying up the rock. The fulcrum stays in the same position. How has the mechanical advantage of the board changed? How does it change your work?

27. SYNTHESIZE What is the difference between a single fixed pulley and a single movable pulley? Draw a diagram to illustrate the difference.

Use the information in the diagram below to answer the next three questions.

4 m

1.5 m

28. SYNTHESIZE What is the mechanical advantage of the ramp? By how many times does the ramp multiply the man's input force?

29. SYNTHESIZE If the ramp's length were longer, what effect would this have on its mechanical advantage? Would this require the man to exert more or less input force?

30. INFER If the ramp's length stayed the same but the height was raised, how would this change the input force required?

Complete the following calculations.

31. You swing a hockey stick with a force of 10 N. The stick applies 5 N of force on the puck. What is the mechanical advantage of the hockey stick?

32. Your input work on a manual lawn mower is 125,000 J. The output work is 90,000 J. What is the efficiency of the lawn mower?

33. If a car engine has a 20 percent efficiency, what percentage of the input work is lost?

34. A steering wheel has a radius of 21 cm. The steering column on which it turns has a radius of 3 cm. What is the mechanical advantage of this wheel and axle?

35. Two gears with the same diameter form a gear system. Each gear has 24 teeth. What is the mechanical advantage of this gear system?

the **BIG** idea

36. DRAW CONCLUSIONS Look back at the photograph on pages 142–143. Name the simple machines you see in the photograph. How do you think they work together to move balls through the sculpture? How has your understanding changed as to the way in which machines help people work?

37. SYNTHESIZE Think of a compound machine you have used recently. Explain which simple machines it includes and how they helped you do work.

38. PREDICT How do you think nanotechnology will be useful in the future? Give several examples.

UNIT PROJECTS

Evaluate all of the data, results, and information from your project folder. Prepare to present your project to the class. Be ready to answer questions posed by your classmates about your results.

Standardized Test Practice

Analyzing Graphics

The Archimedean screw is a mechanical device first used more than 2000 years ago. It consists of a screw inside a cylinder. One end of the device is placed in water. As the screw is turned with a handle, its threads carry water upward. The Archimedean screw is still used in some parts of the world to pump water for irrigating fields. It can also be used to move grain in mills.

Study the illustration of an Archimedean screw. Then answer the questions that follow.

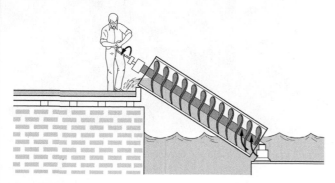

1. Which type of simple machine moves water in the cylinder?

  a. block and tackle   **c.** screw

  b. pulley   **d.** wedge

2. Which type of simple machine is the handle?

  a. wheel and axle   **c.** pulley

  b. inclined plane   **d.** wedge

3. What is the energy source for the Archimedean screw?

  a. the water pressure inside the screw

  b. the person who is turning the handle

  c. falling water that is turning the screw

  d. electrical energy

4. How is the Archimedean screw helping the person in the illustration do work?

  a. by decreasing the input force needed to lift the water

  b. by decreasing the work needed to lift the water

  c. by decreasing the distance over which the input force is applied

  d. by keeping the water from overflowing its banks

5. If the threads on the Archimedean screw are closer together, the input force must be applied over a greater distance. This means that the person using it must turn the handle

  a. with more force

  b. fewer times but faster

  c. in the opposite direction

  d. more times with less effort

Extended Response

Answer the two questions below in detail.

6. A playground seesaw is an example of a lever. The fulcrum is located at the center of the board. People seated at either end take turns applying the force needed to move the other person. If one person weighs more than the other, how can they operate the seesaw? Consider several possibilities in your answer.

7. Picture two gears of different sizes turning together. Suppose you can apply a force to turn the larger gear or the smaller gear, and it will turn the other. Discuss what difference it would make whether you turned the larger or smaller gear. Describe the input work you would do on the gear you are turning and the output work that gear would do on the other gear.

Today's Scientist at Work

Name:	James McLurkin
Degree:	Graduate Student, Massachusetts Institute of Technology
Profession:	Computer Scientist
Location:	Cambridge, Massachusetts

James McLurkin 2003 winner of the $30,000 Lemelson-MIT Student Prize. Photo courtesy of The Lemelson-MIT Program.

If you ever have tried to get a group of your friends to work together on something, you know it's not very easy. Imagine having to get 2,000 people to work on something at the same time. This is similar to the challenge facing computer scientist James McLurkin every day.

McLurkin is trying to get swarms of robots to work together. To do this, he is writing computer algorithms. An algorithm is a list of problem-solving instructions. These instructions enable the machines to "talk" to one another. For example, suppose you want the swarm of robots to form a line. One machine would tell another to "line up behind me and get another machine to line up behind you," and so on. This is similar to the behavior of social insects. McLurkin admits to getting much of his inspiration from watching the behavior of ants. He is quick to say, however, that his robots are far less advanced than insects. "There's a lot of software in those insects, and it has been very heavily tuned over the past 65 million years."

McLurkin made the smallest independent robot of its time. He called it Goliath. The robot was approximately one inch per side.

Photo courtesy of James McLurkin

The future use for these machines is wide open. McLurkin thinks one possibility is earthquake rescue. Armies of small and large robots could go into an area damaged by an earthquake. They could do everything from detecting signs of life to figuring out how to get people to safety. Achieving this goal may be decades or even centuries away. However, this doesn't stop McLurkin from working toward it.

Student Resource Handbooks

Scientific Thinking Handbook

Making Observations

An **observation** is an act of noting and recording an event, characteristic, behavior, or anything else detected with an instrument or with the senses.

Observations allow you to make informed hypotheses and to gather data for experiments. Careful observations often lead to ideas for new experiments. There are two categories of observations:

- **Quantitative observations** can be expressed in numbers and include records of time, temperature, mass, distance, and volume.

- **Qualitative observations** include descriptions of sights, sounds, smells, and textures.

EXAMPLE

A student dissolved 30 grams of Epsom salts in water, poured the solution into a dish, and let the dish sit out uncovered overnight. The next day, she made the following observations of the Epsom salt crystals that grew in the dish.

Table 1. Observations of Epsom Salt Crystals

To determine the mass, the student found the mass of the dish before and after growing the crystals and then used subtraction to find the difference.

The student measured several crystals and calculated the mean length. (To learn how to calculate the mean of a data set, see page R36.)

Quantitative Observations	Qualitative Observations
• mass = 30 g • mean crystal length = 0.5 cm • longest crystal length = 2 cm	• Crystals are clear. • Crystals are long, thin, and rectangular. • White crust has formed around edge of dish.

Photographs or sketches are useful for recording qualitative observations.

Epsom salt crystals

MORE ABOUT OBSERVING

- Make quantitative observations whenever possible. That way, others will know exactly what you observed and be able to compare their results with yours.

- It is always a good idea to make qualitative observations too. You never know when you might observe something unexpected.

Predicting and Hypothesizing

A **prediction** is an expectation of what will be observed or what will happen. A **hypothesis** is a tentative explanation for an observation or scientific problem that can be tested by further investigation.

EXAMPLE

Suppose you have made two paper airplanes and you wonder why one of them tends to glide farther than the other one.

1. Start by asking a question.

2. Make an educated guess. After examination, you notice that the wings of the airplane that flies farther are slightly larger than the wings of the other airplane.

3. Write a prediction based upon your educated guess, in the form of an "If . . . , then . . ." statement. Write the independent variable after the word *if,* and the dependent variable after the word *then*.

4. To make a hypothesis, explain why you think what you predicted will occur. Write the explanation after the word *because*.

1. Why does one of the paper airplanes glide farther than the other?

2. The size of an airplane's wings may affect how far the airplane will glide.

3. Prediction: If I make a paper airplane with larger wings, then the airplane will glide farther.

To read about independent and dependent variables, see page R30.

4. Hypothesis: If I make a paper airplane with larger wings, then the airplane will glide farther, because the additional surface area of the wing will produce more lift.

Notice that the part of the hypothesis after *because* adds an explanation of why the airplane will glide farther.

MORE ABOUT HYPOTHESES

• The results of an experiment cannot prove that a hypothesis is correct. Rather, the results either support or do not support the hypothesis.

• Valuable information is gained even when your hypothesis is not supported by your results. For example, it would be an important discovery to find that wing size is not related to how far an airplane glides.

• In science, a hypothesis is supported only after many scientists have conducted many experiments and produced consistent results.

Inferring

An **inference** is a logical conclusion drawn from the available evidence and prior knowledge. Inferences are often made from observations.

EXAMPLE

A student observing a set of acorns noticed something unexpected about one of them. He noticed a white, soft-bodied insect eating its way out of the acorn.

The student recorded these observations.

Observations

- There is a hole in the acorn, about 0.5 cm in diameter, where the insect crawled out.
- There is a second hole, which is about the size of a pinhole, on the other side of the acorn.
- The inside of the acorn is hollow.

Here are some inferences that can be made on the basis of the observations.

Inferences

- The insect formed from the material inside the acorn, grew to its present size, and ate its way out of the acorn.
- The insect crawled through the smaller hole, ate the inside of the acorn, grew to its present size, and ate its way out of the acorn.
- An egg was laid in the acorn through the smaller hole. The egg hatched into a larva that ate the inside of the acorn, grew to its present size, and ate its way out of the acorn.

When you make inferences, be sure to look at all of the evidence available and combine it with what you already know.

MORE ABOUT INFERENCES

Inferences depend both on observations and on the knowledge of the people making the inferences. Ancient people who did not know that organisms are produced only by similar organisms might have made an inference like the first one. A student today might look at the same observations and make the second inference. A third student might have knowledge about this particular insect and know that it is never small enough to fit through the smaller hole, leading her to the third inference.

Identifying Cause and Effect

In a **cause-and-effect relationship,** one event or characteristic is the result of another. Usually an effect follows its cause in time.

There are many examples of cause-and-effect relationships in everyday life.

Cause	Effect
Turn off a light.	Room gets dark.
Drop a glass.	Glass breaks.
Blow a whistle.	Sound is heard.

Scientists must be careful not to infer a cause-and-effect relationship just because one event happens after another event. When one event occurs after another, you cannot infer a cause-and-effect relationship on the basis of that information alone. You also cannot conclude that one event caused another if there are alternative ways to explain the second event. A scientist must demonstrate through experimentation or continued observation that an event was truly caused by another event.

EXAMPLE

Make an Observation

Suppose you have a few plants growing outside. When the weather starts getting colder, you bring one of the plants indoors. You notice that the plant you brought indoors is growing faster than the others are growing. You cannot conclude from your observation that the change in temperature was the cause of the increased plant growth, because there are alternative explanations for the observation. Some possible explanations are given below.

- The humidity indoors caused the plant to grow faster.

- The level of sunlight indoors caused the plant to grow faster.

- The indoor plant's being noticed more often and watered more often than the outdoor plants caused it to grow faster.

- The plant that was brought indoors was healthier than the other plants to begin with.

To determine which of these factors, if any, caused the indoor plant to grow faster than the outdoor plants, you would need to design and conduct an experiment.

See pages R28–R35 for information about designing experiments.

Recognizing Bias

Television, newspapers, and the Internet are full of experts claiming to have scientific evidence to back up their claims. How do you know whether the claims are really backed up by good science?

Bias is a slanted point of view, or personal prejudice. The goal of scientists is to be as objective as possible and to base their findings on facts instead of opinions. However, bias often affects the conclusions of researchers, and it is important to learn to recognize bias.

When scientific results are reported, you should consider the source of the information as well as the information itself. It is important to critically analyze the information that you see and read.

SOURCES OF BIAS

There are several ways in which a report of scientific information may be biased. Here are some questions that you can ask yourself:

1. **Who is sponsoring the research?**

   Sometimes, the results of an investigation are biased because an organization paying for the research is looking for a specific answer. This type of bias can affect how data are gathered and interpreted.

2. **Is the research sample large enough?**

   Sometimes research does not include enough data. The larger the sample size, the more likely that the results are accurate, assuming a truly random sample.

3. **In a survey, who is answering the questions?**

   The results of a survey or poll can be biased. The people taking part in the survey may have been specifically chosen because of how they would answer. They may have the same ideas or lifestyles. A survey or poll should make use of a random sample of people.

4. **Are the people who take part in a survey biased?**

   People who take part in surveys sometimes try to answer the questions the way they think the researcher wants them to answer. Also, in surveys or polls that ask for personal information, people may be unwilling to answer questions truthfully.

SCIENTIFIC BIAS

It is also important to realize that scientists have their own biases because of the types of research they do and because of their scientific viewpoints. Two scientists may look at the same set of data and come to completely different conclusions because of these biases. However, such disagreements are not necessarily bad. In fact, a critical analysis of disagreements is often responsible for moving science forward.

Identifying Faulty Reasoning

Faulty reasoning is wrong or incorrect thinking. It leads to mistakes and to wrong conclusions. Scientists are careful not to draw unreasonable conclusions from experimental data. Without such caution, the results of scientific investigations may be misleading.

EXAMPLE

Scientists try to make generalizations based on their data to explain as much about nature as possible. If only a small sample of data is looked at, however, a conclusion may be faulty. Suppose a scientist has studied the effects of the El Niño and La Niña weather patterns on flood damage in California from 1989 to 1995. The scientist organized the data in the bar graph below.

The scientist drew the following conclusions:

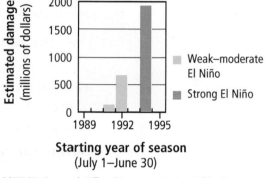

Flood and Storm Damage in California

SOURCE: *Governor's Office of Emergency Services, California*

1. The La Niña weather pattern has no effect on flooding in California.

2. When neither weather pattern occurs, there is almost no flood damage.

3. A weak or moderate El Niño produces a small or moderate amount of flooding.

4. A strong El Niño produces a lot of flooding.

For the six-year period of the scientist's investigation, these conclusions may seem to be reasonable. However, a six-year study of weather patterns may be too small of a sample for the conclusions to be supported. Consider the following graph, which shows information that was gathered from 1949 to 1997.

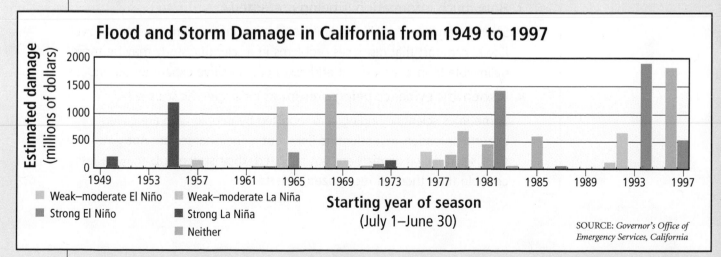

Flood and Storm Damage in California from 1949 to 1997

SOURCE: *Governor's Office of Emergency Services, California*

The only one of the conclusions that all of this information supports is number 3: a weak or moderate El Niño produces a small or moderate amount of flooding. By collecting more data, scientists can be more certain of their conclusions and can avoid faulty reasoning.

Analyzing Statements

To **analyze** a statement is to examine its parts carefully. Scientific findings are often reported through media such as television or the Internet. A report that is made public often focuses on only a small part of research. As a result, it is important to question the sources of information.

Evaluate Media Claims

To **evaluate** a statement is to judge it on the basis of criteria you've established. Sometimes evaluating means deciding whether a statement is true.

Reports of scientific research and findings in the media may be misleading or incomplete. When you are exposed to this information, you should ask yourself some questions so that you can make informed judgments about the information.

1. **Does the information come from a credible source?**

   Suppose you learn about a new product and it is stated that scientific evidence proves that the product works. A report from a respected news source may be more believable than an advertisement paid for by the product's manufacturer.

2. **How much evidence supports the claim?**

   Often, it may seem that there is new evidence every day of something in the world that either causes or cures an illness. However, information that is the result of several years of work by several different scientists is more credible than an advertisement that does not even cite the subjects of the experiment.

3. **How much information is being presented?**

   Science cannot solve all questions, and scientific experiments often have flaws. A report that discusses problems in a scientific study may be more believable than a report that addresses only positive experimental findings.

4. **Is scientific evidence being presented by a specific source?**

   Sometimes scientific findings are reported by people who are called experts or leaders in a scientific field. But if their names are not given or their scientific credentials are not reported, their statements may be less credible than those of recognized experts.

Differentiate Between Fact and Opinion

Sometimes information is presented as a fact when it may be an opinion. When scientific conclusions are reported, it is important to recognize whether they are based on solid evidence. Again, you may find it helpful to ask yourself some questions.

1. **What is the difference between a fact and an opinion?**

   A **fact** is a piece of information that can be strictly defined and proved true. An **opinion** is a statement that expresses a belief, value, or feeling. An opinion cannot be proved true or false. For example, a person's age is a fact, but if someone is asked how old they feel, it is impossible to prove the person's answer to be true or false.

2. **Can opinions be measured?**

   Yes, opinions can be measured. In fact, surveys often ask for people's opinions on a topic. But there is no way to know whether or not an opinion is the truth.

HOW TO DIFFERENTIATE FACT FROM OPINION

Opinions

Notice words or phrases that express beliefs or feelings. The words *unfortunately* and *careless* show that opinions are being expressed.

Opinion

Look for statements that speculate about events. These statements are opinions, because they cannot be proved.

Human Activities and the Environment

Unfortunately, human use of fossil fuels is one of the most significant developments of the past few centuries. Humans rely on fossil fuels, a non-renewable energy resource, for more than 90 percent of their energy needs.

This careless misuse of our planet's resources has resulted in pollution, global warming, and the destruction of fragile ecosystems. For example, oil pipelines carry more than one million barrels of oil each day across tundra regions. Transporting oil across such areas can only result in oil spills that poison the land for decades.

Facts

Statements that contain statistics tend to be facts. Writers often use facts to support their opinions.

Lab Handbook

Safety Rules

Before you work in the laboratory, read these safety rules twice. Ask your teacher to explain any rules that you do not completely understand. Refer to these rules later on if you have questions about safety in the science classroom.

Directions

- Read all directions and make sure that you understand them before starting an investigation or lab activity. If you do not understand how to do a procedure or how to use a piece of equipment, ask your teacher.
- Do not begin any investigation or touch any equipment until your teacher has told you to start.
- Never experiment on your own. If you want to try a procedure that the directions do not call for, ask your teacher for permission first.
- If you are hurt or injured in any way, tell your teacher immediately.

Dress Code

goggles

apron

gloves

- Wear goggles when
  — using glassware, sharp objects, or chemicals
  — heating an object
  — working with anything that can easily fly up into the air and hurt someone's eye
- Tie back long hair or hair that hangs in front of your eyes.
- Remove any article of clothing—such as a loose sweater or a scarf—that hangs down and may touch a flame, chemical, or piece of equipment.
- Observe all safety icons calling for the wearing of eye protection, gloves, and aprons.

Heating and Fire Safety

fire safety

heating safety

- Keep your work area neat, clean, and free of extra materials.
- Never reach over a flame or heat source.
- Point objects being heated away from you and others.
- Never heat a substance or an object in a closed container.
- Never touch an object that has been heated. If you are unsure whether something is hot, treat it as though it is. Use oven mitts, clamps, tongs, or a test-tube holder.
- Know where the fire extinguisher and fire blanket are kept in your classroom.
- Do not throw hot substances into the trash. Wait for them to cool or use the container your teacher puts out for disposal.

Electrical Safety

electrical safety

- Never use lamps or other electrical equipment with frayed cords.
- Make sure no cord is lying on the floor where someone can trip over it.
- Do not let a cord hang over the side of a counter or table so that the equipment can easily be pulled or knocked to the floor.
- Never let cords hang into sinks or other places where water can be found.
- Never try to fix electrical problems. Inform your teacher of any problems immediately.
- Unplug an electrical cord by pulling on the plug, not the cord.

Chemical Safety

chemical safety

poison

fumes

- If you spill a chemical or get one on your skin or in your eyes, tell your teacher right away.
- Never touch, taste, or sniff any chemicals in the lab. If you need to determine odor, waft. Wafting consists of holding the chemical in its container 15 centimeters (6 in.) away from your nose, and using your fingers to bring fumes from the container to your nose.
- Keep lids on all chemicals you are not using.
- Never put unused chemicals back into the original containers. Throw away extra chemicals where your teacher tells you to.
- Pour chemicals over a sink or your work area, not over the floor.
- If you get a chemical in your eye, use the eyewash right away.
- Always wash your hands after handling chemicals, plants, or soil.

Wafting

Glassware and Sharp-Object Safety

sharp objects

- If you break glassware, tell your teacher right away.
- Do not use broken or chipped glassware. Give these to your teacher.
- Use knives and other cutting instruments carefully. Always wear eye protection and cut away from you.

Animal Safety

- Never hurt an animal.
- Touch animals only when necessary. Follow your teacher's instructions for handling animals.
- Always wash your hands after working with animals.

Cleanup

disposal

- Follow your teacher's instructions for throwing away or putting away supplies.
- Clean your work area and pick up anything that has dropped to the floor.
- Wash your hands.

Using Lab Equipment

Different experiments require different types of equipment. But even though experiments differ, the ways in which the equipment is used are the same.

Beakers

- Use beakers for holding and pouring liquids.
- Do not use a beaker to measure the volume of a liquid. Use a graduated cylinder instead. (See page R16.)
- Use a beaker that holds about twice as much liquid as you need. For example, if you need 100 milliliters of water, you should use a 200- or 250-milliliter beaker.

Test Tubes

- Use test tubes to hold small amounts of substances.
- Do not use a test tube to measure the volume of a liquid.
- Use a test tube when heating a substance over a flame. Aim the mouth of the tube away from yourself and other people.
- Liquids easily spill or splash from test tubes, so it is important to use only small amounts of liquids.

Test-Tube Holder

- Use a test-tube holder when heating a substance in a test tube.
- Use a test-tube holder if the substance in a test tube is dangerous to touch.
- Make sure the test-tube holder tightly grips the test tube so that the test tube will not slide out of the holder.
- Make sure that the test-tube holder is above the surface of the substance in the test tube so that you can observe the substance.

Test-Tube Rack

- Use a test-tube rack to organize test tubes before, during, and after an experiment.

- Use a test-tube rack to keep test tubes upright so that they do not fall over and spill their contents.

- Use a test-tube rack that is the correct size for the test tubes that you are using. If the rack is too small, a test tube may become stuck. If the rack is too large, a test tube may lean over, and some of its contents may spill or splash.

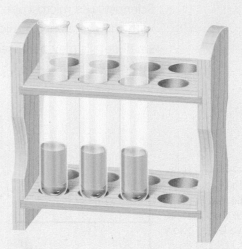

Forceps

- Use forceps when you need to pick up or hold a very small object that should not be touched with your hands.

- Do not use forceps to hold anything over a flame, because forceps are not long enough to keep your hand safely away from the flame. Plastic forceps will melt, and metal forceps will conduct heat and burn your hand.

Hot Plate

- Use a hot plate when a substance needs to be kept warmer than room temperature for a long period of time.

- Use a hot plate instead of a Bunsen burner or a candle when you need to carefully control temperature.

- Do not use a hot plate when a substance needs to be burned in an experiment.

- Always use "hot hands" safety mitts or oven mitts when handling anything that has been heated on a hot plate.

Microscope

Scientists use microscopes to see very small objects that cannot easily be seen with the eye alone. A microscope magnifies the image of an object so that small details may be observed. A microscope that you may use can magnify an object 400 times—the object will appear 400 times larger than its actual size.

LAB HANDBOOK

Body The body separates the lens in the eyepiece from the objective lenses below.

Nosepiece The nosepiece holds the objective lenses above the stage and rotates so that all lenses may be used.

High-Power Objective Lens This is the largest lens on the nosepiece. It magnifies an image approximately 40 times.

Stage The stage supports the object being viewed.

Diaphragm The diaphragm is used to adjust the amount of light passing through the slide and into an objective lens.

Mirror or Light Source Some microscopes use light that is reflected through the stage by a mirror. Other microscopes have their own light sources.

Eyepiece Objects are viewed through the eyepiece. The eyepiece contains a lens that commonly magnifies an image 10 times.

Coarse Adjustment This knob is used to focus the image of an object when it is viewed through the low-power lens.

Fine Adjustment This knob is used to focus the image of an object when it is viewed through the high-power lens.

Low-Power Objective Lens This is the smallest lens on the nosepiece. It magnifies an image approximately 10 times.

Arm The arm supports the body above the stage. Always carry a microscope by the arm and base.

Stage Clip The stage clip holds a slide in place on the stage.

Base The base supports the microscope.

VIEWING AN OBJECT

1. Use the coarse adjustment knob to raise the body tube.

2. Adjust the diaphragm so that you can see a bright circle of light through the eyepiece.

3. Place the object or slide on the stage. Be sure that it is centered over the hole in the stage.

4. Turn the nosepiece to click the low-power lens into place.

5. Using the coarse adjustment knob, slowly lower the lens and focus on the specimen being viewed. Be sure not to touch the slide or object with the lens.

6. When switching from the low-power lens to the high-power lens, first raise the body tube with the coarse adjustment knob so that the high-power lens will not hit the slide.

7. Turn the nosepiece to click the high-power lens into place.

8. Use the fine adjustment knob to focus on the specimen being viewed. Again, be sure not to touch the slide or object with the lens.

MAKING A SLIDE, OR WET MOUNT

1 Place the specimen in the center of a clean slide.

2 Place a drop of water on the specimen.

Place a cover slip on the slide. Put one edge of the cover slip into the drop of water and slowly lower it over the specimen.

4 Remove any air bubbles from under the cover slip by gently tapping the cover slip.

5 Dry any excess water before placing the slide on the microscope stage for viewing.

Spring Scale (Force Meter)

- Use a spring scale to measure a force pulling on the scale.
- Use a spring scale to measure the force of gravity exerted on an object by Earth.
- To measure a force accurately, a spring scale must be zeroed before it is used. The scale is zeroed when no weight is attached and the indicator is positioned at zero.
- Do not attach a weight that is either too heavy or too light to a spring scale. A weight that is too heavy could break the scale or exert too great a force for the scale to measure. A weight that is too light may not exert enough force to be measured accurately.

Graduated Cylinder

- Use a graduated cylinder to measure the volume of a liquid.
- Be sure that the graduated cylinder is on a flat surface so that your measurement will be accurate.
- When reading the scale on a graduated cylinder, be sure to have your eyes at the level of the surface of the liquid.
- The surface of the liquid will be curved in the graduated cylinder. Read the volume of the liquid at the bottom of the curve, or meniscus (muh-NIHS-kuhs).
- You can use a graduated cylinder to find the volume of a solid object by measuring the increase in a liquid's level after you add the object to the cylinder.

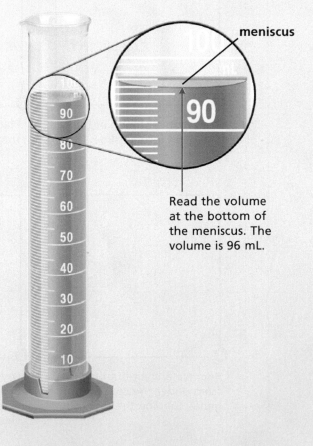

meniscus

90

Read the volume at the bottom of the meniscus. The volume is 96 mL.

Metric Rulers

- Use metric rulers or meter sticks to measure objects' lengths.

- Do not measure an object from the end of a metric ruler or meter stick, because the end is often imperfect. Instead, measure from the 1-centimeter mark, but remember to subtract a centimeter from the apparent measurement.

- Estimate any lengths that extend between marked units. For example, if a meter stick shows centimeters but not millimeters, you can estimate the length that an object extends between centimeter marks to measure it to the nearest millimeter.

- **Controlling Variables** If you are taking repeated measurements, always measure from the same point each time. For example, if you're measuring how high two different balls bounce when dropped from the same height, measure both bounces at the same point on the balls—either the top or the bottom. Do not measure at the top of one ball and the bottom of the other.

EXAMPLE

How to Measure a Leaf

1. Lay a ruler flat on top of the leaf so that the 1-centimeter mark lines up with one end. Make sure the ruler and the leaf do not move between the time you line them up and the time you take the measurement.

2. Look straight down on the ruler so that you can see exactly how the marks line up with the other end of the leaf.

3. Estimate the length by which the leaf extends beyond a marking. For example, the leaf below extends about halfway between the 4.2-centimeter and 4.3-centimeter marks, so the apparent measurement is about 4.25 centimeters.

4. Remember to subtract 1 centimeter from your apparent measurement, since you started at the 1-centimeter mark on the ruler and not at the end. The leaf is about 3.25 centimeters long (4.25 cm − 1 cm = 3.25 cm).

Triple-Beam Balance

This balance has a pan and three beams with sliding masses, called riders. At one end of the beams is a pointer that indicates whether the mass on the pan is equal to the masses shown on the beams.

1. Make sure the balance is zeroed before measuring the mass of an object. The balance is zeroed if the pointer is at zero when nothing is on the pan and the riders are at their zero points. Use the adjustment knob at the base of the balance to zero it.

2. Place the object to be measured on the pan.

3. Move the riders one notch at a time away from the pan. Begin with the largest rider. If moving the largest rider one notch brings the pointer below zero, begin measuring the mass of the object with the next smaller rider.

4. Change the positions of the riders until they balance the mass on the pan and the pointer is at zero. Then add the readings from the three beams to determine the mass of the object.

300 g	position of largest rider
90 g	position of middle rider
+ 3 g	position of smallest rider
393 g	mass of beaker

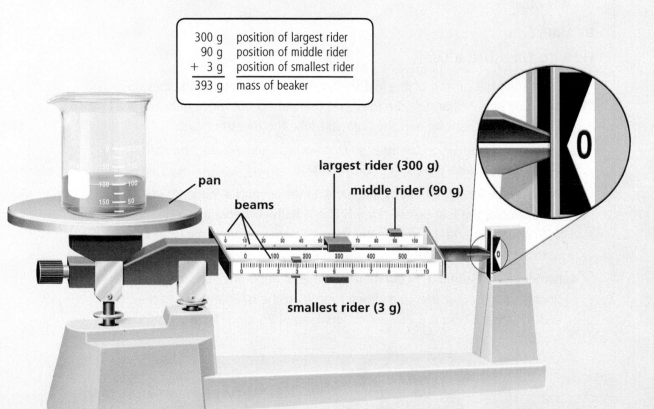

pan

beams

largest rider (300 g)

middle rider (90 g)

smallest rider (3 g)

Double-Pan Balance

This type of balance has two pans. Between the pans is a pointer that indicates whether the masses on the pans are equal.

1. Make sure the balance is zeroed before measuring the mass of an object. The balance is zeroed if the pointer is at zero when there is nothing on either of the pans. Many double-pan balances have sliding knobs that can be used to zero them.

2. Place the object to be measured on one of the pans.

3. Begin adding standard masses to the other pan. Begin with the largest standard mass. If this adds too much mass to the balance, begin measuring the mass of the object with the next smaller standard mass.

4. Add standard masses until the masses on both pans are balanced and the pointer is at zero. Then add the standard masses together to determine the mass of the object being measured.

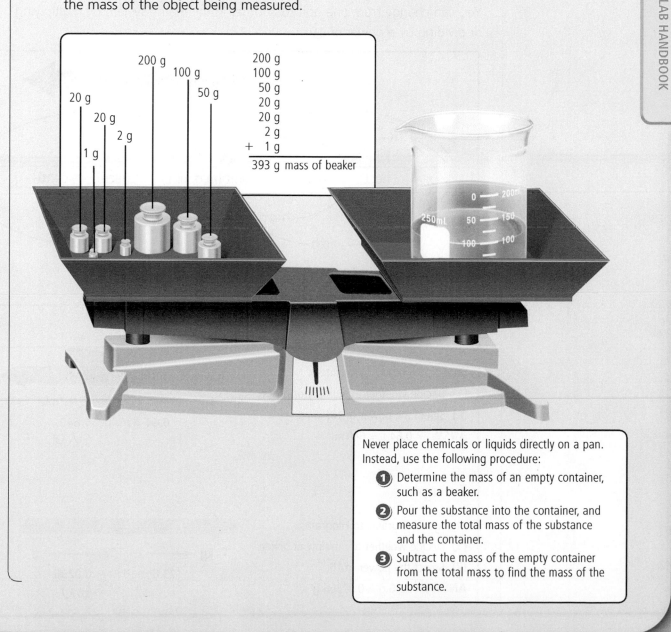

```
            200 g
    200 g   100 g       200 g
            100 g       100 g
                50 g     50 g
20 g                     20 g
        20 g             20 g
                 2 g      2 g
    1 g               +   1 g
                       _____
                       393 g mass of beaker
```

Never place chemicals or liquids directly on a pan. Instead, use the following procedure:

❶ Determine the mass of an empty container, such as a beaker.

❷ Pour the substance into the container, and measure the total mass of the substance and the container.

❸ Subtract the mass of the empty container from the total mass to find the mass of the substance.

LAB HANDBOOK

The Metric System and SI Units

Scientists use International System (SI) units for measurements of distance, volume, mass, and temperature. The International System is based on multiples of ten and the metric system of measurement.

Basic SI Units		
Property	Name	Symbol
length	meter	m
volume	liter	L
mass	kilogram	kg
temperature	kelvin	K

SI Prefixes		
Prefix	Symbol	Multiple of 10
kilo-	k	1000
hecto-	h	100
deca-	da	10
deci-	d	$0.1 \left(\frac{1}{10}\right)$
centi-	c	$0.01 \left(\frac{1}{100}\right)$
milli-	m	$0.001 \left(\frac{1}{1000}\right)$

Changing Metric Units

You can change from one unit to another in the metric system by multiplying or dividing by a power of 10.

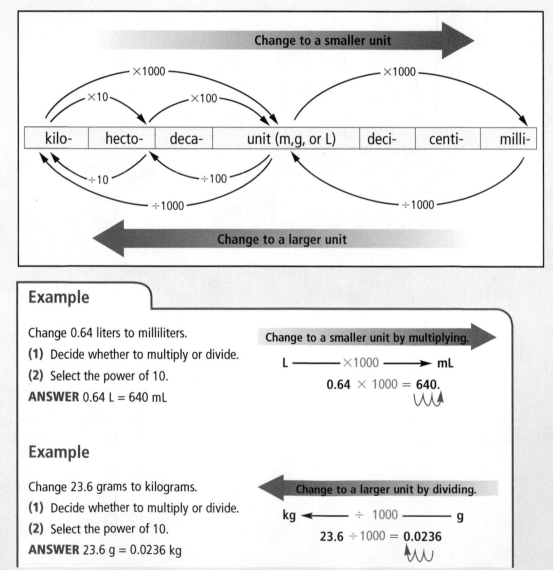

Example

Change 0.64 liters to milliliters.

(1) Decide whether to multiply or divide.
(2) Select the power of 10.
ANSWER 0.64 L = 640 mL

Change to a smaller unit by multiplying.

$$L \xrightarrow{\times 1000} mL$$
$$0.64 \times 1000 = 640.$$

Example

Change 23.6 grams to kilograms.

(1) Decide whether to multiply or divide.
(2) Select the power of 10.
ANSWER 23.6 g = 0.0236 kg

Change to a larger unit by dividing.

$$kg \xleftarrow{\div 1000} g$$
$$23.6 \div 1000 = 0.0236$$

Temperature Conversions

Even though the kelvin is the SI base unit of temperature, the degree Celsius will be the unit you use most often in your science studies. The formulas below show the relationships between temperatures in degrees Fahrenheit (°F), degrees Celsius (°C), and kelvins (K).

$$°C = \frac{5}{9}(°F - 32)$$

$$°F = \frac{9}{5}°C + 32$$

$$K = °C + 273$$

See page R42 for help with using formulas.

Examples of Temperature Conversions		
Condition	**Degrees Celsius**	**Degrees Fahrenheit**
Freezing point of water	0	32
Cool day	10	50
Mild day	20	68
Warm day	30	86
Normal body temperature	37	98.6
Very hot day	40	104
Boiling point of water	100	212

Converting Between SI and U.S. Customary Units

Use the chart below when you need to convert between SI units and U.S. customary units.

SI Unit	From SI to U.S. Customary			From U.S. Customary to SI		
Length	**When you know**	**multiply by**	**to find**	**When you know**	**multiply by**	**to find**
kilometer (km) = 1000 m	kilometers	0.62	miles	miles	1.61	kilometers
meter (m) = 100 cm	meters	3.28	feet	feet	0.3048	meters
centimeter (cm) = 10 mm	centimeters	0.39	inches	inches	2.54	centimeters
millimeter (mm) = 0.1 cm	millimeters	0.04	inches	inches	25.4	millimeters
Area	**When you know**	**multiply by**	**to find**	**When you know**	**multiply by**	**to find**
square kilometer (km²)	square kilometers	0.39	square miles	square miles	2.59	square kilometers
square meter (m²)	square meters	1.2	square yards	square yards	0.84	square meters
square centimeter (cm²)	square centimeters	0.155	square inches	square inches	6.45	square centimeters
Volume	**When you know**	**multiply by**	**to find**	**When you know**	**multiply by**	**to find**
liter (L) = 1000 mL	liters	1.06	quarts	quarts	0.95	liters
	liters	0.26	gallons	gallons	3.79	liters
	liters	4.23	cups	cups	0.24	liters
	liters	2.12	pints	pints	0.47	liters
milliliter (mL) = 0.001 L	milliliters	0.20	teaspoons	teaspoons	4.93	milliliters
	milliliters	0.07	tablespoons	tablespoons	14.79	milliliters
	milliliters	0.03	fluid ounces	fluid ounces	29.57	milliliters
Mass	**When you know**	**multiply by**	**to find**	**When you know**	**multiply by**	**to find**
kilogram (kg) = 1000 g	kilograms	2.2	pounds	pounds	0.45	kilograms
gram (g) = 1000 mg	grams	0.035	ounces	ounces	28.35	grams

Precision and Accuracy

When you do an experiment, it is important that your methods, observations, and data be both precise and accurate.

low precision

precision, but not accuracy

precision and accuracy

Precision

In science, **precision** is the exactness and consistency of measurements. For example, measurements made with a ruler that has both centimeter and millimeter markings would be more precise than measurements made with a ruler that has only centimeter markings. Another indicator of precision is the care taken to make sure that methods and observations are as exact and consistent as possible. Every time a particular experiment is done, the same procedure should be used. Precision is necessary because experiments are repeated several times and if the procedure changes, the results will change.

EXAMPLE

Suppose you are measuring temperatures over a two-week period. Your precision will be greater if you measure each temperature at the same place, at the same time of day, and with the same thermometer than if you change any of these factors from one day to the next.

Accuracy

In science, it is possible to be precise but not accurate. **Accuracy** depends on the difference between a measurement and an actual value. The smaller the difference, the more accurate the measurement.

EXAMPLE

Suppose you look at a stream and estimate that it is about 1 meter wide at a particular place. You decide to check your estimate by measuring the stream with a meter stick, and you determine that the stream is 1.32 meters wide. However, because it is hard to measure the width of a stream with a meter stick, it turns out that you didn't do a very good job. The stream is actually 1.14 meters wide. Therefore, even though your estimate was less precise than your measurement, your estimate was actually more accurate.

Making Data Tables and Graphs

Data tables and graphs are useful tools for both recording and communicating scientific data.

Making Data Tables

You can use a **data table** to organize and record the measurements that you make. Some examples of information that might be recorded in data tables are frequencies, times, and amounts.

EXAMPLE

Suppose you are investigating photosynthesis in two elodea plants. One sits in direct sunlight, and the other sits in a dimly lit room. You measure the rate of photosynthesis by counting the number of bubbles in the jar every ten minutes.

1. Title and number your data table.

2. Decide how you will organize the table into columns and rows.

3. Any units, such as seconds or degrees, should be included in column headings, not in the individual cells.

Table 1. Number of Bubbles from Elodea

◄ Always number and title data tables.

Time (min)	Sunlight	Dim Light
0	0	0
10	15	5
20	25	8
30	32	7
40	41	10
50	47	9
60	42	9

The data in the table above could also be organized in a different way.

Table 1. Number of Bubbles from Elodea

◄ Put units in column heading.

Light Condition	Time (min)						
	0	10	20	30	40	50	60
Sunlight	0	15	25	32	41	47	42
Dim light	0	5	8	7	10	9	9

Making Line Graphs

You can use a **line graph** to show a relationship between variables. Line graphs are particularly useful for showing changes in variables over time.

EXAMPLE

Suppose you are interested in graphing temperature data that you collected over the course of a day.

Table 1. Outside Temperature During the Day on March 7

	Time of Day						
	7:00 A.M.	9:00 A.M.	11:00 A.M.	1:00 P.M.	3:00 P.M.	5:00 P.M.	7:00 P.M.
Temp (°C)	8	9	11	14	12	10	6

1. Use the vertical axis of your line graph for the variable that you are measuring—temperature.

2. Choose scales for both the horizontal axis and the vertical axis of the graph. You should have two points more than you need on the vertical axis, and the horizontal axis should be long enough for all of the data points to fit.

3. Draw and label each axis.

4. Graph each value. First find the appropriate point on the scale of the horizontal axis. Imagine a line that rises vertically from that place on the scale. Then find the corresponding value on the vertical axis, and imagine a line that moves horizontally from that value. The point where these two imaginary lines intersect is where the value should be plotted.

5. Connect the points with straight lines.

Be sure to add a number and a title to your graph.

vertical axis

horizontal axis

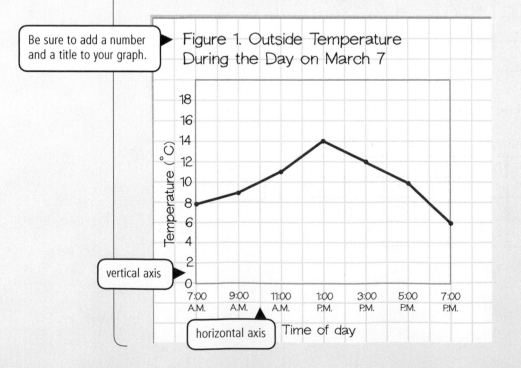

Figure 1. Outside Temperature During the Day on March 7

Making Circle Graphs

You can use a **circle graph,** sometimes called a pie chart, to represent data as parts of a circle. Circle graphs are used only when the data can be expressed as percentages of a whole. The entire circle shown in a circle graph is equal to 100 percent of the data.

EXAMPLE

Suppose you identified the species of each mature tree growing in a small wooded area. You organized your data in a table, but you also want to show the data in a circle graph.

1. To begin, find the total number of mature trees.

    $56 + 34 + 22 + 10 + 28 = 150$

2. To find the degree measure for each sector of the circle, write a fraction comparing the number of each tree species with the total number of trees. Then multiply the fraction by 360°.

    Oak: $\frac{56}{150} \times 360° = 134.4°$

3. Draw a circle. Use a protractor to draw the angle for each sector of the graph.

4. Color and label each sector of the graph.

5. Give the graph a number and title.

Table 1. Tree Species in Wooded Area

Species	Number of Specimens
Oak	56
Maple	34
Birch	22
Willow	10
Pine	28

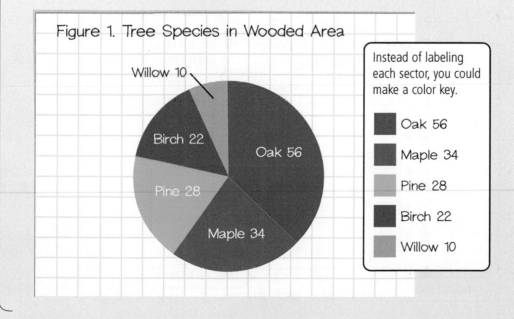

Figure 1. Tree Species in Wooded Area

Willow 10
Birch 22
Oak 56
Pine 28
Maple 34

Instead of labeling each sector, you could make a color key.

Oak 56
Maple 34
Pine 28
Birch 22
Willow 10

Bar Graph

A **bar graph** is a type of graph in which the lengths of the bars are used to represent and compare data. A numerical scale is used to determine the lengths of the bars.

EXAMPLE

To determine the effect of water on seed sprouting, three cups were filled with sand, and ten seeds were planted in each. Different amounts of water were added to each cup over a three-day period.

Table 1. Effect of Water on Seed Sprouting

Daily Amount of Water (mL)	Number of Seeds That Sprouted After 3 Days in Sand
0	1
10	4
20	8

1. Choose a numerical scale. The greatest value is 8, so the end of the scale should have a value greater than 8, such as 10. Use equal increments along the scale, such as increments of 2.

2. Draw and label the axes. Mark intervals on the vertical axis according to the scale you chose.

3. Draw a bar for each data value. Use the scale to decide how long to make each bar.

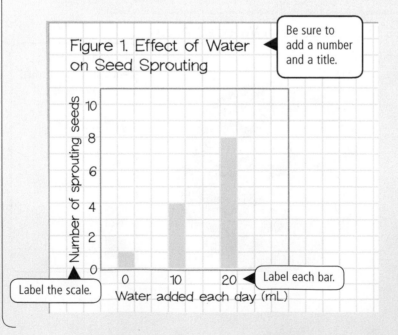

Figure 1. Effect of Water on Seed Sprouting

Be sure to add a number and a title.

Label the scale.

Label each bar.

Double Bar Graph

A **double bar graph** is a bar graph that shows two sets of data. The two bars for each measurement are drawn next to each other.

EXAMPLE

The seed-sprouting experiment was done using both sand and potting soil. The data for sand and potting soil can be plotted on one graph.

1. Draw one set of bars, using the data for sand, as shown below.

2. Draw bars for the potting-soil data next to the bars for the sand data. Shade them a different color. Add a key.

Table 2. Effect of Water and Soil on Seed Sprouting

Daily Amount of Water (mL)	Number of Seeds That Sprouted After 3 Days in Sand	Number of Seeds That Sprouted After 3 Days in Potting Soil
0	1	2
10	4	5
20	8	9

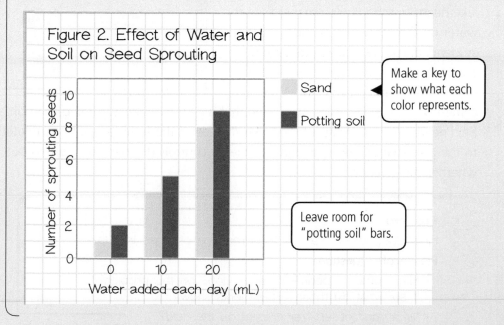

Figure 2. Effect of Water and Soil on Seed Sprouting

Make a key to show what each color represents.

Leave room for "potting soil" bars.

LAB HANDBOOK

Designing an Experiment

Use this section when designing or conducting an experiment.

Determining a Purpose

You can find a purpose for an experiment by doing research, by examining the results of a previous experiment, or by observing the world around you. An **experiment** is an organized procedure to study something under controlled conditions.

1. Write the purpose of your experiment as a question or problem that you want to investigate.

2. Write down research questions and begin searching for information that will help you design an experiment. Consult the library, the Internet, and other people as you conduct your research.

> Don't forget to learn as much as possible about your topic before you begin.

EXAMPLE

Middle school students observed an odor near the lake by their school. They also noticed that the water on the side of the lake near the school was greener than the water on the other side of the lake. The students did some research to learn more about their observations. They discovered that the odor and green color in the lake

came from algae. They also discovered that a new fertilizer was being used on a field nearby. The students inferred that the use of the fertilizer might be related to the presence of the algae and designed a controlled experiment to find out whether they were right.

Problem

How does fertilizer affect the presence of algae in a lake?

Research Questions

• Have other experiments been done on this problem? If so, what did those experiments show?

• What kind of fertilizer is used on the field? How much?

• How do algae grow?

• How do people measure algae?

• Can fertilizer and algae be used safely in a lab? How?

> **Research**
> As you research, you may find a topic that is more interesting to you than your original topic, or learn that a procedure you wanted to use is not practical or safe. It is OK to change your purpose as you research.

Writing a Hypothesis

A **hypothesis** is a tentative explanation for an observation or scientific problem that can be tested by further investigation. You can write your hypothesis in the form of an "If . . . , then . . . , because . . ." statement.

Hypothesis

If the amount of fertilizer in lake water is increased, then the amount of algae will also increase, because fertilizers provide nutrients that algae need to grow.

Hypotheses
For help with hypotheses, refer to page R3.

Determining Materials

Make a list of all the materials you will need to do your experiment. Be specific, especially if someone else is helping you obtain the materials. Try to think of everything you will need.

Materials
- 1 large jar or container
- 4 identical smaller containers
- rubber gloves that also cover the arms
- sample of fertilizer-and-water solution
- eyedropper
- clear plastic wrap
- scissors
- masking tape
- marker
- ruler

Determining Variables and Constants

EXPERIMENTAL GROUP AND CONTROL GROUP

An experiment to determine how two factors are related always has two groups—a control group and an experimental group.

1. Design an experimental group. Include as many trials as possible in the experimental group in order to obtain reliable results.

2. Design a control group that is the same as the experimental group in every way possible, except for the factor you wish to test.

Experimental Group: two containers of lake water with one drop of fertilizer solution added to each

Control Group: two containers of lake water with no fertilizer solution added

Go back to your materials list and make sure you have enough items listed to cover both your experimental group and your control group.

VARIABLES AND CONSTANTS

Identify the variables and constants in your experiment. In a controlled experiment, a **variable** is any factor that can change. **Constants** are all of the factors that are the same in both the experimental group and the control group.

1. Read your hypothesis. The **independent variable** is the factor that you wish to test and that is manipulated or changed so that it can be tested. The independent variable is expressed in your hypothesis after the word *if*. Identify the independent variable in your laboratory report.

2. The **dependent variable** is the factor that you measure to gather results. It is expressed in your hypothesis after the word *then*. Identify the dependent variable in your laboratory report.

Hypothesis
If the amount of fertilizer in lake water is increased, then the amount of algae will also increase, because fertilizers provide nutrients that algae need to grow.

Table 1. Variables and Constants in Algae Experiment

Independent Variable	Dependent Variable	Constants
Amount of fertilizer in lake water	Amount of algae that grow	• Where the lake water is obtained • Type of container used • Light and temperature conditions where water will be stored

Set up your experiment so that you will test only one variable.

MEASURING THE DEPENDENT VARIABLE

Before starting your experiment, you need to define how you will measure the dependent variable. An **operational definition** is a description of the one particular way in which you will measure the dependent variable.

Your operational definition is important for several reasons. First, in any experiment there are several ways in which a dependent variable can be measured. Second, the procedure of the experiment depends on how you decide to measure the dependent variable. Third, your operational definition makes it possible for other people to evaluate and build on your experiment.

EXAMPLE 1

An operational definition of a dependent variable can be qualitative. That is, your measurement of the dependent variable can simply be an observation of whether a change occurs as a result of a change in the independent variable. This type of operational definition can be thought of as a "yes or no" measurement.

Table 2. Qualitative Operational Definition of Algae Growth

Independent Variable	Dependent Variable	Operational Definition
Amount of fertilizer in lake water	Amount of algae that grow	Algae grow in lake water

A qualitative measurement of a dependent variable is often easy to make and record. However, this type of information does not provide a great deal of detail in your experimental results.

EXAMPLE 2

An operational definition of a dependent variable can be quantitative. That is, your measurement of the dependent variable can be a number that shows how much change occurs as a result of a change in the independent variable.

Table 3. Quantitative Operational Definition of Algae Growth

Independent Variable	Dependent Variable	Operational Definition
Amount of fertilizer in lake water	Amount of algae that grow	Diameter of largest algal growth (in mm)

A quantitative measurement of a dependent variable can be more difficult to make and analyze than a qualitative measurement. However, this type of data provides much more information about your experiment and is often more useful.

Writing a Procedure

Write each step of your procedure. Start each step with a verb, or action word, and keep the steps short. Your procedure should be clear enough for someone else to use as instructions for repeating your experiment.

> If necessary, go back to your materials list and add any materials that you left out.

Procedure

1. Put on your gloves. Use the large container to obtain a sample of lake water.

2. Divide the sample of lake water equally among the four smaller containers.

> **Controlling Variables**
> The same amount of fertilizer solution must be added to two of the four containers.

3. Use the eyedropper to add one drop of fertilizer solution to two of the containers.

4. Use the masking tape and the marker to label the containers with your initials, the date, and the identifiers "Jar 1 with Fertilizer," "Jar 2 with Fertilizer," "Jar 1 without Fertilizer," and "Jar 2 without Fertilizer."

5. Cover the containers with clear plastic wrap. Use the scissors to punch ten holes in each of the covers.

> **Controlling Variables**
> All four containers must receive the same amount of light.

6. Place all four containers on a window ledge. Make sure that they all receive the same amount of light.

7. Observe the containers every day for one week.

8. Use the ruler to measure the diameter of the largest clump of algae in each container, and record your measurements daily.

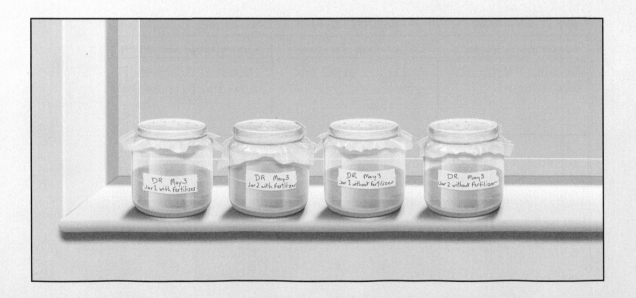

Recording Observations

Once you have obtained all of your materials and your procedure has been approved, you can begin making experimental observations. Gather both quantitative and qualitative data. If something goes wrong during your procedure, make sure you record that too.

Observations
For help with making qualitative and quantitative observations, refer to page R2.

For more examples of data tables, see page R23.

Table 4. Fertilizer and Algae Growth

Date and Time	Experimental Group		Control Group		Observations
	Jar 1 with Fertilizer (diameter of algae in mm)	Jar 2 with Fertilizer (diameter of algae in mm)	Jar 1 without Fertilizer (diameter of algae in mm)	Jar 2 without Fertilizer (diameter of algae in mm)	
5/3 4:00 P.M.	0	0	0	0	condensation in all containers
5/4 4:00 P.M.	0	3	0	0	tiny green blobs in jar 2 with fertilizer
5/5 4:15 P.M.	4	5	0	3	green blobs in jars 1 and 2 with fertilizer and jar 2 without fertilizer
5/6 4:00 P.M.	5	6	0	4	water light green in jar 2 with fertilizer
5/7 4:00 P.M.	8	10	0	6	water light green in jars 1 and 2 with fertilizer and in jar 2 without fertilizer
5/8 3:30 P.M.	10	18	0	6	cover off jar 2 with fertilizer
5/9 3:30 P.M.	14	23	0	8	drew sketches of each container

Notice that on the sixth day, the observer found that the cover was off one of the containers. It is important to record observations of unintended factors because they might affect the results of the experiment.

Drawings of Samples Viewed Under Microscope on 5/9 at 100x

Use technology, such as a microscope, to help you make observations when possible.

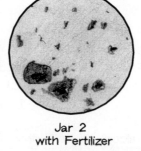
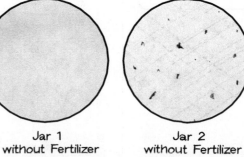

| Jar 1 with Fertilizer | Jar 2 with Fertilizer | Jar 1 without Fertilizer | Jar 2 without Fertilizer |

LAB HANDBOOK

Summarizing Results

To summarize your data, look at all of your observations together. Look for meaningful ways to present your observations. For example, you might average your data or make a graph to look for patterns. When possible, use spreadsheet software to help you analyze and present your data. The two graphs below show the same data.

EXAMPLE 1

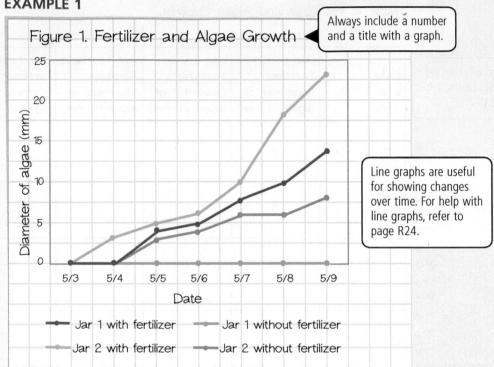

Figure 1. Fertilizer and Algae Growth

> Always include a number and a title with a graph.

> Line graphs are useful for showing changes over time. For help with line graphs, refer to page R24.

EXAMPLE 2

> Bar graphs are useful for comparing different data sets. This bar graph has four bars for each day. Another way to present the data would be to calculate averages for the tests and the controls, and to show one test bar and one control bar for each day.

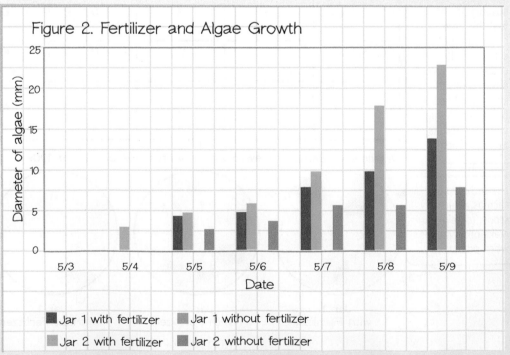

Figure 2. Fertilizer and Algae Growth

Drawing Conclusions

RESULTS AND INFERENCES

To draw conclusions from your experiment, first write your results. Then compare your results with your hypothesis. Do your results support your hypothesis? Be careful not to make inferences about factors that you did not test.

> For help with making inferences, see page R4.

Results and Inferences

The results of my experiment show that more algae grew in lake water to which fertilizer had been added than in lake water to which no fertilizer had been added. My hypothesis was supported. I infer that it is possible that the growth of algae in the lake was caused by the fertilizer used on the field.

> Notice that you cannot conclude from this experiment that the presence of algae in the lake was due only to the fertilizer.

QUESTIONS FOR FURTHER RESEARCH

Write a list of questions for further research and investigation. Your ideas may lead you to new experiments and discoveries.

Questions for Further Research

• What is the connection between the amount of fertilizer and algae growth?
• How do different brands of fertilizer affect algae growth?
• How would algae growth in the lake be affected if no fertilizer were used on the field?
• How do algae affect the lake and the other life in and around it?
• How does fertilizer affect the lake and the life in and around it?
• If fertilizer is getting into the lake, how is it getting there?

Math Handbook

Describing a Set of Data

Means, medians, modes, and ranges are important math tools for describing data sets such as the following widths of fossilized clamshells.

13 mm   25 mm   14 mm   21 mm   16 mm   23 mm   14 mm

Mean

The **mean** of a data set is the sum of the values divided by the number of values.

> **Example**
>
> To find the mean of the clamshell data, add the values and then divide the sum by the number of values.
>
> $$\frac{13 \text{ mm} + 25 \text{ mm} + 14 \text{ mm} + 21 \text{ mm} + 16 \text{ mm} + 23 \text{ mm} + 14 \text{ mm}}{7} = \frac{126 \text{ mm}}{7} = 18 \text{ mm}$$
>
> **ANSWER** The mean is 18 mm.

Median

The **median** of a data set is the middle value when the values are written in numerical order. If a data set has an even number of values, the median is the mean of the two middle values.

> **Example**
>
> To find the median of the clamshell data, arrange the values in order from least to greatest. The median is the middle value.
>
> 13 mm   14 mm   14 mm   16 mm   21 mm   23 mm   25 mm
>
> **ANSWER** The median is 16 mm.

Mode

The **mode** of a data set is the value that occurs most often.

Example

To find the mode of the clamshell data, arrange the values in order from least to greatest and determine the value that occurs most often.

13 mm   14 mm   14 mm   16 mm   21 mm   23 mm   25 mm

ANSWER The mode is 14 mm.

A data set can have more than one mode or no mode. For example, the following data set has modes of 2 mm and 4 mm:

2 mm   2 mm   **3 mm**   4 mm   4 mm

The data set below has no mode, because no value occurs more often than any other.

2 mm   3 mm   4 mm   5 mm

Range

The **range** of a data set is the difference between the greatest value and the least value.

Example

To find the range of the clamshell data, arrange the values in order from least to greatest.

13 mm   14 mm   14 mm   16 mm   21 mm   23 mm   25 mm

Subtract the least value from the greatest value.

13 mm is the least value.
25 mm is the greatest value.

25 mm − 13 mm = 12 mm

ANSWER The range is 12 mm.

Using Ratios, Rates, and Proportions

You can use ratios and rates to compare values in data sets. You can use proportions to find unknown values.

Ratios

A **ratio** uses division to compare two values. The ratio of a value a to a nonzero value b can be written as $\frac{a}{b}$.

Example

The height of one plant is 8 centimeters. The height of another plant is 6 centimeters. To find the ratio of the height of the first plant to the height of the second plant, write a fraction and simplify it.

$$\frac{8 \text{ cm}}{6 \text{ cm}} = \frac{4 \times \overset{1}{\cancel{2}}}{3 \times \underset{1}{\cancel{2}}} = \frac{4}{3}$$

ANSWER The ratio of the plant heights is $\frac{4}{3}$.

You can also write the ratio $\frac{a}{b}$ as "a to b" or as $a:b$. For example, you can write the ratio of the plant heights as "4 to 3" or as $4:3$.

Rates

A **rate** is a ratio of two values expressed in different units. A unit rate is a rate with a denominator of 1 unit.

Example

A plant grew 6 centimeters in 2 days. The plant's rate of growth was $\frac{6 \text{ cm}}{2 \text{ days}}$. To describe the plant's growth in centimeters per day, write a unit rate.

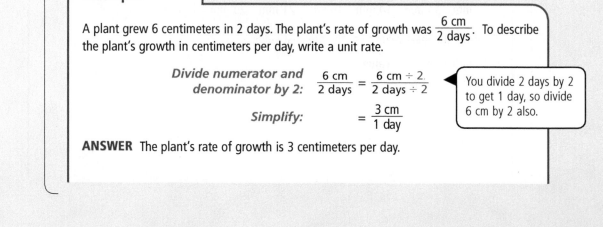

Divide numerator and denominator by 2: $\quad \frac{6 \text{ cm}}{2 \text{ days}} = \frac{6 \text{ cm} \div 2}{2 \text{ days} \div 2}$

You divide 2 days by 2 to get 1 day, so divide 6 cm by 2 also.

Simplify: $\quad = \frac{3 \text{ cm}}{1 \text{ day}}$

ANSWER The plant's rate of growth is 3 centimeters per day.

Proportions

A **proportion** is an equation stating that two ratios are equivalent. To solve for an unknown value in a proportion, you can use cross products.

Example

If a plant grew 6 centimeters in 2 days, how many centimeters would it grow in 3 days (if its rate of growth is constant)?

Write a proportion: $\dfrac{6 \text{ cm}}{2 \text{ days}} = \dfrac{x}{3 \text{ days}}$

Set cross products: $6 \text{ cm} \cdot 3 = 2x$

Multiply 6 and 3: $18 \text{ cm} = 2x$

Divide each side by 2: $\dfrac{18 \text{ cm}}{2} = \dfrac{2x}{2}$

Simplify: $9 \text{ cm} = x$

ANSWER The plant would grow 9 centimeters in 3 days.

Using Decimals, Fractions, and Percents

Decimals, fractions, and percentages are all ways of recording and representing data.

Decimals

A **decimal** is a number that is written in the base-ten place value system, in which a decimal point separates the ones and tenths digits. The values of each place is ten times that of the place to its right.

Example

A caterpillar traveled from point A to point C along the path shown.

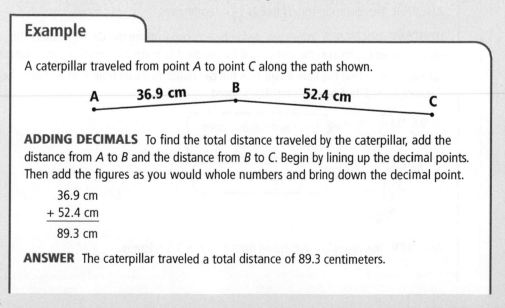

ADDING DECIMALS To find the total distance traveled by the caterpillar, add the distance from A to B and the distance from B to C. Begin by lining up the decimal points. Then add the figures as you would whole numbers and bring down the decimal point.

$$
\begin{array}{r}
36.9 \text{ cm} \\
+\ 52.4 \text{ cm} \\
\hline
89.3 \text{ cm}
\end{array}
$$

ANSWER The caterpillar traveled a total distance of 89.3 centimeters.

SUBTRACTING DECIMALS To find how much farther the caterpillar traveled on the second leg of the journey, subtract the distance from *A* to *B* from the distance from *B* to *C*.

$$\begin{array}{r} 52.4 \text{ cm} \\ -\,36.9 \text{ cm} \\ \hline 15.5 \text{ cm} \end{array}$$

ANSWER The caterpillar traveled 15.5 centimeters farther on the second leg of the journey.

Example

A caterpillar is traveling from point *D* to point *F* along the path shown. The caterpillar travels at a speed of 9.6 centimeters per minute.

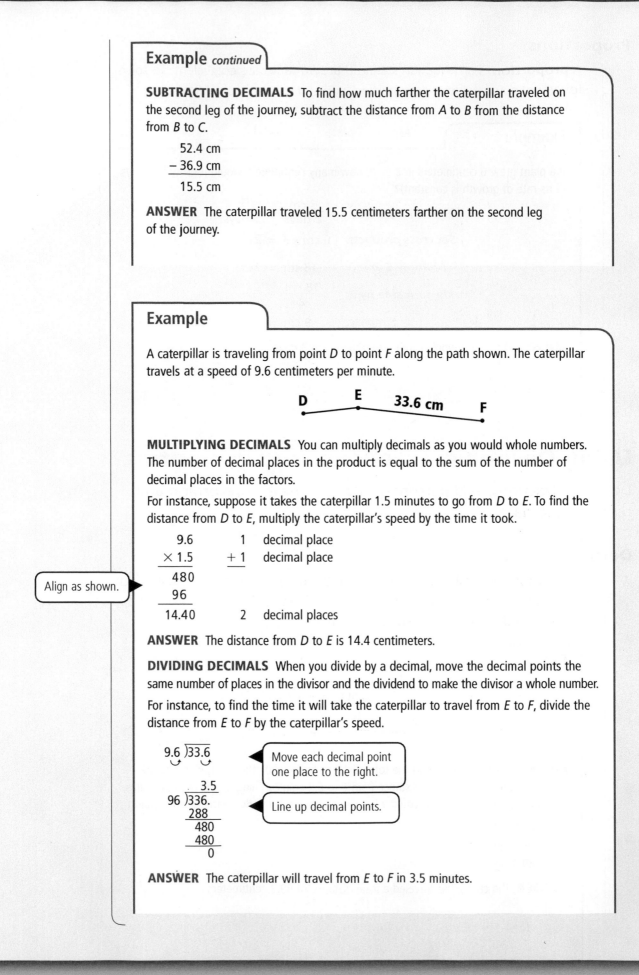

D   E   **33.6 cm**   F

MULTIPLYING DECIMALS You can multiply decimals as you would whole numbers. The number of decimal places in the product is equal to the sum of the number of decimal places in the factors.

For instance, suppose it takes the caterpillar 1.5 minutes to go from *D* to *E*. To find the distance from *D* to *E*, multiply the caterpillar's speed by the time it took.

Align as shown. ►

$$\begin{array}{rl} 9.6 & \quad 1 \quad \text{decimal place} \\ \times\,1.5 & +\,1 \quad \text{decimal place} \\ \hline 480 & \\ 96 & \\ \hline 14.40 & \quad 2 \quad \text{decimal places} \end{array}$$

ANSWER The distance from *D* to *E* is 14.4 centimeters.

DIVIDING DECIMALS When you divide by a decimal, move the decimal points the same number of places in the divisor and the dividend to make the divisor a whole number.

For instance, to find the time it will take the caterpillar to travel from *E* to *F*, divide the distance from *E* to *F* by the caterpillar's speed.

$$9.6 \overline{\smash{)}33.6}$$

Move each decimal point one place to the right.

$$\begin{array}{r} 3.5 \\ 96 \overline{\smash{)}336.} \\ \underline{288} \\ 480 \\ \underline{480} \\ 0 \end{array}$$

Line up decimal points.

ANSWER The caterpillar will travel from *E* to *F* in 3.5 minutes.

Fractions

A **fraction** is a number in the form $\frac{a}{b}$, where b is not equal to 0. A fraction is in **simplest form** if its numerator and denominator have a greatest common factor (GCF) of 1. To simplify a fraction, divide its numerator and denominator by their GCF.

Example

A caterpillar is 40 millimeters long. The head of the caterpillar is 6 millimeters long. To compare the length of the caterpillar's head with the caterpillar's total length, you can write and simplify a fraction that expresses the ratio of the two lengths.

$$\text{Write the ratio of the two lengths:} \quad \frac{\text{Length of head}}{\text{Total length}} = \frac{6 \text{ mm}}{40 \text{ mm}}$$

$$\text{Write numerator and denominator as products of numbers and the GCF:} \quad = \frac{3 \times 2}{20 \times 2}$$

$$\text{Divide numerator and denominator by the GCF:} \quad = \frac{3 \times \overset{1}{\cancel{2}}}{20 \times \underset{1}{\cancel{2}}}$$

$$\text{Simplify:} \quad = \frac{3}{20}$$

ANSWER In simplest form, the ratio of the lengths is $\frac{3}{20}$.

Percents

A **percent** is a ratio that compares a number to 100. The word *percent* means "per hundred" or "out of 100." The symbol for *percent* is %.

For instance, suppose 43 out of 100 caterpillars are female. You can represent this ratio as a percent, a decimal, or a fraction.

Percent	Decimal	Fraction
43%	0.43	$\frac{43}{100}$

Example

In the preceding example, the ratio of the length of the caterpillar's head to the caterpillar's total length is $\frac{3}{20}$. To write this ratio as a percent, write an equivalent fraction that has a denominator of 100.

$$\text{Multiply numerator and denominator by 5:} \quad \frac{3}{20} = \frac{3 \times 5}{20 \times 5}$$

$$= \frac{15}{100}$$

$$\text{Write as a percent:} \quad = 15\%$$

ANSWER The caterpillar's head represents 15 percent of its total length.

Using Formulas

A **formula** is an equation that shows the general relationship between two or more quantities.

The term *variable* is also used in science to refer to a factor that can change during an experiment.

In science, a formula often has a word form and a symbolic form. The formula below expresses Ohm's law.

Word Form

$$\text{Current} = \frac{\text{voltage}}{\text{resistance}}$$

Symbolic Form

$$I = \frac{V}{R}$$

In this formula, *I*, *V*, and *R* are variables. A mathematical **variable** is a symbol or letter that is used to represent one or more numbers.

Example

Suppose that you measure a voltage of 1.5 volts and a resistance of 15 ohms. You can use the formula for Ohm's law to find the current in amperes.

Write the formula for Ohm's law: $\quad I = \dfrac{V}{R}$

Substitute 1.5 volts for V and 15 ohms for R: $\quad I = \dfrac{1.5 \text{ volts}}{15 \text{ ohms}}$

Simplify: $\quad I = 0.1 \text{ amp}$

ANSWER The current is 0.1 ampere.

If you know the values of all variables but one in a formula, you can solve for the value of the unknown variable. For instance, Ohm's law can be used to find a voltage if you know the current and the resistance.

Example

Suppose that you know that a current is 0.2 amperes and the resistance is 18 ohms. Use the formula for Ohm's law to find the voltage in volts.

Write the formula for Ohm's law: $\quad I = \dfrac{V}{R}$

Substitute 0.2 amp for I and 18 ohms for R: $\quad 0.2 \text{ amp} = \dfrac{V}{18 \text{ ohms}}$

Multiply both sides by 18 ohms: $\quad 0.2 \text{ amp} \cdot 18 \text{ ohms} = V$

Simplify: $\quad 3.6 \text{ volts} = V$

ANSWER The voltage is 3.6 volts.

Finding Areas

The area of a figure is the amount of surface the figure covers.

Area is measured in square units, such as square meters (m^2) or square centimeters (cm^2). Formulas for the areas of three common geometric figures are shown below.

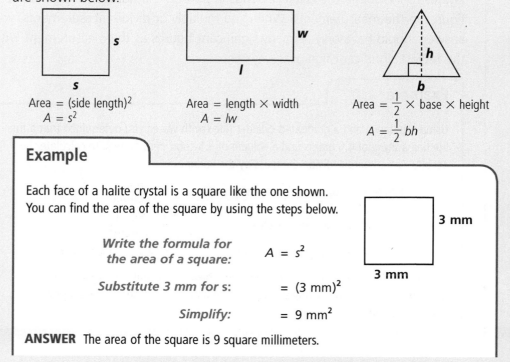

Area = (side length)²
$A = s^2$

Area = length × width
$A = lw$

Area = $\frac{1}{2}$ × base × height
$A = \frac{1}{2} bh$

Example

Each face of a halite crystal is a square like the one shown. You can find the area of the square by using the steps below.

3 mm

3 mm

Write the formula for the area of a square:	$A = s^2$
Substitute 3 mm for s:	$= (3\ mm)^2$
Simplify:	$= 9\ mm^2$

ANSWER The area of the square is 9 square millimeters.

Finding Volumes

The volume of a solid is the amount of space contained by the solid.

Volume is measured in cubic units, such as cubic meters (m^3) or cubic centimeters (cm^3). The volume of a rectangular prism is given by the formula shown below.

Volume = length × width × height
$V = lwh$

Example

A topaz crystal is a rectangular prism like the one shown. You can find the volume of the prism by using the steps below.

10 mm

12 mm

20 mm

Write the formula for the volume of a rectangular prism:	$V = lwh$
Substitute dimensions:	$= 20\ mm \times 12\ mm \times 10\ mm$
Simplify:	$= 2400\ mm^3$

ANSWER The volume of the rectangular prism is 2400 cubic millimeters.

Using Significant Figures

The **significant figures** in a decimal are the digits that are warranted by the accuracy of a measuring device.

When you perform a calculation with measurements, the number of significant figures to include in the result depends in part on the number of significant figures in the measurements. When you multiply or divide measurements, your answer should have only as many significant figures as the measurement with the fewest significant figures.

Example

Using a balance and a graduated cylinder filled with water, you determined that a marble has a mass of 8.0 grams and a volume of 3.5 cubic centimeters. To calculate the density of the marble, divide the mass by the volume.

Write the formula for density: $\text{Density} = \dfrac{\text{mass}}{\text{Volume}}$

Substitute measurements: $= \dfrac{8.0 \text{ g}}{3.5 \text{ cm}^3}$

Use a calculator to divide: $\approx 2.285714286 \text{ g/cm}^3$

ANSWER Because the mass and the volume have two significant figures each, give the density to two significant figures. The marble has a density of 2.3 grams per cubic centimeter.

Using Scientific Notation

Scientific notation is a shorthand way to write very large or very small numbers. For example, 73,500,000,000,000,000,000,000 kg is the mass of the Moon. In scientific notation, it is 7.35×10^{22} kg.

Example

You can convert from standard form to scientific notation.

Standard Form	Scientific Notation
720,000	7.2×10^5
5 decimal places left	Exponent is 5.
0.000291	2.91×10^{-4}
4 decimal places right	Exponent is −4.

You can convert from scientific notation to standard form.

Scientific Notation	Standard Form
4.63×10^7	46,300,000
Exponent is 7.	7 decimal places right
1.08×10^{-6}	0.00000108
Exponent is −6.	6 decimal places left

Note-Taking Handbook

Note-Taking Strategies

Taking notes as you read helps you understand the information. The notes you take can also be used as a study guide for later review. This handbook presents several ways to organize your notes.

Content Frame

1. Make a chart in which each column represents a category.
2. Give each column a heading.
3. Write details under the headings.

NAME	GROUP	CHARACTERISTICS	DRAWING
snail	mollusks	mantle, shell	
ant	arthropods	six legs, exoskeleton	
earthworm	segmented worms	segmented body, circulatory and digestive systems	
heartworm	roundworms	digestive system	
sea star	echinoderms	spiny skin, tube feet	
jellyfish	cnidarians	stinging cells	

categories

details

Combination Notes

1. For each new idea or concept, write an informal outline of the information.
2. Make a sketch to illustrate the concept, and label it.

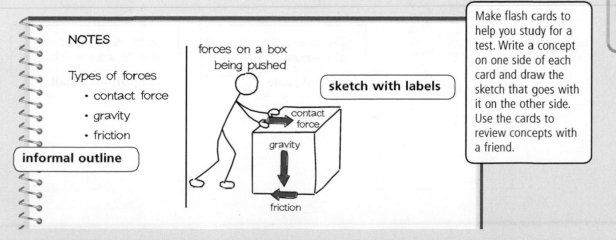

NOTES

Types of forces
• contact force
• gravity
• friction

informal outline

forces on a box being pushed

sketch with labels

contact force

gravity

friction

Make flash cards to help you study for a test. Write a concept on one side of each card and draw the sketch that goes with it on the other side. Use the cards to review concepts with a friend.

NOTE–TAKING HANDBOOK

Main Idea and Detail Notes

1. In the left-hand column of a two-column chart, list main ideas. The blue headings express main ideas throughout this textbook.

2. In the right-hand column, write details that expand on each main idea.

You can shorten the headings in your chart. Be sure to use the most important words.

When studying for tests, cover up the detail notes column with a sheet of paper. Then use each main idea to form a question—such as "How does latitude affect climate?" Answer the question, and then uncover the detail notes column to check your answer.

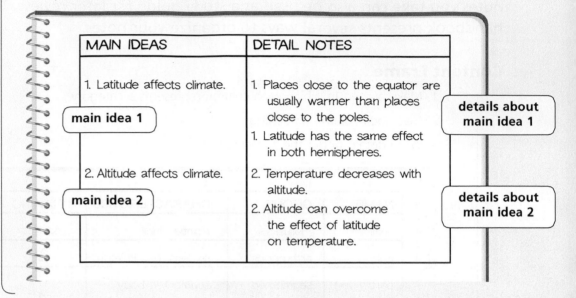

MAIN IDEAS	DETAIL NOTES
1. Latitude affects climate.	1. Places close to the equator are usually warmer than places close to the poles.
	1. Latitude has the same effect in both hemispheres.
2. Altitude affects climate.	2. Temperature decreases with altitude.
	2. Altitude can overcome the effect of latitude on temperature.

main idea 1

main idea 2

details about main idea 1

details about main idea 2

Main Idea Web

1. Write a main idea in a box.

2. Add boxes around it with related vocabulary terms and important details.

You can find definitions near highlighted terms.

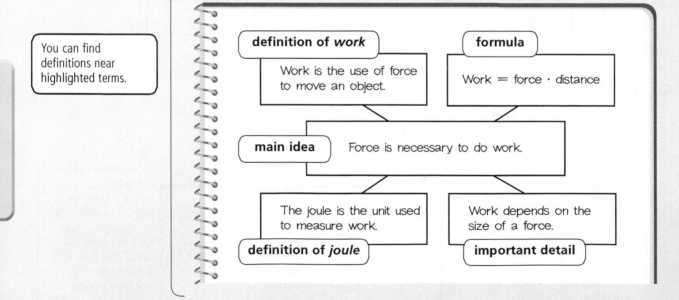

definition of *work*

Work is the use of force to move an object.

formula

Work = force · distance

main idea

Force is necessary to do work.

The joule is the unit used to measure work.

definition of *joule*

Work depends on the size of a force.

important detail

Mind Map

1. Write a main idea in the center.

2. Add details that relate to one another and to the main idea.

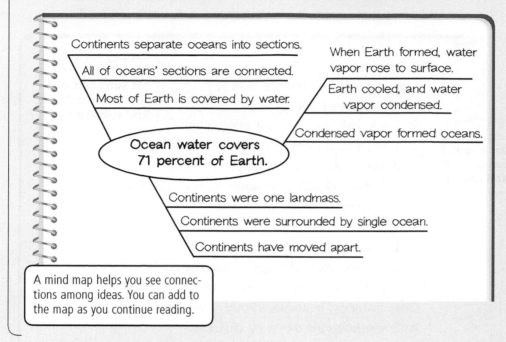

Continents separate oceans into sections.

All of oceans' sections are connected.

Most of Earth is covered by water.

When Earth formed, water vapor rose to surface.

Earth cooled, and water vapor condensed.

Condensed vapor formed oceans.

Ocean water covers 71 percent of Earth.

Continents were one landmass.

Continents were surrounded by single ocean.

Continents have moved apart.

A mind map helps you see connections among ideas. You can add to the map as you continue reading.

Supporting Main Ideas

1. Write a main idea in a box.

2. Add boxes underneath with information—such as reasons, explanations, and examples—that supports the main idea.

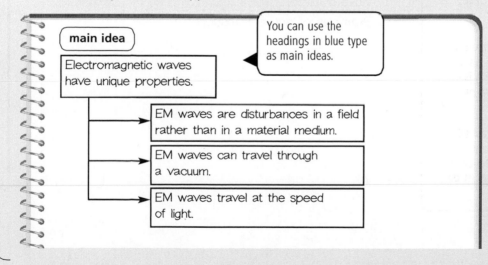

main idea

Electromagnetic waves have unique properties.

You can use the headings in blue type as main ideas.

EM waves are disturbances in a field rather than in a material medium.

EM waves can travel through a vacuum.

EM waves travel at the speed of light.

Outline

1. Copy the chapter title and headings from the book in the form of an outline.
2. Add notes that summarize in your own words what you read.

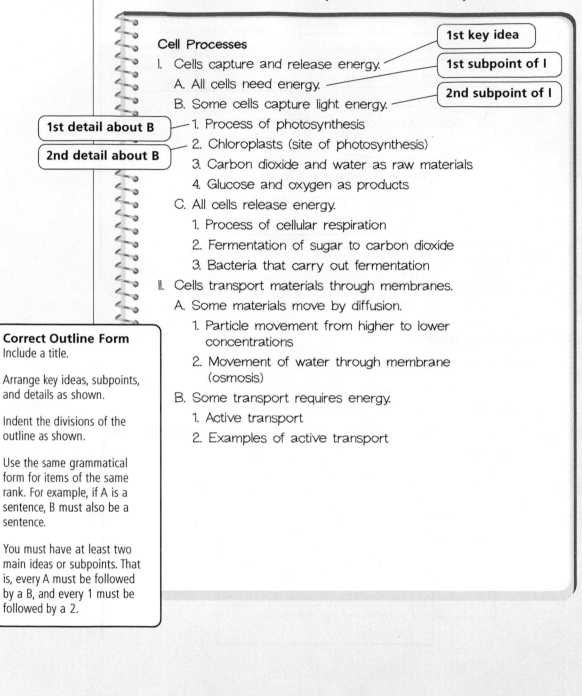

Cell Processes

I. Cells capture and release energy.   **1st key idea**
    A. All cells need energy.   **1st subpoint of I**
    B. Some cells capture light energy.   **2nd subpoint of I**
       1. Process of photosynthesis   **1st detail about B**
       2. Chloroplasts (site of photosynthesis)   **2nd detail about B**
       3. Carbon dioxide and water as raw materials
       4. Glucose and oxygen as products
    C. All cells release energy.
       1. Process of cellular respiration
       2. Fermentation of sugar to carbon dioxide
       3. Bacteria that carry out fermentation
II. Cells transport materials through membranes.
    A. Some materials move by diffusion.
       1. Particle movement from higher to lower concentrations
       2. Movement of water through membrane (osmosis)
    B. Some transport requires energy.
       1. Active transport
       2. Examples of active transport

Correct Outline Form

Include a title.

Arrange key ideas, subpoints, and details as shown.

Indent the divisions of the outline as shown.

Use the same grammatical form for items of the same rank. For example, if A is a sentence, B must also be a sentence.

You must have at least two main ideas or subpoints. That is, every A must be followed by a B, and every 1 must be followed by a 2.

Concept Map

1. Write an important concept in a large oval.
2. Add details related to the concept in smaller ovals.
3. Write linking words on arrows that connect the ovals.

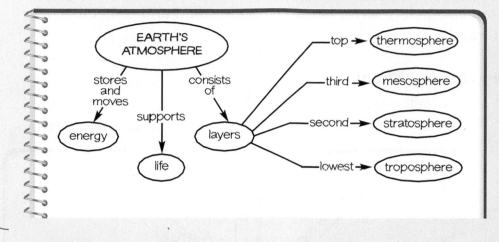

The main ideas or concepts can often be found in the blue headings. An example is "The atmosphere stores and moves energy." Use nouns from these concepts in the ovals, and use the verb or verbs on the lines.

Venn Diagram

1. Draw two overlapping circles, one for each item that you are comparing.
2. In the overlapping section, list the characteristics that are shared by both items.
3. In the outer sections, list the characteristics that are peculiar to each item.
4. Write a summary that describes the information in the Venn diagram.

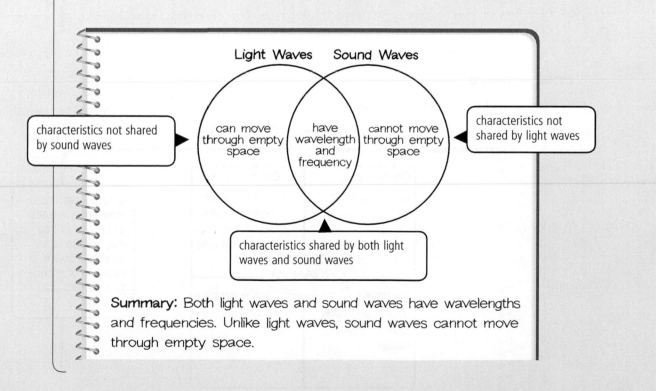

Summary: Both light waves and sound waves have wavelengths and frequencies. Unlike light waves, sound waves cannot move through empty space.

Vocabulary Strategies

Important terms are highlighted in this book. A definition of each term can be found in the sentence or paragraph where the term appears. You can also find definitions in the Glossary. Taking notes about vocabulary terms helps you understand and remember what you read.

Description Wheel

1. Write a term inside a circle.
2. Write words that describe the term on "spokes" attached to the circle.

When studying for a test with a friend, read the phrases on the spokes one at a time until your friend identifies the correct term.

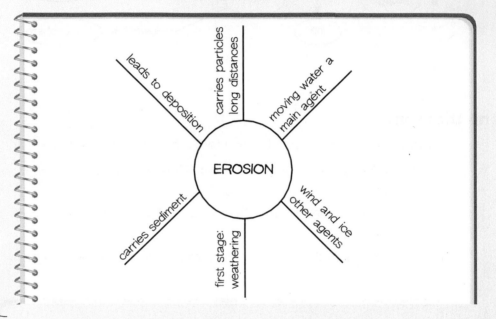

Four Square

1. Write a term in the center.
2. Write details in the four areas around the term.

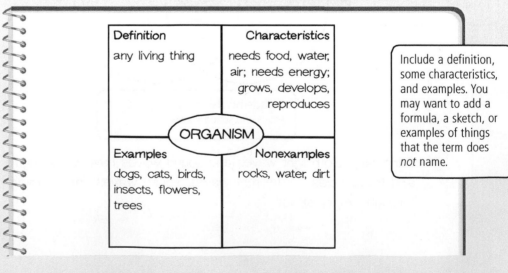

Include a definition, some characteristics, and examples. You may want to add a formula, a sketch, or examples of things that the term does *not* name.

Frame Game

1. Write a term in the center.
2. Frame the term with details.

Include examples, descriptions, sketches, or sentences that use the term in context. Change the frame to fit each new term.

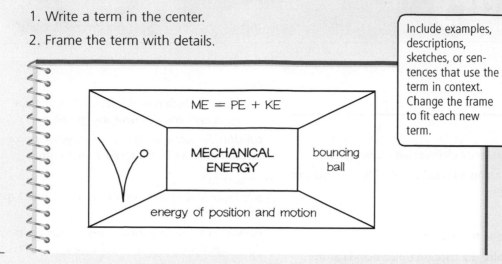

$$ME = PE + KE$$

MECHANICAL ENERGY

bouncing ball

energy of position and motion

Magnet Word

1. Write a term on the magnet.
2. On the lines, add details related to the term.

You can also use phrases or sentences on the lines.

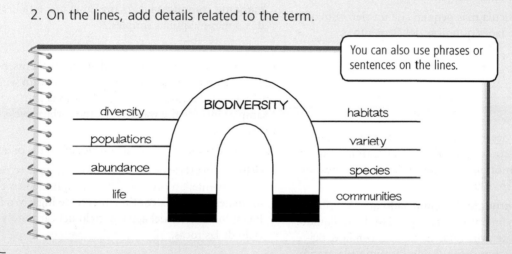

BIODIVERSITY

diversity

populations

abundance

life

habitats

variety

species

communities

Word Triangle

1. Write a term and its definition in the bottom section.
2. In the middle section, write a sentence in which the term is used correctly.
3. In the top section, draw a small picture to illustrate the term.

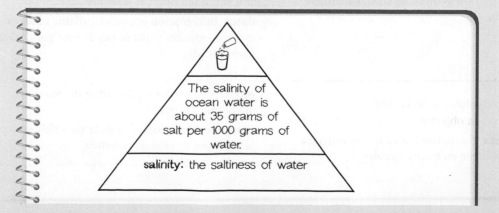

The salinity of ocean water is about 35 grams of salt per 1000 grams of water.

salinity: the saltiness of water

Glossary

A

acceleration
The rate at which velocity changes over time. (p. 25)

> **aceleración** La razón a la cual la velocidad cambia con respecto al tiempo.

air resistance
The fluid friction due to air. (p. 89)

> **resistencia del aire** La fricción fluida debida al aire.

atom
The smallest particle of an element that has the chemical properties of that element. (p. xv)

> **átomo** La partícula más pequeña de un elemento que tiene las propiedades químicas del elemento.

B

Bernoulli's principle
A statement that describes the effects of movement on fluid pressure. According to this principle, an increase in the speed of the motion of a fluid decreases the pressure within the fluid. (p. 100)

> **principio de Bernoulli** Un enunciado que describe los efectos del movimiento sobre la presión de un líquido. De acuerdo a este principio, un aumento en la velocidad del movimiento de un fluido disminuye la presión dentro del líquido

buoyant force
The upward force on objects in a fluid; often called buoyancy. (p. 98)

> **fuerza flotante** La fuerza hacia arriba que ejerce un fluido sobre un objeto inmerso en él, a menudo llamada flotación.

C

centripetal force (sehn-TRIHP-ih-tuhl)
Any force that keeps an object moving in a circle. (p. 54)

> **fuerza centrípeta** Cualquier fuerza que mantiene a un objeto moviéndose en forma circular.

collision
A situation in which two objects in close contact exchange energy and momentum. (p. 66)

> **colisión** Situación en la cual dos objetos en contacto cercano intercambian energía y momento.

compound
A substance made up of two or more different types of atoms bonded together.

> **compuesto** Una sustancia formada por dos o más diferentes tipos de átomos enlazados.

compound machine
A machine that is made up of two or more simple machines. (p. 164)

> **máquina compuesta** Una máquina que está hecha de dos o más máquinas simples.

cycle
n. A series of events or actions that repeat themselves regularly; a physical and/or chemical process in which one material continually changes locations and/or forms. Examples include the water cycle, the carbon cycle, and the rock cycle.

v. To move through a repeating series of events or actions.

> **ciclo** *s.* Una serie de eventos o acciones que se repiten regularmente; un proceso físico y/o químico en el cual un material cambia continuamente de lugar y/o forma. Ejemplos: el ciclo del agua, el ciclo del carbono y el ciclo de las rocas.

D

data
Information gathered by observation or experimentation that can be used in calculating or reasoning. *Data* is a plural word; the singular is *datum*.

> **datos** Información reunida mediante observación o experimentación y que se puede usar para calcular o para razonar.

density
A property of matter representing the mass per unit volume. (p. 99)

> **densidad** Una propiedad de la materia que representa la masa por unidad de volumen.

E

efficiency
The percentage of the input work done on a machine that the machine can return in output work. A machine's output work divided by its input work and multiplied by 100. (p. 150)

eficiencia El porcentaje del trabajo de entrada suministrado a una máquina que la máquina puede devolver como trabajo de salida. El trabajo de salida de una máquina dividido por su trabajo de entrada y multiplicado por cien.

element
A substance that cannot be broken down into a simpler substance by ordinary chemical changes. An element consists of atoms of only one type. (p. xv)

elemento Una sustancia que no puede descomponerse en otra sustancia más simple por medio de cambios químicos normales. Un elemento consta de átomos de un solo tipo.

energy
The ability to do work or to cause a change. For example, the energy of a moving bowling ball knocks over pins; energy from food allows animals to move and to grow; and energy from the Sun heats Earth's surface and atmosphere, which causes air to move. (p. xix)

energía La capacidad para trabajar o causar un cambio. Por ejemplo, la energía de una bola de boliche en movimiento tumba los pinos; la energía proveniente de su alimento permite a los animales moverse y crecer; la energía del Sol calienta la superficie y la atmósfera de la Tierra, lo que ocasiona que el aire se mueva.

experiment
An organized procedure to study something under controlled conditions. (p. xxiv)

experimento Un procedimiento organizado para estudiar algo bajo condiciones controladas.

F

fluid
A substance that can flow easily, such as a gas or a liquid. (p. 88)

fluido Una sustancia que fluye fácilmente, como por ejemplo un gas o un líquido.

force
A push or a pull; something that changes the motion of an object. (p. 41)

fuerza Un empuje o un jalón; algo que cambia el movimiento de un objeto.

friction
A force that resists the motion between two surfaces in contact. (p. 85)

fricción Una fuerza que resiste el movimiento entre dos superficies en contacto.

fulcrum
A fixed point around which a lever rotates. (p. 155)

fulcro Un punto fijo alrededor del cual gira una palanca.

G

gravity
The force that objects exert on each other because of their masses. (p. 77)

gravedad La fuerza que los objetos ejercen entre sí debido a sus masas.

H

horizontal
Parallel to the horizon; level.

horizontal Paralelo al horizonte; nivelado.

horsepower hp
The unit of measurement of power for engines and motors. One horsepower equals 745 watts. (p. 132)

caballos de fuerza La unidad de medición de potencia para máquinas y motores. Un caballo de fuerza es igual a 745 vatios.

hypothesis
A tentative explanation for an observation or phenomenon. A hypothesis is used to make testable predictions. (p. xxiv)

hipótesis Una explicación provisional de una observación o de un fenómeno. Una hipótesis se usa para hacer predicciones que se pueden probar.

I

inclined plane
A simple machine that is a sloping surface, such as a ramp. (p. 158)

plano inclinado Una máquina simple que es una superficie en pendiente, como por ejemplo una rampa.

inertia (ih-NUR-shuh)

The resistance of an object to a change in the speed or the direction of its motion. (p. 46)

inercia La resistencia de un objeto al cambio de la velocidad o de la dirección de su movimiento.

J

joule (jool) J

A unit used to measure energy and work. One calorie is equal to 4.18 joules of energy; one joule of work is done when a force of one newton moves an object one meter. (p. 117)

julio Una unidad que se usa para medir la energía y el trabajo. Una caloría es igual a 4.18 julios de energía; se hace un joule de trabajo cuando una fuerza de un newton mueve un objeto un metro.

K

kinetic energy (kuh-NEHT-ihk)

The energy of motion. A moving object has the most kinetic energy at the point where it moves the fastest. (p. 122)

energía cinética La energía de movimiento. Un objeto en movimiento tiene la mayor energía cinética en el punto en donde se mueve más rápidamente.

L

law

In science, a rule or principle describing a physical relationship that always works in the same way under the same conditions. The law of conservation of energy is an example.

ley En las ciencias, una regla o un principio que describe una relación física que siempre funciona de la misma manera bajo las mismas condiciones. La ley de la conservación de la energía es un ejemplo.

law of conservation of energy

A law stating that no matter how energy is transferred or transformed, all of the energy is still present in one form or another. (p. 126)

ley de la conservación de la energía Una ley que establece que no importa cómo se transfiera o transmita la energía, toda la energía sigue presente de una forma o de otra.

law of conservation of momentum

A law stating that the amount of momentum a system of objects has does not change as long as there are no outside forces acting on that system. (p. 67)

ley de la conservación del momento Una ley que establece que la cantidad de momento que tiene un sistema de objetos no cambia mientras no haya fuerzas externas actuando sobre el sistema.

lever

A solid bar that rotates, or turns, around a fixed point (fulcrum); one of the six simple machines. (p. 155)

palanca Una barra sólida que da vueltas o gira alrededor de un punto fijo (el fulcro); una de las seis máquinas simples.

M

machine

Any device that makes doing work easier. (p. 145)

máquina Cualquier aparato que facilita el trabajo.

mass

A measure of how much matter an object is made of. (p. xv)

masa Una medida de la cantidad de materia de la que está compuesto un objeto.

matter

Anything that has mass and volume. Matter exists ordinarily as a solid, a liquid, or a gas. (p. xv)

materia Todo lo que tiene masa y volumen. Generalmente la materia existe como sólido, líquido o gas.

mechanical advantage

The number of times a machine multiplies the input force; output force divided by input force (p. 147)

ventaja mecánica El número de veces que una máquina multiplica la fuerza de entrada; la fuerza de salida dividida por la fuerza de entrada.

mechanical energy

A combination of the kinetic energy and potential energy an object has. (p. 125)

energía mecánica La combinación de la energía cinética y la energía potencial que tiene un objeto.

meter m

The international standard unit of length, about 39.37 inches.

metro La unidad estándar internacional de longitud, aproximadamente 39.37 pulgadas.

molecule

A group of atoms that are held together by covalent bonds so that they move as a single unit. (p. xv)

molécula Un grupo de átomos que están unidos mediante enlaces covalentes de tal manera que se mueven como una sola unidad.

momentum (moh-MEHN-tuhm)

A measure of mass in motion. The momentum of an object is the product of its mass and velocity. (p. 64)

momento Una medida de la masa en movimiento. El momento de un objeto es el producto de su masa y su velocidad.

motion

A change of position over time. (p. 11)

movimiento Un cambio de posición a través del tiempo.

N

nanotechnology

The science and technology of building electronic circuits and devices from single atoms and molecules. (p. 167)

nanotecnología La ciencia y tecnología de fabricar circuitos y aparatos electrónicos a partir de átomos y moléculas individuales.

net force

The overall force acting on an object when all of the forces acting on it are combined. (p. 43)

fuerza neta La fuerza resultante que actúa sobre un objeto cuando todas las fuerzas que actúan sobre él son combinadas .

Newton's first law

A scientific law stating that objects at rest remain at rest, and objects in motion remain in motion with the same velocity, unless acted on by an unbalanced force. (p. 45)

primera ley de Newton Una ley científica que establece que los objetos en reposo permanecen en reposo, y que los objetos en movimiento permanecen en movimiento con la misma velocidad, a menos que actúe sobre ellos una fuerza no balanceada.

Newton's second law

A scientific law stating that the acceleration of an object increases with increased force and decreases with increased mass. (p. 50)

segunda ley de Newton Una ley científica que establece que la aceleración de un objeto aumenta al incrementar la fuerza que actúa sobre él y disminuye al incrementar su masa.

Newton's third law

A scientific law stating that every time one object exerts a force on another object, the second object exerts a force that is equal in size and opposite in direction back on the first object. (p. 57)

tercera ley de Newton Una ley científica que establece que cada vez que un objeto ejerce una fuerza sobre otro objeto, el segundo objeto ejerce una fuerza de la misma magnitud y en dirección opuesta sobre el primer objeto.

O

orbit

The elliptical path one celestial body follows around another celestial body. An object in orbit has a centripetal force acting on it that keeps the object moving in a circle or other ellipse. (p. 80)

órbita El camino elíptico que un cuerpo celeste sigue alrededor de otro cuerpo celeste. La fuerza centrípeta actúa sobre un objeto en órbita y lo mantiene en un movimiento circular o elíptico.

P, Q

pascal Pa

The unit used to measure pressure. One pascal is the pressure exerted by one newton of force on an area of one square meter, or one N/m^2. (p. 92)

pascal La unidad utilizada para medir presión. Un pascal es la presión ejercida por un newton de fuerza sobre un área de un metro cuadrado, o un N/m^2.

Pascal's principle

A statement that says when an outside pressure is applied at any point to a fluid in a container, that pressure is transmitted throughout the fluid with equal strength. (p. 102)

principio de Pascal Un enunciado que dice que cuando una presión externa es aplicada a cualquier punto de un líquido en un contenedor, esta presión es transmitida a través del fluido con igual fuerza.

position

An object's location. (p. 9)

posición La ubicación de un objeto.

potential energy

Stored energy; the energy an object has due to its position, molecular arrangement, or chemical composition. (p. 122)

energía potencial Energía almacenada; o la energía que tiene un objeto debido a su posición, arreglo molecular o composición química.

power

The rate at which work is done. (p. 130)

potencia La razón a la cual se hace el trabajo.

pressure

A measure of how much force is acting on a certain area; how concentrated a force is. Pressure is equal to the force divided by area. (p. 91)

presión Una medida de cuánta fuerza actúa sobre cierta área; el nivel de concentración de la fuerza. La presión es igual a la fuerza dividida entre el área.

pulley

A wheel with a grooved rim that turns on an axle; one of the six simple machines. (p. 156)

polea Una rueda con un canto acanalado que gira sobre un eje; una de las seis máquinas simples.

R

reference point

A location to which another location is compared. (p. 10)

punto de referencia Una ubicación con la cual se compara otra ubicación.

relative motion

The idea that the observation of motion depends on the observer. (p. 13)

movimiento relativo La idea de que la observación del movimiento depende del observador.

robot

A machine that works automatically or by remote control. (p. 169)

robot Una máquina que funciona automáticamente o por control remoto.

S

screw

A simple machine that is an inclined plane wrapped around a cylinder. A screw can be used to raise and lower weights as well as to fasten objects. (p. 159)

tornillo Una máquina simple que es un plano inclinado enrollado alrededor de un cilindro. Un tornillo se puede usar para levantar o bajar pesos y también para sujetar objetos.

second s

A unit of time equal to one-sixtieth of a minute.

segundo Una unidad de tiempo igual a una sesentava parte de un minuto.

simple machine

One of the basic machines on which all other mechanical machines are based. The six simple machines are the lever, inclined plane, wheel and axle, pulley, wedge, and screw. (p. 154)

máquina simple Una de las máquinas básicas sobre las cuales están basadas todas las demás máquinas mecánicas. Las seis máquinas simples son la palanca, el plano inclinado, la rueda y eje, la polea, la cuña y el tornillo.

speed

A measure of how fast something moves through a particular distance over a definite time period. Speed is distance divided by time. (p. 16)

rapidez Una medida del desplazamiento de un objeto a lo largo de una distancia específica en un período de tiempo definido. La rapidez es la distancia dividida entre el tiempo.

system

A group of objects or phenomena that interact. A system can be as simple as a rope, a pulley, and a mass. It also can be as complex as the interaction of energy and matter in the four parts of the Earth system.

sistema Un grupo de objetos o fenómenos que interactúan. Un sistema puede ser algo tan sencillo como una cuerda, una polea y una masa. También puede ser algo tan complejo como la interacción de la energía y la materia en las cuatro partes del sistema de la Tierra.

T, U

technology

The use of scientific knowledge to solve problems or engineer new products, tools, or processes.

tecnología El uso de conocimientos científicos para resolver problemas o para diseñar nuevos productos, herramientas o procesos.

terminal velocity

The final, maximum velocity of a falling object. (p. 89)

velocidad terminal La velocidad máxima final de un objeto en caída libre.

theory

In science, a set of widely accepted explanations of observations and phenomena. A theory is a well-tested explanation that is consistent with all available evidence.

teoría En las ciencias, un conjunto de explicaciones de observaciones y fenómenos que es ampliamente aceptado. Una teoría es una explicación bien probada que es consecuente con la evidencia disponible.

V

variable
Any factor that can change in a controlled experiment, observation, or model. (p. R30)

variable Cualquier factor que puede cambiar en un experimento controlado, en una observación o en un modelo.

vector
A quantity that has both size and direction. (p. 22)

vector Una cantidad que tiene magnitud y dirección.

velocity
A speed in a specific direction. (p. 22)

velocidad Una rapidez en una dirección específica.

vertical
Going straight up or down from a level surface.

vertical Que está dispuesto hacia arriba o hacia abajo de una superficie nivelada.

volume
An amount of three-dimensional space, often used to describe the space that an object takes up. (p. xv)

volumen Una cantidad de espacio tridimensional; a menudo se usa este término para describir el espacio que ocupa un objeto.

W, X, Y, Z

watt W
The unit of measurement for power, which is equal to one joule of work done or energy transferred in one second. For example, a 75 W light bulb converts electrical energy into heat and light at a rate of 75 joules per second. (p. 131)

vatio La unidad de medición de la potencia, el cual es igual a un julio de trabajo realizado o energía transferida en un segundo. Por ejemplo, una bombilla de 75 W convierte energía eléctrica a calor y luz a un ritmo de 75 julios por segundo.

wedge
A simple machine that has a thick end and a thin end. A wedge is used to cut, split, or pierce objects, or to hold objects together. (p. 158)

cuña Una máquina simple que tiene un extremo grueso y otro extremo delgado. Una cuña se usa para cortar, partir o penetrar objetos, o para mantener objetos juntos.

weight
The force of gravity on an object. (p. 79)

peso La fuerza de gravedad sobre un objeto.

wheel and axle
A simple machine that is a wheel attached to a shaft, or axle. (p. 156)

rueda y eje Una máquina simple que es una rueda unida a una flecha, o a un eje.

work
The use of force to move an object over a distance. (p. 115)

trabajo El uso de fuerza para mover un objeto una distancia.

Index

Page numbers for definitions are printed in **boldface** type.
Page numbers for illustrations, maps, and charts are printed in *italics*.

INDEX

E

Earth
  curvature of, 80, *81*
  gravity of, 78, 79
  mass and weight on, *80*
  orbit around Sun, 80
efficiency, **150,** *150,* 150–152, *153*
  calculating, 150, *153*
  friction and, *150,* 151, 156
  ideal mechanical advantage and, 160
Einstein, Albert, 84, 111
electricity, 128, 135, 146, 151
electromagnetic energy, 128
elements, xv
ellipse, *80*
energy, xviii, **xix,** 121–128, 138
  chemical, xviii, 128
  conservation of, xix, **126,** *126, 127,* 128, *138*
  efficiency and, 151, 152
  elastic potential, 122
  electrical, xviii, 128, 135, 146, 151
  electromagnetic, 128
  forms of, xviii, 128
  kinetic, **122,** *122, 124,* 125–128, *127, 138*
  mechanical, **125,** 125–128, *127,* 146, 151
  nuclear, 128
  potential, **122,** *122, 123,* 125–128, *127, 138,* 148, *149*
  power, time, and, 133–136
  radiant, 128
  sources of, xix
  thermal, 128, 151
  transfer of, 121–128, *122,* 133–135, *134, 135, 149*
  transformation of, 121, 122, 125–128, *127*
engine. *See also* motor.
  efficiency of car, 151, 152
  power of different types, 132
  steam, 109–110, *109, 110,* 132
equator, *10*
evaluating, **R8**
  media claims, R8
evidence, collection of, xxiv
experiment, **xxiv.** *See also* lab.
  conclusions, drawing, R35
  constants, determining, R30
  controlled, **R28,** R30
  designing, R28–R35
  hypothesis, writing, R29
  materials, determining, R29
  observations, recording, R33
  procedure, writing, R32
  purpose, determining, R28
  results, summarizing, R34
  variables, R30–R31, R32
experimental group, R30

F

fact, **R9**
  different from opinion, R9
faulty reasoning, **R7**
first law of motion. *See* Newton's laws of motion.
floating. *See* buoyancy.
fluids, **88,** 88–89, *93,* 93–95, 98–103
  friction in, 88–89, *89*
  pressure in, *93,* 93–95
  transmission of force through, 102–103, 104
force, **xxi,** 38–70, **41,** *42*
  acceleration, mass, and, *50, 51, 52, 53,* 56, *67,* 70, *86*
  action and reaction, 57–60, *59, 60,* 66, *70,* 85, 158
  applied, *116*
  area and, 91–95, 104
  balanced, *43,* 43–47, *45,* 59, *86*
  buoyancy, **98**
  centripetal, **54,** *55,* 80, *81*
  changing direction of, 42, 43, 147, *149*
  contact, **xxi,** *42*
  direction of motion changed by, 53–55
  distance, work, and, 115–119, *116, 118,* 138
  electrical, xxi
  friction, xxi, **85,** *85–89*
  gravitational, **xxi,** 42, *42,* 77–84
  input, 146–147, *146,* 149–153, *155,* 160–162
  Internet activity, 39
  machines, work, and, 145–152, *146, 147,* 155–162, *155, 172*
  magnetic, xxi
  mass, distance, and, 77–85, *78,* 104
  multiplication of, 146, 147
  needed to overcome friction, *86, 87, 104*
  net, **43,** 44, *93,* 98, *99,* 149
  output, 146–147, *146,* 150–153, *155,* 160–162
  physical, xx–xxi
  strong, 111
  transmission through fluids, 102–103
  types of, 42
  unbalanced, *43,* 43–47, *45, 47,* 70
formulas, **R42**
fractions, **R41**
frame of reference, *13. See also* motion, observing.
free fall, 83, 90
friction, xxi, *42,* 44, **85,** 85–89, *86, 87,* 110.
  air resistance, **89,** *89,* 152
  compound machines and, 165
  efficiency and, *150,* 151, 152, 156
  fluids and, 88–89, *89*
  force needed to overcome, *86, 87, 104*
  heat and, *87*
  reducing, 152
  surfaces and, 86–88
  weight and, *87*
fuel cell, xxvii, *xxvii*
fulcrum, 109, **155,** *155, 162,* 163, *172*

INDEX

INDEX

Acknowledgments

Photography

Cover © Brett Froomer/Getty Images; **i** © Brett Froomer/Getty Images; **iii** *left (top to bottom)* Photograph of James Trefil by Evan Cantwell; Photograph of Rita Ann Calvo by Joseph Calvo; Photograph of Linda Carnine by Amilcar Cifuentes; Photograph of Sam Miller by Samuel Miller; *right (top to bottom)* Photograph of Kenneth Cutler by Kenneth A. Cutler; Photograph of Donald Steely by Marni Stamm; Photograph of Vicky Vachon by Redfern Photographics; **vi** © Arthur Tilley/Getty Images; **vii** © Mike Chew/Corbis; **ix** Photographs by Sharon Hoogstraten; **xiv–xv** © Larry Hamill/age fotostock america, inc.; **xvi–xvii** © Fritz Poelking/age fotostock america, inc.; **xviii–xix** © Galen Rowell/Corbis; **xx–xxi** © Jack Affleck/SuperStock; **xxii** AP/Wide World Photos; **xxiii** © David Parker/IMI/University of Birmingham High, TC Consortium/Photo Researchers; **xxiv** *left* AP/Wide World Photos; *right Washington University Record;* **xxv** *top* © Kim Steele/Getty Images; *bottom* Reprinted with permission from S. Zhou et al., *SCIENCE* 291:1944–47. © 2001 AAAS; **xxvi–xxvii** © Mike Fiala/Getty Images; **xxvii** *left* © Derek Trask/Corbis; *right* AP/Wide World Photos; **xxxii** © The Chedd-Angier Production Company; **2–3** Courtesy of NASA/JPL/Caltech; **3** © Stocktrek/Corbis; **4** *top* Courtesy of NASA/JPL/Caltech; *bottom* © The Chedd-Angier Production Company; **6–7** © Lester Lefkowitz/Corbis; **7** Photographs by Sharon Hoogstraten; **9** © Royalty-Free/Corbis; **11** © Globus, Holway & Lobel/Corbis; **12** *top* Photograph by Sharon Hoogstraten; *bottom* © The Image Bank/Getty Images; **14** *top* © Georgina Bowater/Corbis; *bottom* © SuperStock; **15** © Graham Wheatley/ The Military Picture Library/Corbis; **16, 17** Photographs by Sharon Hoogstraten; **18** © Gunter Marx Photography/Corbis; **19** Photograph by Sharon Hoogstraten; **21** © Tom Brakefield/Corbis; **22** © David M. Dennis/Animals Animals; **23** © Kelly-Mooney Photography/Corbis; **24** © Gallo Images/Corbis; **25** © 1986 Richard Megna/Fundamental Photographs, NYC; **27** Photograph by Sharon Hoogstraten; **28** © Royalty-Free/Corbis; **29** Courtesy of NASA/JPL/Caltech; **30** © Robert Essel NYC/Corbis; **32** *top* © Mark Jenkinson/Corbis; *bottom* Photographs by Sharon Hoogstraten; **34** *top* © Globus, Holway & Lobel/Corbis; *center* Photograph by Sharon Hoogstraten; **36** © David M. Dennis/Animals Animals; **38–39** © Arthur Tilley/Getty Images; **39, 41** Photographs by Sharon Hoogstraten; **42** © John Kelly/Getty Images; **43** *left* © AFP/Corbis; *right* © Reuters NewMedia Inc./Corbis; **44** © Michael Kevin Daly/Corbis; **45** *left* © Jim Cummins/Getty Images; *right* © Piecework Productions/ Getty Images; **46** Photograph by Sharon Hoogstraten; **47** © Jeffrey Lynch/Mendola, Ltd.; **48** *left, inset* © Bill Ross/Corbis; *right* Dr. Paula Messina, San Jose State University; **49, 50** Photographs by Sharon Hoogstraten; **52** AP/Wide World Photos; **53** NASA; **54** Photograph by Sharon Hoogstraten; **55** AP/Wide World Photos; **56** *top* Clare Hirn, Jewish Hospital, University of Louisville and ABIOMED; *bottom* John Lair, Jewish Hospital, University of Louisville and ABIOMED; **57** © Danny Lehman/Corbis; **58, 59** Photographs by Sharon Hoogstraten; **60** © Photodisc/Getty Images; *background* © David C. Fritts/Animals Animals; **62** *top* Digital image © 1996 Corbis/Original image courtesy of NASA/Corbis; *bottom* Photographs by Sharon Hoogstraten; **64, 66** Photographs by Sharon Hoogstraten; **68** © TRL Ltd./Photo Researchers; **69** © Charles O'Rear/Corbis; **70** *top* © Photodisc/Getty Images; *bottom* Photographs by Sharon Hoogstraten; **71** © Siede Preis/ Getty Images; **72** Photographs by Sharon Hoogstraten; **74–75** © Mike Chew/Corbis; **75, 77** Photographs by Sharon Hoogstraten; **80, 81** Photographs of models by Sharon Hoogstraten; **80** *left* NASA; *right* © Photodisc/Getty Images; **81** *top, bottom, background* NASA; **82** Photograph by Sharon Hoogstraten; **83** NASA; **84** *left* © Royalty-Free/Corbis; *right* NASA/ESA; **85** © John Beatty/Getty Images; **86, 87** Photographs by Sharon Hoogstraten; **88** *top* © Al Francekevich/Corbis; *bottom* Photograph by Sharon Hoogstraten; **89** © Joe McBride/Getty Images; **90** © NatPhotos/Tony Sweet/Digital Vision; *inset* © Michael S. Yamashita/Corbis; **91** Photograph by Sharon Hoogstraten; **92** © Wilson Goodrich/Index Stock; **93** © Royalty-Free/Corbis; **94** © Philip & Karen Smith/Getty Images; **95** © Ralph A. Clevenger/Corbis; **96** *top* © Stephen Frink/Corbis; *bottom* Photographs by Sharon Hoogstraten; **98, 99, 100** Photographs by Sharon Hoogstraten; **101** Photograph of prairie dogs © W. Perry Conway/Corbis; **103** © Omni Photo Communications Inc./Index Stock; **104** *top, bottom* Photographs by Sharon Hoogstraten; *center* © Royalty-Free/Corbis; **105** Photograph by Sharon Hoogstraten; **106** *left* © Joe McBride/Getty Images; *right* Photograph by Sharon Hoogstraten; **108** *top* © Erich Lessing/Art Resource, New York; *bottom* © Dagli Orti/The Art Archive; **109** *top left* © SPL/Photo Researchers; *top right* Sam Fogg Rare Books & Manuscripts; *bottom* © Dorling Kindersley; **110** *left* © Victoria & Albert Museum, London/Art Resource, New York; *top right* Photo Franca Principe, Institute and Museum of the History of Science; *center right* © Scala/Art Resource, New York; *bottom right* © Dorling Kindersley; **111** *top left* © Gerald L. Schad/Photo Researchers; *top right* Courtesy Claudia Alexander/JPL; *bottom* NASA; **112–113** © Digital Vision; **113** *top* Image Club Graphics; *center* Photograph by Sharon Hoogstraten; **115, 116** Photographs by Sharon Hoogstraten; **117** © Rob Lewine/Corbis; **118** Photograph by Sharon Hoogstraten; **119** © Reinhard Eisele/Corbis; **120** © Roger Allyn Lee/ SuperStock; **121** Chris Wipperman/KCPDSA; **123** © Patrik Giardino/Corbis; **124** © Tony Anderson/Getty Images; **125** Photograph by Sharon Hoogstraten; **126** © 1988 Paul Silverman/ Fundamental Photographs, NYC; **127** © Tony Donaldson/Icon Sports Media; **129** © AFP/Corbis; **130** Photograph by Sharon Hoogstraten; **131** © Pete Saloutos/Corbis; **132** © Digital Vision; **133** Photograph by Sharon Hoogstraten; **134** © Walter Hodges/Corbis; **135** © Grantpix/Index Stock; **136** *top* © David Young-Wolff/PhotoEdit; *bottom* Photographs by Sharon Hoogstraten; **138** © Pete Saloutos/Corbis; **140** Photographs by Sharon Hoogstraten; **142–143** © Balthazar Korab; **145** Photograph by Sharon Hoogstraten; **146** © David Young-Wolff/PhotoEdit; **147** © Joseph Sohm/ ChromoSohm Inc./Corbis; **149** © Brad Wrobleski/Masterfile; **150** © Michael Macor/San Francisco Chronicle/Corbis SABA; **151** Photograph by Sharon Hoogstraten; **152** © Jean-Yves Ruszniewski/Corbis; **153** © Royalty-Free/Corbis; *inset* © Felicia Martinez/ PhotoEdit; **154, 155** Photographs by Sharon Hoogstraten; **156** © Tom Stewart/Corbis; **157** Photograph by Sharon Hoogstraten; **158** *top* © David Butow/Corbis SABA; *bottom* © Peter Beck/Corbis; **159** © Henryk T. Kaiser/Index Stock; **160** © Tony Freeman/ PhotoEdit; **161** © Todd A. Gipstein/Corbis; **163** AP/Wide World Photos; **164** © Tony Freeman/PhotoEdit; **165** © Lester Lefkowitz/ Corbis; **166** Hurst Jaws of Life; **167** © David Parker/Photo Researchers; **168** *top* AP/Wide World Photos; *bottom* © Robert Caputo/Stock Boston; *background* © Royalty-Free/Corbis; **170** *top* © Photodisc/Getty Images; *bottom* Photograph by Sharon Hoogstraten; **172** © ThinkStock/SuperStock; **173** *top left* Photograph by Sharon Hoogstraten; **174** © Tony Freeman/ PhotoEdit; **R28** © Photodisc/Getty Images.

Illustrations and Maps

Accurate Art, Inc. **107, 175**; Steve Cowden **122**; Ampersand Design Group **15**; MapQuest.com, Inc. **10, 60, 129, 168**; Tony Randazzo/American Artists Rep. Inc. **13**; Dan Stuckenschneider **102, 135, 156, 157, 158, 159, 162, 165, 172, 173, R11–R19, R22, R32**; Dan Stukenschneider based on an illustration by Matt Cioffi **168**.

4500675358-0607-2017

Printed in the U.S.A